Praise f

"Anxiety is at epidemic levels today. In *Feed Your Calm*, Ann Silvers gives readers an approachable antidote to this epidemic."

Megan DeBell, MD (Integrative and Functional Medicine),
Seattle, WA

"Ann nailed it in her book, *Feed You Calm*!

Feed Your Calm is inviting, well researched with the most up to date information, interactive, and easy to refer back to."

Heidi Crawford, MSW, LICSW
Confluence Health, Wenatchee, WA

"The connection between nutrition and mental well-being is crucial, and author Ann Silvers brings much-needed clarity to this subject. She expertly guides you through what to eat and, just as importantly, what not to eat, so that you can better deal with stress. *Feed Your Calm* needs to be a part of everyone's health library."

Dr. Lori Shemek, PhD, CNC, Bestselling Author:
How to Fight FATflammation! and *Fire-Up Your Fat Burn!*

"Many of my clients know they need to change their diets and eat healthier to feel better and improve their anxiety, but in this age of fads and conflicting advice it is difficult for them to know how to begin. Ann Silvers really breaks it down in her book *Feed Your Calm*, providing science-based information that is not only easy to understand, but easy to utilize. The charts and tables that are scattered throughout the chapters help facilitate learning and can be used for easy reference. The worksheets at the end of the book are perfect for planning, keeping track, and staying focused on getting well.

Thank you, Ann, for creating such a valuable resource."

Kathleen O'Rourke, MA, LMHC
True Compass Counseling, Warwick, RI

Feed Your
Calm

Anti-Anxiety Anti-Stress Diet *and* Supplement Tips *for* Stress Resilience

ANN SILVERS, MA

SILVERSPUBLISHING

Ann Silvers is a counselor, hypnotherapist, relationship coach, and author living in Washington State. Among her credentials are a Master's Degree in Counseling and a Certificate in Integrative Medicine for Mental Health. She has written self-help books and created hypnosis recordings addressing anxiety and many other topics.

Ann hasn't always been a counselor. During her first career, she was a Medical Lab Tech working in hospital microbiology labs. After experiencing the benefits of counseling when she sought out therapy for the emotional scars from being raised by two alcoholics, she wanted to help other people improve their lives too, so she returned to school to acquire the university degrees and training to become a counselor.

Anxiety became one of Ann's specialties in her counseling private practice. She has helped clients relieve everything from a worn-out stressed feeling to general anxiety to fear of flying. She also dealt with anxiety herself for many years. Her particular mix of academic study of the topic, work experience, and personal experience gives her unique insight into what anxiety feels like, what it's all about, and how to reduce it.

Having been attentive to nutrition for several decades in her own life and to growing degrees in the lives of her clients, Ann has been excited to see a burgeoning appreciation for the impact physical health has on mental health, and the development of training and associations of helping professionals to advance understanding of how we can engage physical systems and natural remedies to improve mood. Getting a Certificate in Integrative Medicine for Mental Health brought Ann's career path full circle, bringing together her medical and mental health training and experience.

v

Anxiety Mini-Book

A Quick Look at Anxiety: Simple Powerful Anti-Anxiety Tips for Stress, Anxiety, and Panic Attack Relief

Journal/Workbooks

Discovering How Foods Affect Me, Silver Lining Elimination Diet Journal helps you plan an elimination diet and track how you feel physically and mentally so you can uncover food intolerances, sensitivities, and allergies that could be contributing to anxiety and stress.

Learn, Let Go, and Lighten Up, Silver Lining Emotional Detox Journal and Workbook can help you process emotional baggage including sources of anxiety.

Hypnosis Recordings (Available at annsilvers.com)

Hypnosis is a powerful anti-anxiety stress relief tool. My downloadable mp3 hypnosis recordings are designed to listen to anytime you have about a half-hour to relax or as you are going to sleep. Many people report that listening to my recordings at bedtime improves their sleep. I have recordings on a variety of issues, including:

- *Release and Refresh: Emotional Detox Hypnosis*
- *Discover Calm: Anti-Anxiety Hypnosis*

Contents

My own experience as to the widespread issue that is anxiety in our society started a few years out of medical school when I was practicing at a naturopathic primary care clinic. I didn't have intentions of focusing on anxiety management in my practice; I anticipated naturopathic primary care to be about medication and supplement management, ordering routine lab work, making referrals to specialists, and offering naturopathic alternatives to mainstream treatment plans. It quickly became obvious to me, however, that nearly every patient that walked in my door was struggling with anxiety. Often, I was finding, it was probably at the root of their illness too, whether that was heart disease, eczema, digestive issues, or migraines.

As a naturopath, I am trained to dig deep into an individual's history to find when and where the symptoms started and to find a common thread that may point to the underlying cause for illness. As I dug and dug to get to the "root cause" of the issue with my patients, an astonishing number of times it came down to either a major stressor in their lives (a divorce, moving, a physical trauma, etc.) or a longstanding presence of stress in their lives (a job, a family situation, a relationship, etc.).

While the obvious solution is to change the stressor to reduce the stress, I would often find that by simply eliminating or changing the stressor, people were not experiencing the relief I expected. Or, sometimes they weren't able to completely modify that stressor in their life (they had to keep working a job they disliked because they needed the money, for example). This presented a new problem: How could we create the best situation in their body for handling stress? How could I help reduce the total amount of stressors impacting their body?

Naturopaths often look closely at the foods people eat. We believe that food affects us probably as much as, or sometimes more than, most other things we take or do. We eat food all throughout the day, every day. It's undeniable that many physical and mental symptoms are directly connected to the fuel being fed to the body. We've all heard the old adage, "garbage in = garbage out"—well, it's literally the same with our bodies. We have to put the good stuff in to get the good stuff out.

While this much was already ingrained in me from my naturopathic medical school training, I often found myself wondering, "What foods are the most problematic and/ or beneficial for anxiety specifically?" I was making some headway with patients in anxiety reduction through supplement prescription but was searching for more ways to help through diet specifically. I knew about foods that would trigger joint pain or foods that were more likely to stress the digestive tract. But aside from avoiding caffeine, I did not have a clear understanding of the exact foods that would be the *best* for keeping anxiety at bay and decreasing the brain chemicals that feed the anxiety response in our bodies.

About this time, I became acquainted with Ann Silvers' work with anxiety. At a networking luncheon, she provided me with some samples of her booklets and hypnosis recordings related to anxiety. We then began working together with some mutual patients to treat their anxiety from different clinical angles, and I saw that Ann really believes in the principles of naturopathy—namely, that what we put into our bodies impacts how our brain works. Encouraged by the gains she was seeing in her anxiety clients when they made diet and supplement adjustments, Ann started on the journey to uncover more nutritional advice for these clients to best set them up for a healthy and steady mood. I was excited when

I heard that she had begun working on a book based on this research that would discuss some of the nutrients and foods that are best suited for anxiety.

This book, *Feed Your Calm*, contains the fruits of her labor. She researched and wrote about how so much of what's going on in your body—from gut function to inflammation—influences your brain and stress response. She dove deep into learning what foods could be strategically eaten to enhance certain nutrient levels in our bodies so as to decrease our overall experience of anxiety.

Ann has created quite a masterpiece: a book that not only explains stress and its impact on the body but is also a comprehensive resource on anxiety and nutrition that can serve as a reference for both patients and practitioners. This book is complete in its explanation of each nutrient's impact on your body, which are the best for "feeding your calm," and which ones will make you more "stress resilient" in the long run. She discusses the pros and cons of supplements that have stress- and anxiety-relieving potential and gives references for recommended daily intakes of those that are especially helpful. For practitioners and patients alike, there's a section on labs that can be checked to examine the impact stress has had on one's body and which nutrients might be most deficient.

As a practitioner, I am particularly excited to have this resource available for myself and my patients. People are hungry for more information on how they can improve their lives and reduce their stress. They also want to know which supplements to take and how much. This book can serve as a tool that is easy to follow, easy to implement, and handy to reference as you make real changes.

Dr. Jessica Corbeille Harris, ND

Listen to your bodies.
You are constantly receiving information
from your body
about how to care for it and yourself.

– Claudia Black

Anxiety can suck the life out of life.

It is draining, distracting, and sometimes debilitating. It revs you up and wears you out. It can make you immobile, irritable, and irrational. It can interfere with your job performance, reduce your quality of life, and undermine your relationships.

Anxiety ranges in intensity from a stressed-out overwhelmed feeling to a full-blown panic attack that sends you to the emergency room for a heart check. Different types of anxiety include generalized anxiety (GAD), panic, social anxiety, phobias such as fear of flying, obsessive-compulsive disorder (OCD), and post-traumatic stress disorder (PTSD). Anxiety is often found in combination with other mental challenges such as depression.

If you have anxiety now or have experienced it in the past, you are not alone. The National Institute of Mental Health estimates that 30% of the adult population of the United States will experience an anxiety disorder.

Sources of stress are going to be part of your life. You are going to be running late sometimes. You are going to have disagreements with people. You are going to have deadlines, whether it is getting dinner on the table before the kids' baseball practice or transporting a kidney before it expires. The level of stress you experience in response to each of these threats is determined by your mental and physical state. Managing stress so that it doesn't turn into anxiety requires stress resilience: the ability to withstand stress, recover quickly, and spring back into shape.

> **Stress Resilience** is the ability to withstand stress, recover quickly, and spring back into shape.

Anxiety is emotional and physical

Anxiety is both emotional and physical. You feel the emotion of anxiety and you feel the physical sensation of being anxious. Your body and mind are connected, and each affects the other: your biochemistry can alter your mood and your mood can alter your biochemistry.

As a therapist, I've helped many people overcome anxiety with psychological interventions such as emotion skill-building, getting at the root causes of the individual's anxiety, relaxation skills training, hypnosis, and other therapeutic approaches. I believe these are important avenues for managing stress. I have written other books and articles about ways to understand and deal with the mental and emotional aspects of anxiety, and I expect to write more on those topics in the future, but they are not the focus of this book.

I have also seen that physical interventions help reduce anxiety and increase stress resilience. In thinking about whether you should address your anxiety physically or psychologically, it's not necessarily an either/or thing. I think it's a both/and thing; addressing anxiety from a psychological perspective and a physical perspective is a great combination that reaps many benefits and boosts both the speed and level of improvement.

The emotion of anxiety

Anxiety is a member of the fear family of emotions. Other members of the fear family include panic, nervousness, worry, and concern. Any of them may be felt as, or labeled as, *stress*.

All emotions are information. The information in fear is "danger": "danger to myself, something, or someone."

Sometimes the level of fear felt is warranted by your current situation and it is important to make adjustments to deal with the feared thing. Sometimes you are overreacting to whatever is going on right now and experiencing an exaggerated amount of discomfort. In that case, you would do well to figure out what part of the fear is really about now and address that issue, while you also work at uncovering why you tend to overreact.

There is a hierarchy of fear, from more intense to less intense:

- panic
- anxiety
- nervousness/worry
- concern

Concern is the sweat spot for fear. At concern, you can logically identify what you are afraid of, consider your options for dealing with the feared thing, make a plan of action, and put the plan into action. At the higher levels of fear, your mind tends to spin or be distracted. The higher levels of fear get in the way of being clearheaded and logical. Instead of addressing the feared thing and moving forward, there is a tendency to stay stuck in fear or ramp up the intensity.

The physical symptoms of anxiety

When fear provokes the fight, flight, or freeze response, it commands your body to perform specific chemical processes that are meant to keep you safe in times of danger. Some of the resulting physical changes are felt as the symptoms of anxiety.

Anxiety's physical manifestations are different for different people. One person might sweat, another person might have diarrhea, another constipation. Your particular body and the intensity of your anxiety will determine your symptoms.

There is an overlap between what is commonly called "anxiety" and what is labeled "panic," with panic being more physically intense. Anxiety can last for long periods (days, weeks, months, or years) with symptoms that are sometimes worse than other times. It can come over you slowly or quickly, stimulated by situations or thoughts, or it can be in the background most of the time. Panic attacks appear suddenly with a surge of symptoms that usually peak within ten minutes, and while they range in duration from seconds to hours, they typically subside within a half hour. Some people with anxiety never experience a panic attack, while others may have had years of anxiety peppered with a few or many panic episodes.

Anxiety may have any of these physical symptoms:

- difficulty thinking
- brain fog
- muscle tension
- sweating
- trembling or shaking
- tightness in the throat
- crackling or unsteady voice
- dry mouth
- nausea or stomach upset
- intestinal problems (diarrhea, constipation, bloating, gas, cramps)
- headaches/migraines
- increased heart rate
- skin rashes or hives

Anxiety that has reached panic levels may have any of the symptoms listed on the previous page plus any of these more intense symptoms:

- dizziness or faintness
- chills or hot flashes
- racing heart
- heart palpitations
- chest pain
- vision changes
- numbness or tingling
- shortness of breath
- hyperventilation
- difficulty moving

I've experienced a couple of panic attacks myself. With the second one, I was so worried that I was going to pass out that I laid myself down on the floor so if I passed out I had nowhere to fall.

Helping your body deal with stress

A common method to address the physical aspect of anxiety is prescription of pharmaceutical drugs like Xanax and Valium. Pharmaceuticals are one possible way to address the physicality of anxiety, but they aren't the only way. There are many potentially helpful natural physical anti-anxiety interventions that can be used in conjunction with pharmaceuticals or as an alternative approach. Non-pharmaceutical ways to help your body cope with stress include getting enough exercise, seeing a massage therapist or acupuncturist, and using essential oils. That's just a beginning of a list of natural remedies for anxiety. This book will focus on another natural anxiety remedy: diet.

Food and supplements contribute to your body chemistry's potential as an anxiety inducer or stress mitigator. As Integrative Medicine for Mental Health specialist Dr. Leslie Korn succinctly describes it: "Mood follows food."[1] Some foods make anxiety worse by stressing your physical systems and introducing destructive biochemicals that interfere with your organs, glands, and cells doing their jobs. Other foods offer up amino acids, antioxidants, fats, and minerals that fuel your body and brain to cope with stress and repair damage done so that your body and mind can get a boost.

"Mood follows food."
—Dr. Leslie Korn

Feeding your calm involves giving your body what it needs to deal with stress and avoiding inputting foods that add to your stress load. My goal in helping you manage stress and anxiety with diet and supplements is to maximize your body's ability to handle stressors and the fear reaction.

About referenced research

I have been frustrated with books and articles by authors who make claims about natural remedies for anxiety and other issues but don't back their declarations with research. I decided to go the extra many miles of effort to track where I got information so you can see the sources for yourself if you are so inclined. If research is boring or unimportant to you, just skip over the little reference numbers.

Even if the background information isn't interesting to you personally, the references may be helpful when you are talking to your doctors and other medical professionals about any of these topics.

I have attempted to present information that can stand up to scientific scrutiny. Most of the human studies referenced in the Encouraging Research sections in the chapters of Part Two: What Helps Your Calm used placebo-controlled double-blind methods with significant numbers of subjects. For the most part, I have avoided referencing studies that are based on small samples of participants or the observation of practitioners.

You may be wondering what all that research jargon means.

Placebo-controlled studies use at least two groups of participants: a subject group of people who are doing what the study is studying (e.g., taking a specific dose of a certain supplement) and a control group of similar people that are not doing that thing but think they are, or at least potentially are, doing it (e.g., taking a placebo that looks like the supplement being studied). *Blind studies* are set up so that the participants don't know if they are in the subject or control group. *Double-blind studies* leave the researchers as well as the participants in the dark about who is in the control and subject groups until they are analyzing the data.

Another type of study that is well respected is research of data gathered about large groups of people over extended time periods. These projects are known as *longitudinal studies*.

The reality is that there isn't as much scientific research on natural remedies compared to pharmaceutical medications because there isn't as much financial incentive to run the research. This means there are limited resources to draw from to back up natural approaches to health. Throughout the book, I note what I found with a few details to help you assess the various studies' value for yourself.

Besides studies that look at natural remedies for anxiety, I have also included relevant depression-related research because there is a high percentage of crossover between these conditions, with many people experiencing both anxiety and depression simultaneously.

In research for the effectiveness of remedies—both natural and pharmaceutical—for anxiety and other mood conditions, researchers often start with animal studies. This approach has led to the creation of standardized study methods to assess the level of anxiety-related behavior in mice and rats. I found them very interesting, and you might find them interesting too, for their parallels with how anxiety shows up for people.

These are examples of standardized rodent anxiety tests:

- **The Open Field Exploration Test:** Researchers place a single animal in a square box-like chamber for five minutes and monitor how much time it spends in the center area. Spending more time close to the walls is characteristic of increased anxiety behavior (an interesting parallel with the potential of anxiety decreasing adventurous behavior in people).

- **The Elevated Plus-Maze:** Individual mice are placed in a maze elevated off the floor. Some of the arms of the maze are closed and dark, and some are open and exposed to bright light. More-anxious mice spend more time in the sheltered dark areas where they feel more secure. Less-anxious mice are more adventurous and spend more time exploring the open areas.

Book overview

Before presenting my lists of foods and supplements to help you manage stress and reduce anxiety in Parts Four and Five of *Feed Your Calm*, I'll explain what is happening in your body when you are stressed (Part One), how different nutrients assist the physical processes we're targeting for stress resilience (Part Two), and what you might be consuming that is adding to your stress load (Part Three).

Part One: Your Body on Stress

- I'll explain what is happening in your body when you are stressed and introduce you to the physical mechanisms we are targeting to optimize your stress resilience and reduce anxiety.

Part Two: What Helps Your Calm

- We'll look at how specific minerals, vitamins, fats, probiotics, amino acids, and herbs can assist your body's stress response and what can get in the way of them doing their anti-anxiety jobs.

Part Three: What Hurts Your Calm

- Without knowing it, you may be consuming foods that are contributing to your stress load, taxing your body's stress response, decreasing your ability to deal with emotional stressors, and contributing to your anxiety. I'll point out five foods and groups of food to watch out for.

Part Four: Stress Resilience Foods

- A dozen foods to improve your chances of taking stress in stride will be discussed as well as general advice for anti-stress eating.

Part Five: Stress Resilience Supplements

- I'll describe the variety of forms available for each of my top 10 supplements and recommendations for which forms might be best for stress management and anxiety relief.

Part Six: Bringing It All Together

- This part provides a place for you to track your thoughts and insights. It's there as an option to help you more easily make connections between material presented throughout the book, feel less overwhelmed by the information, set priorities, and build a plan of action to take steps towards a calmer, more stress-resilient you.

- You may want to tag this part with a sticky note or paper clip for easy access and quick reference.

- The first chapter in each part of *Feed Your Calm* ends with a section entitled Notes for Bringing It All Together, which suggests topics that you may want to consider noting on the pages of Part Six.

- For a pdf workbook version of Part Six, go to: annsilvers.com/pages/feed-your-calm-workbook

Appendix: Lab Tests

- A few relevant lab tests will be discussed and I'll point toward some resources that you may find helpful for acquiring testing.

Feed Your Calm is a summary of information I have found about the topics I present and my interpretation of what I've learned from research, education, and experience. I am not a medical doctor. This book is not intended to replace individualized medical advice you can get from health professionals in person. I hope that the subjects I present spark new ideas of how you might improve your life and that the included references assist both you and your medical team to investigate the topics further.

If you are currently on a pharmaceutical medication for anxiety, depression, or other psychological conditions, it is important that you *not* take yourself off of your meds. Consult with your physician about how to utilize what you learn about natural remedies while you maintain or change your medications. Most psychological medications require a weaning process if you decide to stop taking them. Some supplements have been shown to improve the results of anti-anxiety pharmaceuticals. I'll make note of these as we're talking about what helps your calm in Part Two.

If you feel overwhelmed by all the information and possibilities to consider, take a breath and remind yourself that even one small change can make a difference. You are an individual with individual circumstances. Starting where you are, with what you have to work with, is OK. You might not know yet how wonderful you'll feel when you put into action some of the suggested dietary additions or subtractions. Let's get started on helping you learn how to feed your calm.

Part One

Your Body on Stress

In order to trust your body as a guide,
the first step is to begin to understand it.

– Deepak Chopra

Introduction to Your Body on Stress

Your body has to deal with a wide range of physical stressors every day: noise, chemicals, injury, illness, inflammation, and hormone fluctuations, to name a few. It also has to deal with emotional stress from problems big and small. All these stressors, both physical and emotional, tax the physical mechanisms that are engaged in the stress response.

To help you understand what foods and supplements might be helpful for reducing anxiety and relieving a stressed-out feeling, this first part of *Feed Your Calm* will explain what is going on in your body as it deals with stress. We'll focus on six areas of interest that are central to your body's response to stress and its ability to cope with stressors:

1. Adrenal glands
2. Nerves
3. Neurotransmitters
4. Relaxation
5. Your gut
6. Glucose (blood sugar)

In the upcoming chapters, I'll explain how each of these physical aspects connects to anxiety and how you can use food and supplements to improve your stress resilience.

Notes for Bringing It All Together

As you read the chapters of Part One, keep a lookout for connections between the physical systems mentioned and symptoms you experience related to anxiety or other health issues. This information may help you decide your priorities for foods and supplements on the recommended lists in Parts Four and Five and foods suggested for elimination or reduction in Part Three.

You may want to note your insights on the pages set aside in Part Six: Bringing It All Together.

2 The Adrenals, Your Stress Glands

Anxiety is intense fear. Fear's message to you is, "Danger!" That message can stimulate the fight-or-flight response. And that will get your adrenal glands involved.

Fight-or-flight puts your adrenal glands to work producing and releasing hormones:

- Adrenaline (aka adrenalin or epinephrine)
- Noradrenaline (aka noradrenalin or norepinephrine)
- Cortisol

These hormones tell your body and brain what to do next. They boost your fight responses or prep you to make a speedy getaway, and they suppress other body functions that aren't necessary for high-level protective maneuvers.

Adrenaline and noradrenaline are the first-wave threat response team.[1] They exert their force in a flash: your heart rate increases, you become hyper-alert, your digestion slows down, and your blood sugar goes up. You might recognize these as physical symptoms that accompany anxiety.

Cortisol is the second-wave responder, keeping some of these reactions going and changing others to help you deal with prolonged stress. It impacts when the stress response will be turned off.[2]

Cortisol

Cortisol is considered the primary stress hormone. It helps you deal with stressors of all kinds, from noise to infections and toxic chemicals to psychological stresses.

In healthy conditions, your cortisol ebbs and flows throughout the day. It goes up in the morning so you feel perky and down at night so you feel relaxed in preparation for sleep. It spikes in response to emergencies and then stands down when the emergency passes.

> Healthy cortisol goes up in the morning and down at night.

Cortisol can be helpful when you encounter a stressor. It focuses your physical forces away from unnecessary functions and toward dealing with the threat. Cortisol can help you battle the lion at the cave door or be "on" for a speech.

Cortisol also acts as an anti-inflammatory agent. (That's why doctors give cortisone shots to fight inflammation.) When your adrenal glands are clicking along producing healthy amounts of cortisol, it can reduce the likelihood you'll get any of the myriad of illnesses that inflammation causes, contributes to, or exacerbates.

In a healthy response to a threat, cortisol[3]

- mobilizes fats and glucose to increase energy supply,
- suppresses immune response,
- decreases inflammation,
- increases heart rate and blood pressure,
- reduces the perception of pain, and
- suppresses growth and reproduction.

That's all well and good when there is an acute threat to your safety or even something you need to be alert to deal with, like that speech or getting your taxes done on time. Unfortunately, repeated or prolonged exposure to stressors, or dwelling on stress, or even anticipating stress, can result in chronically high cortisol levels.[4] That has lots of downsides.

Chronically high cortisol levels can[5]

- negatively impact working memory,
- increase blood pressure,
- decrease immune function,
- interfere with reproduction and libido,
- create insulin resistance, and
- contribute to weight gain (especially around your middle).

Cortisol that stays high for too long contributes to a jittery, wired, anxious feeling. But, when it comes to your cortisol being off-kilter because of stress, too high isn't the only option.

Ever since Hans Selye proposed the concept of fight-or-flight and described the impact that increased cortisol has on our bodies and minds in the 1930s, focus has been on this particular response to stress. In the last couple of decades, however, researchers noticed that some people who have experienced trauma or are under chronic stress don't have high cortisol—they have unusually low cortisol.[6]

Chronically low cortisol has a negative impact on your health and well-being. Your body misses cortisol's perk-you-up and anti-inflammatory qualities. In 2001, Dr. James Wilson, who has doctorate degrees in naturopathy, chiropathy, and nutrition, wrote about the symptoms of low cortisol as part of a condition he calls *adrenal fatigue*. His concept of the adrenal glands getting worn down by long-term stress is strongly objected to by some and adamantly embraced by others. (The fact that my 2015 copy of his book *Adrenal Fatigue: The 21st Century Stress Syndrome* says it is the 26th printing attests to its popularity.)[7]

Whether you are for or against the idea of the adrenals getting worn out from stress, there is no denying that the adrenal glands produce cortisol in response to stress, your adrenals are forced to work hard if you are dealing with stress in a big or extended way, there is growing scientific evidence that stress can cause either high or low cortisol levels for abnormally long periods, and both ends of the cortisol continuum have negative symptoms.

Chronically low cortisol can cause[8]

- a run-down fatigued feeling,
- difficulty thinking,
- increased inflammation, and
- increased pain sensitivity.

Extended periods of low cortisol levels appear common in chronic pain conditions such as fibromyalgia, debilitating low-energy illnesses such as chronic fatigue syndrome, and inflammatory or autoimmune disorders like arthritis and asthma. It is also implicated in idiopathic pain—that is, pain that doesn't have a physical explanation. Many studies about low cortisol have been performed on people with PTSD because it is a common, though not universal, finding with this disorder.[9]

Another potential outcome of stress is an everyday cortisol pattern that, rather than being consistently high or consistently low, is the opposite of healthy: it can be blunted in the morning, when it is supposed to be increasing so you feel motivated and ready to deal with your day, and increased at night, countering your ability to sleep.[10]

To recap: stress can make your cortisol go all wonky (technically called *dysregulation*). A wonky dysregulated cortisol level—chronically high, chronically low, or high and low at the wrong times of day—can result in increased anxious feelings. It begins with exposure to stress or trauma and it contributes to feeling stressed out and anxious. It's a vicious feel-bad circle.

When we're looking at natural remedies for anxiety, we want to help your body regulate its cortisol level. We want to make sure you have the nutrients you may burn through as your adrenal glands respond to stress and support these glands so they can create healthy levels of feel-good anti-inflammatory cortisol.

Stress Gets on Your Nerves

When you're anxious, does it feel like you can't think straight? Does it feel like something—or everything—is getting on your nerves?

To deal with stress, you need to feed your nerve cells (aka neurons), including the billions in your brain. Nerve health is important for dealing with stress and anxiety. When it comes to anxiety, your brain matters. And when it comes to your brain, nerves matter.

Your brain runs your body. It's the computer that is in constant communication with your organs and physical systems and it helps you figure out what to think, do, and feel. Your nerves can be likened to wires that connect your brain to the rest of your body and function as the vehicle of information inside your brain. That information is transmitted two ways: electrically and chemically. Electrical signals (nerve impulses) and chemicals are transferred to other nerve cells, muscles, and glands that turn movement, hormones, and other biochemicals on and off.

Your brain has about 100 billion nerve cells. You continue to make new nerve cells in your brain even as an adult.[1] Those nerve cells are largely made up of fat. About two-thirds of the dry weight of your brain is fat.

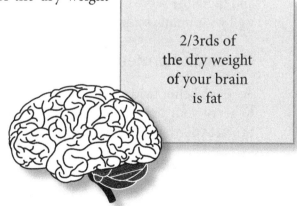

2/3rds of
the dry weight
of your brain
is fat

Fatty acids are present in two major parts of each nerve cell:

1. The membrane that coats the exterior of the cell controlling what biochemicals get in and go out

2. The *myelin sheath* that forms an outer covering along the nerve cell's arm-like *axon* to facilitate the flow of electrical impulses

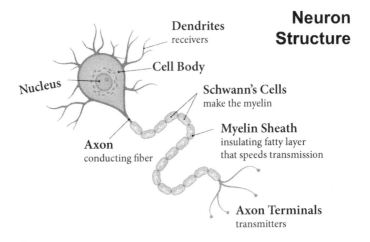

Neuron Structure

Dendrites
receivers

Cell Body

Nucleus

Schwann's Cells
make the myelin

Myelin Sheath
insulating fatty layer
that speeds transmission

Axon
conducting fiber

Axon Terminals
transmitters

The nutrients you take in, including what type of fat you eat, and therefore serve up to your nerves and brain, impact how well your brain works and how well it deals with stress.

Serve and protect

To deal better with stress, and reduce anxiety, you need to serve your brain the nutrients it needs and you need to protect your brain's nerve cells.

You need to protect your brain cells from two potential sources of assault:

1. Oxidative stress
2. Inflammation

1. Oxidative Stress

Your body's cells can be under attack by *free radicals*: junk molecules that you take into your body or create inside your body. You breathe in, absorb, and eat free radicals from your environment, food, and activities like smoking. You also create free radicals as leftovers from normal metabolic reactions in your body. You may be familiar with the concept of dangerous chemicals posing a threat to your body, but less familiar with the fact that you also have to play cleanup for the billions of routine biochemical processes that your body is going through every minute.

Antioxidants are your body's clean-up team. They swoop in and sweep up those free radicals. As long as you have enough antioxidants to deal with your load of pollutants and chemical reaction leftovers, your body will do relatively well. But, if you have more free radicals than you can clean up, those molecules will mess with your cells and their ability to function. That stresses out your body and can stress *you* out.

Even the term for not having enough antioxidants to play cleanup has *stress* in the title. It's called *oxidative stress*.

> **Oxidative stress** happens when you don't have enough antioxidants to clean up free radical molecules from pollutants and biochemical reaction leftovers.

Several things make your brain particularly vulnerable to oxidative stress, including nerve cells' high fat content and the fact that your brain is one of the most active organs in your body.[2] All that activity creates a large amount of free radical reaction leftovers. Stress potentially increases your brain's free radical load even further.[3]

Over the last decade, more and more research is pointing toward oxidative stress as a potential contributor to anxiety.[4] Mental/emotional stress can lead to oxidative stress and oxidative stress can contribute to mental/emotional stress. It's a vicious circle that you can help break with the care and feeding of your brain.

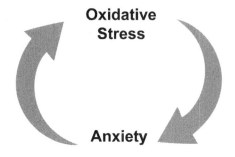

2. Inflammation

> Chronic inflammation is your immune system on overdrive.

Your body's immune system has a number of mechanisms to jump in and defend you against viruses, threatening bacteria, toxic chemicals, and anything it considers a foreign object. That's a good thing. However, when your immune system goes into overdrive, it can cause problems associated with chronic inflammation.

You may be familiar with inflammation's connection to illnesses like arthritis. Inflammation can also be connected to many other physical conditions, and, as is being revealed more recently, even to depression, anxiety, and other mental conditions. In arthritis, inflammation is impacting your joints. In depression and anxiety, inflammation may be impacting your nerve cells and brain function.

There has been quite a lot of research attention given to the association between depression and inflammation. That's important to many people with anxiety because there is a strong overlap between the two conditions: many people who experience anxiety also experience depression and vice versa. There also is strengthening research pointing toward inflammation as a potential contributor to anxiety.

Published in 2012, the 88th volume of the book series *Advances in Protein Chemistry and Structural Biology*, containing chapters by academics considered experts in their fields, is subtitled *Inflammation in Neuropsychiatric Disorders*. The title itself seems to back up the idea that there is growing acceptance of the connection between your mental state and the amount of inflammation in your body. *Advances in Protein Chemistry and Structural Biology: Inflammation in Neuropsychiatric Disorders* includes chapters about depression, schizophrenia, Parkinson's, and anxiety. The fact that the book opens with the "Inflammation in Anxiety" chapter strikes me as more evidence that inflammation must be a consideration when discussing causes of anxiety.[5]

The mechanisms behind inflammation's contribution to depression and anxiety are not yet well understood, but pro-inflammatory cytokines appear to be at the center of most theories.[6] Cytokines are proteins that signal cells to turn on and off immune responses.

Pro-inflammatory cytokines turn on your immune system and anti-inflammatory cytokines turn it off. Prolonged increases in pro-inflammatory cytokines can mess with your brain and may contribute to anxiety by causing oxidative stress and negatively impacting brain nerve cell health, production, and function. Certain foods and biochemicals cause increases in pro-inflammatory cytokines. Others stimulate the production of anti-inflammatory cytokines.

As with oxidative stress and anxiety, there appears to be a two-way connection between inflammation and anxiety. Inflammation may contribute to anxiety, and anxiety may stimulate inflammation.[7]

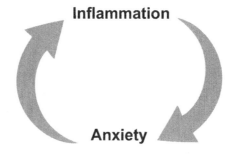

Inflammation

Anxiety

While we look at what helps and hurts your stress resilience, I'll be pointing out nutrients that take care of your nerve cells by supplying their building blocks or reducing oxidative stress and inflammation. I'll also identify food components that may damage nerve cells by contributing bad fats or elements that create oxidative stress and inflammation.

Neurotransmitters Tell Your Body to Calm Down or Rev Up

Neurotransmitters are produced by nerve cells (neurons) to stimulate your body's cells to do what they are supposed to do—or at least to do what the neurotransmitters are designed to make your body's cells do.

You've probably heard of some of the neurotransmitters by name: serotonin, adrenaline, and GABA are a few examples of this group of biochemicals. Neurotransmitters are the focus of anti-anxiety pharmaceutical medications, but there are also natural approaches to help your body get your neurotransmitter house in order.

Some neurotransmitters rev things up and some calm things down

Neurotransmitters are divided into two groups: *excitatory* neurotransmitters rev you up and *inhibitory* neurotransmitters calm you down. Some of the neurotransmitters serve multiple functions in your body and can be excitatory for some of their duties and inhibitory for others.

What your neurotransmitters do:

- serotonin is calming
- GABA is calming
- glycine is calming
- glutamate revs things up
- aspartate revs things up
- adrenaline generally revs things up
- noradrenaline generally revs things up
- acetylcholine usually revs up muscles
- dopamine goes both ways

You may have noticed that adrenaline was mentioned as an adrenal gland hormone earlier and a neurotransmitter here. That's because it is both a hormone and a neurotransmitter. It is considered a hormone when it is released by the adrenal gland and a neurotransmitter when it is released by nerve cells.

You need some of the revving-up neurotransmitters some of the time so you can focus and feel energetic, but too much and you feel jittery and your brain bounces around. If you have too much of the revving up going on, you make your body create too much of the compensating neurotransmitters that are trying to calm you down and you wear out your ability to perform the balancing act.

To reduce anxiety, you may have to reduce your intake of excitatory neurotransmitter sources like the artificial sweetener aspartame, which contains aspartate, and give an extra boost to the calming neurotransmitters with foods and supplements that provide the building blocks for their production.

How neurotransmitters work

Nerve cells release neurotransmitters through their axon terminal into a gap, known as the *synapse*, which is created between it and another nerve cell. Once the neurotransmitter is released by one nerve cell, it will only be picked up by another if receptors for that particular neurotransmitter are ready, waiting, and able to receive it.

There are take-backs with neurotransmitters. If the receiving cell doesn't absorb the neurotransmitter when it's released, it can be reabsorbed into the originating cell.

There are several steps that facilitate having neurotransmitters available when you need them and impact your ability to use them:

1. **Creation:** Most neurotransmitters need to be created using elements like amino acids from proteins, along with enzymes, vitamins, and minerals.

2. **Release:** The neurotransmitters are passed out the end of a nerve cell into the synapse and hang out near the nerve cells, sort of waiting to be picked up.

3. **Reception:** The receiving nerve cell has to have a receptor for that neurotransmitter in order for the transfer to take place.

4. **Reuptake:** Neurotransmitters that are hanging out in the synapse between nerve cells can be taken back into the original nerve if the receiving nerve doesn't accept it.

Neurotransmitter Movement Between Nerve Cells

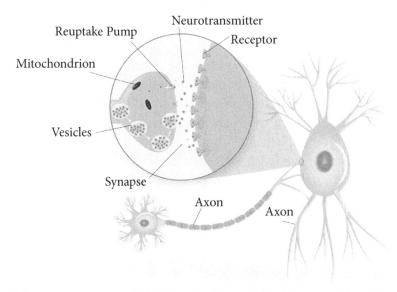

Pharmaceutical drugs for depression and anxiety typically target the reception and reuptake steps of the neurotransmitter system:

- Benzodiazepines such as Valium and Xanax are used to stimulate receptors for the calming neurotransmitter GABA, and

- SSRIs such as Prozac, Zoloft, Celexa, and Lexapro are Selective Serotonin Reuptake Inhibitors that potentially prolong serotonin's ability to hang out in the synapses and be picked up by receptors.

Natural remedies can maximize nerve cell health including optimizing receptor and reuptake function and ensuring that the elements you need to produce and use neurotransmitters are available in your body and brain.

The blood-brain barrier

When it comes to getting the building blocks for neurotransmitters into your brain, you have to contend with the blood-brain barrier (BBB). The BBB acts as a gatekeeper. It is on guard to only let certain molecules in and control the amounts of substances coming and going.

It has been widely believed that the calming neurotransmitters GABA, serotonin, and dopamine cannot cross into your brain from your bloodstream because of the BBB. The predominant school of thought has been that there can be no benefit from foods or supplements containing these neurotransmitters because they can't get into your brain to do their thing. But there are some medical professionals and researchers that are questioning whether (a) it is true that they can't get past the BBB and (b) whether it is the only route to effectiveness.[1] I'll leave it at that for now; we'll be talking much more about the blood-brain barrier and natural anxiety relief throughout the book.

Relaxing Your Mind and Body

Relaxation is central to dealing with anxiety. It's the opposite of what you feel when you're anxious, and it's what you crave. You want to be able to relax away the tension in your mind and your body, but it isn't as simple as wishing and making it so.

Anxious tension can make it difficult to feel relaxed, and it can interfere with sleep. Getting physically tense can also up your anxiety as you stress out over being tense. You can get anxious about the possibility of getting tense, anxious about whether you'll be able to sleep, anxious about being anxious.

> You can get anxiety about getting anxiety.

Getting help to relax involves a potential crossover between psychological therapy and physical approaches that assist your mind and muscles to wind down and release tension.

Teaching relaxation skills and using hypnosis to quiet the mind are a couple of ways that I work with clients to relieve stressed-out tension and anxiety. (Relaxation information and tools, such as anti-anxiety hypnosis, that I developed over years of helping people one-on-one are available at annsilvers.com.)

Our discussion of natural remedies for relaxation will include both what hinders relaxation and what helps. Some foods, like those containing caffeine, have a tendency to make it difficult to relax your body and mind. Some foods and supplements, such as those containing magnesium, feed your calm by relieving muscle tension, assisting you to relax during the day, and helping you get a better night's sleep.

6

What's Gut Got to Do with It?

Ever have a *gut feeling* about something? Ever have *butterflies in your stomach*? Even worse, do you experience compounding stress as you worry about how your anxious gut is going to behave in public?

Emotions impact your gut, sometimes in very negative ways. Stress and anxiety can cause occasional upset stomach or diarrhea. They can also cause gastrointestinal symptoms that are ongoing, painful, lifestyle-challenging, and embarrassing. Your digestive system has so many nerve cells (several hundred billion) that it is sometimes called the *second brain*. The nerves around your gut have a direct connection to your brain and other organs via the vagus nerve. (What happens in Vagus does *not* stay in Vagus. Oh—different Vegas.)

Stress is recognized as a potential contributing factor to many annoying, and even debilitating, gastrointestinal tract conditions, such as:[1]

- food sensitivities,
- acid reflux (GERD),
- peptic ulcers,
- Inflammatory Bowel Diseases (IBD) such as Crohn's and ulcerative colitis, and
- Irritable Bowel Syndrome (IBS), which can have a wide range of intestinal symptoms including gas, diarrhea, and constipation.

Your gut is the place where your food gets broken down and converted into useable parts that it passes on to the rest of your body to make everything work. When your gut is disturbed and inflamed, it may not be able to do its job. The result is that you may be eating nutrients but not absorbing or processing them well, so they are literally just passing on through.

When we're looking at foods and supplements to help reduce anxiety, we also want to help heal the impact of anxiety by trying to help heal your gut.

Is your gut leaky?

Your intestines are surrounded by a cell structure known as the *intestinal wall*. The intestinal wall decides which components of the foods you eat make their way into your body's systems. There is recent concern about a condition known as *leaky gut* in which the intestinal wall is compromised. Leaky gut happens when your intestinal wall is damaged to the point where it can't do its protector job and harmful stuff that is supposed to be kept out is leaking into your body. Some of the stuff that gets through a leaking gut can contribute to inflammation and anxiety.

Stress has been shown to increase the permeability of the intestinal wall. In other words, it increases the likelihood that you have a leaky gut.[2]

So—stress can cause leaky gut and leaky gut can cause stress. It's another vicious cycle, but the good news is that there are foods and supplements that can intercede and interfere with the cycle.

Your gut-brain axis

There is a lot of talk lately about the *gut-brain axis*.[3] This refers to what appears to be two-way communication between your brain and gut:

1. your brain impacts your gut, and
2. your gut impacts your brain.

As I mentioned earlier, stress and anxiety can affect your gut. It also turns out that what's in your gut can affect your response to stress and your level of anxiety. Many recent studies indicate that the specific bacteria in your intestines affect mental processes including memory, mood, coping, and perception of pain.[4]

Stress and anxiety affect your gut

and

your gut
affects your level of anxiety
in response to stress.

The bacteria in your gut create huge amounts of serotonin and GABA, but it is unknown how these might impact mood because it is unlikely that they can get past the blood-brain barrier. (GABA may cross the BBB in relatively small amounts.) It is possible that these neurotransmitters don't need to get into your brain to have a relaxing effect. There is mounting evidence that the bacteria in your intestinal tract (known as your *microbiome*) "communicate" with your brain through the vagus nerve that connects your brain and gut, and also by altering your immune system, endocrine system (e.g., the adrenal gland), and neurotransmitter-related chemicals.[5]

Both the condition of your gut and its contents are factors in your mental health, including your ability to deal with stress and your level of anxiety. We'll be talking more about specific mood-improving probiotics as well as foods that support gut health and the growth of helpful intestinal bacteria.

The Glucose Balancing Act

An even-keeled glucose (blood sugar) level helps you feel even keeled.

Glucose is your body's main source of fuel. And your brain uses lots of it. David Kennedy of the Brain, Performance and Nutrition Research Centre, Northumbria University, UK describes your brain's voracious need for glucose this way: "The brain is by far the most metabolically active organ in the body, representing only 2% of body weight but accounting for over 20% of the body's total energy expenditure."[1]

Talking about glucose takes us back to where we started: your adrenal glands. The adrenal glands are intimately involved in your use of glucose under stress.

High stress stimulates the release of the adrenal hormones adrenaline and cortisol so that, among other things, they can in turn stimulate a surge of glucose by drawing it out of storage. Under healthy stress-reaction conditions, that surge of adrenal hormones and glucose is helpful. You then use other nutrients like B vitamins and magnesium along with the glucose in your brain and muscles to flee or fight.

Your body is a system of checks and balances. In a healthy system, the sugar spike created by adrenaline and cortisol is checked and balanced by insulin. The adrenal hormones increase your blood glucose level, and insulin decreases it by moving that glucose into cells where you can use it or store it.

Chronic stress can potentially create a stormy-waters glucose sequence of high crests followed by plummeting dives. The glucose crests can produce physical jittery amped-up anxiety symptoms and the dives can result in

> Chronic stress can create sugar crests and dives.

an exhausted energy crash. Those crashes could draw you to sugar or stimulants to try and pull out of the dive. An unnerving pattern of cresting and diving ensues.

The pattern can also have another starting point: low blood sugar can cause your body to secrete adrenaline in an attempt to normalize your glucose level. The adrenaline impacts not only your glucose but other physical reactions that feel like anxiety.[2] Then, you can get anxious that you are feeling anxious.

When you're thinking about foods and supplements for managing stress, you want to consider what will help keep your blood sugar at an even keel, including:

- supplying nutrients so you can use glucose, and

- reducing foods that may create sugar surges and eating habits that result in major sugar dips, while

- ensuring intake of longer-term energy source foods, such as proteins, at regular intervals throughout your waking hours.

Insulin resistance

As I mentioned, you need insulin to be able to use glucose. Insulin is secreted from your pancreas into your bloodstream so that it can connect with glucose and guide it into your body's cells where it participates in chemical reactions. That system doesn't work if you have a condition known as *insulin resistance.*

You may have come across this term connected to its reputation as a factor in people holding extra weight, especially around the abdomen. Insulin resistance is basically a dysfunctional relationship between glucose and insulin. With insulin resistance, you can have lots of glucose and lots of insulin but there is a disconnect and neither can do its job.

Insulin resistance may be both a cause and an effect of anxiety:

> **Insulin resistance** is a dysfunctional relationship between glucose and insulin that can be both a cause and effect of anxiety.

- Chronic stress that leads to chronically high cortisol can contribute to insulin resistance.[3]

- Insulin resistance may contribute to anxiety by negatively impacting both the general use of energy in your brain and also the specific function of neurotransmitters such as dopamine.[4]

Stabilizing your blood glucose and mitigating insulin resistance are things we'll take into consideration as we get into detailing food and supplement remedies for anxiety and stress management.

Your Body on Stress Cheat Sheet

There are six physical areas of interest central to anxiety relief. Here's a summary of the physical areas and the relationship of each to your ability to deal with stress.

	PHYSICAL AREA	RELATIONSHIP TO STRESS AND ANXIETY
1	Adrenal glands	Source of adrenaline and cortisol used in stress response
2	Nerves	Pathways for energy and chemical messages involved with stress response (need healthy fats; negatively impacted by oxidative stress and inflammation)
3	Neurotransmitters	Messengers triggering excitatory or inhibitory biochemical reactions to rev things up or calm things down (i.e., serotonin, GABA, glycine, glutamate, aspartate, adrenaline, noradrenaline, acetylcholine, dopamine)
4	Relaxation	Relaxing our mind and muscles helps relieve stress
5	Gut	What happens in your gut impacts your brain and vice versa
6	Glucose	A balanced blood sugar helps you feel less stressed

Now that you have some background on anxiety-related physical processes and natural remedy targets, we'll take a look at nutritional elements that help the goal areas.

Part Two

What Helps Your Calm

No one can listen to your body for you.
To grow and heal,
you have to take responsibility
for listening to it yourself.

– Jon Kabat-Zinn

Introduction to What Helps

Your body needs things from you so that it can function at its optimum. It needs nutrients for millions of reactions that keep you going and help you deal with stress. It needs proteins, minerals, vitamins, healthy fats, other supportive nutrients, and good-for-you gut bacteria.

Here are the ten elements we are looking for in foods and supplements that feed your calm and reduce anxiety by supporting your body's response to stress:

1. Magnesium
2. Zinc
3. B vitamins
4. Vitamin C
5. Vitamin D
6. Omega-3 fats
7. Amino acids
8. Probiotics
9. Adaptogens
10. Nervine herbs

RDAs and ULs

Throughout this and subsequent chapters, I'll be mentioning nutritional reference amounts with the abbreviations RDA and UL.

The *Recommended Dietary Allowance (RDA)* for nutrients is a guideline set by the Food and Nutrition Board of the National Academy of Sciences' Institute of Medicine in the US. The level is thought to meet the nutrient requirements for healthy people at a level that staves off chronic nutrition-related illness.

The Food and Nutrition Board has also established a *Tolerable Upper Intake Level (UL)* for some nutrients. The board cautions against negative health consequences if your total intake from food and supplements goes over this limit and suggests staying under the limit unless supervised by a doctor.

Doctors often recommend short-term nutrient doses that exceed the RDA and even UL values in order to raise unhealthy low levels up to normal or to compensate for an individual's increased requirements. I'll include common therapeutic dosage recommendations in Part Five when addressing specific supplements.

Notes for Bringing It All Together

As you read the chapters of Part Two, keep a lookout for mention of any symptoms or conditions that you experience. These may appear in the Encouraging Research or Bonuses sections of each chapter. Noting what elements are associated with your personal circumstances might help you focus in on the stress resilience foods and supplements mentioned in Parts Four and Five that have the potential to be most useful to you.

Also note if any deficiency causes mentioned for particular elements resonate as being present in your life.

You may want to note your insights on the pages set aside in Part Six: Bringing It All Together.

How Magnesium Helps

Magnesium is so important to your body's health and happiness that there is a group dedicated to studying the topic: the International Society for the Development of Research on Magnesium. Magnesium is a mineral required for hundreds of your body's chemical reactions, including reactions that get triggered when you are stressed and reactions that help you feel calm and relaxed. Current estimates are that magnesium is a cofactor for 600 enzymes in your body, and an activator for 200 more.[1]

The connection between magnesium and anxiety

> "Magnesium calms the nervous system and relaxes muscle tension, helping reduce anxiety and panic."
> —Dr. Carolyn Dean

Dr. Carolyn Dean, who is both a medical doctor (MD) and a naturopathic doctor (ND), is a leading expert on magnesium. Her book *The Magnesium Miracle* is a great reference for all things magnesium. Anxiety and panic are just a couple of the many challenges Dr. Dean is convinced can be helped by this mineral: "Magnesium calms the nervous system and relaxes muscle tension, helping reduce anxiety and panic."[2]

Magnesium is necessary for everything on the list of anti-anxiety target areas:[3]

- adrenal gland function,
- nerve health,
- creation and use of calming neurotransmitters (serotonin, dopamine, and GABA),
- muscle relaxation,
- restful rejuvenating sleep,
- gut health, and
- control of blood glucose levels.

Among magnesium's many functions in your body, it performs an assist role with biochemical reactions involving vitamin D and B vitamins.[4] These vitamins are other important players in your stress response that I'll be talking more about in upcoming chapters.

Stress creates a magnesium double bind:

- you need magnesium for biochemical reactions that help you cope with the stress, and

- stress uses up your magnesium, leaving you with less magnesium to deal with stress.

Getting enough useable magnesium into your body can boost your ability to cope with big and small stressors and reduce your anxiety. It's a key player in feeding your calm.

Causes of magnesium deficiencies

It is thought that most of our modern food supply has less magnesium to start with than it used to have because of agricultural practices that deplete the mineral constituents of the soil in which our food is grown and increased use of pesticides that bind with magnesium in the plants. Then, the typical American methods of processing foods further extract and destroy nutrients including magnesium. So, you may not be getting very much magnesium into your body. Then, what is taken in may get burned up or flushed out without it being able to participate in the chemical reactions needed to keep you healthily humming along.

There are many factors that can interfere with magnesium absorption into your body or drain it from your body:[5]

- stress
- alcohol (more than seven drinks per week)
- environmental toxins and heavy metals (pesticides, mercury, lead, cadmium...)
- some medications (diuretics, proton pump inhibitors, antacids, steroids, antibiotics, oral contraceptives...)
- too much calcium
- high-dose vitamin D supplementation
- excessive sweat
- low stomach acid
- pregnancy
- gut problems that lead to poor absorption of food nutrients
- high intake of caffeine
- fluoride
- foods with high oxalate or phytate content (I'll explain more about these food elements later)

Calcium-to-magnesium ratio

The ratio of calcium to magnesium in your body is very important. Magnesium is needed to successfully use calcium as it is meant to be used. But, if you have too much calcium relative to magnesium, your magnesium will get consumed dealing with calcium and not be available for the hundreds of other duties it is supposed to perform in your body.

According to Dr. Dean, the ideal calcium-to-magnesium ratio is around 1:1. In contrast, it seems that the typical American diet results in a calcium-to-magnesium ratio closer to 10:1.[6] Add to that the phase of nutrition advice we have been in that has way overemphasized supplementing with calcium, and the ratio becomes even worse.

Studies that looked at tens of thousands of people have associated taking calcium supplements—but not eating calcium-rich foods—with an increased risk for heart disease and stroke.[7] At the same time, other large studies are showing that high calcium supplementation has not improved bone health.[8] Even though calcium is a mineral that, like magnesium, can help you relax, it didn't make it onto my stress resilience nutrients list because of concerns about over-supplementation.

"There should be a **1:1 ratio of calcium to magnesium** not just in supplements but in combination with diet, water, and supplements. Also, I feel that we can get most of our calcium from food. Therefore, it's only magnesium we need to supplement. In some cases people have to take twice the amount of magnesium as calcium to undo damage from calcium buildup, drug intake, stress, and consequent inflammation in the body."[9]

—Dr. Carolyn Dean

Encouraging research

Magnesium research has two confounding problems that have the potential to make magnesium look less effective than it is in practice:

1. **Magnesium level test validity:**
   Testing serum levels of magnesium is the most common way to determine how much magnesium is in someone's body, but the test is not very sensitive. Your body keeps your serum magnesium level in a very narrow range, even when the levels in your cells may be too low for the magnesium to be doing its job. There are more reliable tests, but serum level is the most widely used. (More on this and alternative tests in the Appendix, but for now, I just bring it to your attention because it potentially impacts the validity of research.)[10]

2. **Different magnesium compounds:**
   Magnesium in supplements must be compounded with another element; it cannot be supplemented as just magnesium by itself. There are about a dozen different magnesium combinations commonly used for supplements. The different compounds have different absorption rates. The worst absorption rate is with the most commonly used and cheapest form: magnesium oxide. Tests done with magnesium oxide may show less of a positive result than real-life use of other compounds such as magnesium glycinate. (I'll explain the different compounds further in Part Five: Stress Resilience Supplements.)

That being said, let's look at some of the encouraging research results.

Here's a sampling of relevant **animal studies**:

- Multiple studies have demonstrated that magnesium deficiency increases anxiety-related behavior in mice and rats.[11]

- Danish researchers found that magnesium deficiency changed the bacteria in the guts of mice and increased their anxiety-like and depression-like behavior.[12]

- Polish researchers including Ewa Poleszak used depression and anxiety tests (the forced swim test and elevated plus-maze) to compare stressed mice supplemented with magnesium to those not supplemented. They concluded that magnesium induces both an antidepressant and anti-anxiety effect without the development of tolerance. (Not developing tolerance means that, unlike many pharmaceutical drugs, magnesium can keep working over the long term.)[13]

- In a separate study, Poleszak's group also found that magnesium boosted the effectiveness of the antidepressant drug imipramine.[14]

Some large studies have looked at dietary intake of magnesium and incidence of **depression**:

- Two thousand men included in a twenty-year study in Finland were assessed for magnesium intake from their food over a four-day period and depression rates. Lower magnesium intake was associated with increased risk for depression.[15]

- A similar project in the US, comparing the dietary intake of magnesium and depression rates in more than 8,000 participants in the National Health and Nutrition Examination Survey, found a correlation between low magnesium diets and depression.[16] The journal article publishing these results created a stir. A group from the Netherlands took exception to some of the conclusions drawn and wrote a letter to the editor.[17] The Americans bolstered the strength of their argument by writing their own letter to the editor addressing each of the concerns.[18]

There isn't much research into the use of magnesium as an **anti-anxiety** agent on people. A 2016 review of research for a presentation at the 14th International Magnesium Symposium only came up with a few relevant studies. Still, they concluded that "the efficacy of magnesium in the treatment of anxiety in the mildly anxious and those reporting premenstrual syndrome–related anxiety is suggestive of a beneficial effect of magnesium intake."[19]

While there isn't much human-subject research into the effectiveness of magnesium alone, the impact of using it in combination with other nutrients for stress protection has been studied. Many research projects have demonstrated a reduction in stress when people are given a **multivitamin/ mineral** containing B vitamins, vitamin C, calcium, zinc, and magnesium:

- "Supplementation led to improved ratings of stress, mental health and vigor and improved cognitive performance during intense mental processing" in one British study of 200 healthy men ages 30–55.[20]

- In another British study, a month of supplementation in young men resulted in "significant reductions in anxiety and perceived stress."[21]

- A South African study included as participants only men and women who had high stress scores at the beginning of the study. The 300 participants were divided into two groups: one received the supplement, the other a placebo. The supplemented group had a significant reduction in stress scores compared to the control group.[22]

- During a three-month Australian study, supplemented participants experienced a stronger reduction in perceived work stress compared to those given a placebo.[23]

Magnesium bonuses

Since magnesium is used by so many chemical reactions in your body, low magnesium levels are implicated in many diseases, illnesses, and physical challenges.

Magnesium can potentially help with many problems:[24]

- osteoporosis (you need magnesium to lay down calcium in bone and keep it there)
- gallstones, kidney stones, and tissue calcifications including benign breast lumps (low magnesium causes calcium to be swimming in your blood instead of being in your bones and that excess available calcium can land in your organs and body tissue)
- fatigue
- inflammation

- high blood pressure and heart problems including palpitations
- depression
- headaches and migraines
- muscle cramps, twitches, tics, restless leg syndrome, and TMJ
- fibromyalgia, neck and back pain
- PMS and painful periods
- menopausal symptoms including hot flashes
- weight gain, insulin resistance, and diabetes
- libido and fertility issues (male and female)
- acid reflux and intestinal problems
- arthritis and asthma
- detoxifying heavy metals and other toxic substances
- mental confusion, memory and learning problems, ADHD, Alzheimer's, and Parkinson's
- sensitivity to "loud" noises (what constitutes "loud" can be exaggerated with sound sensitivity)

Clearly, optimizing your magnesium levels has the potential to help in all sorts of ways.

Recommended amounts

Magnesium RDA in mg/day:

- Men 19–30 years old: 400, over 30: 420
- Women 19–30 years old: 310, over 30: 320

No UL has been established for magnesium.

Magnesium food sources

Simply having a lot of magnesium was not the only criterion I looked at in finding magnesium-rich foods to recommend for reducing anxiety. Some of the foods that commonly appear on lists of foods high in magnesium—including those often recommended for anxiety—have components that get in the way of your body utilizing the magnesium from the food or even exacerbate anxiety.

Chocolate doesn't make the recommended foods list because it's high in caffeine, which can make anxiety worse.

Caffeine content makes it necessary to expunge a food from the recommended list because caffeine can jack up your anxiety and interfere with sleep. Thus, alas, chocolate—which is high in magnesium but also high in caffeine and therefore the opposite of helpful for anxiety—got eliminated.

Legumes, nuts, seeds, whole grains, spinach, Swiss chard, and beet greens are all high-magnesium foods. However, they also have high levels of phytates or oxalates, both of which are classified as *antinutrients* that potentially combine with magnesium and prevent you from absorbing and utilizing it. They may also tax your body in anxiety-provoking ways. Sprouting beans and grains removes their antinutrients, so sprouted beans, lentils, rice, and quinoa are on my recommended foods below. Kale, collard, and arugula are greens that are low in oxalate, unlike spinach and the other greens mentioned above. I'll explain more about antinutrients in Chapter 30: Why Not Phytates and Oxalates?

Top magnesium foods for stress resilience

Note: Some of the ranges for the amount of magnesium per serving are pretty big because I found different numbers from different sources. I include them to give you a general idea of relative amounts.

	FOOD	Approx. mg (per serving)
1	Wild-caught salmon, herring, or sardines	40–100 (4 oz.)
2	Oysters or sea scallops	50 (6 of either)
3	Seaweed	40–100 (1/2 cup dried)
4	Kale, collard, or arugula	25–40 (1 cup)
5	Sprouted rice or quinoa	70–100 (1 cup)
6	Sprouted beans or lentils	75–120 (1 cup)
7	Yogurt	50 (1 cup)
8	Potato	50 (1 medium)
9	Summer squash (e.g., zucchini)	45 (1 cup)
10	Banana	30 (1 medium)

How Zinc Helps

Like magnesium, zinc is a mineral that is involved with hundreds of chemical reactions in your body. It helps your skin and hair, sight, taste and smell, immune system, bones, organs, reproductive systems, cell growth, and more.

The connection between zinc and anxiety

Zinc is crucially important to your brain. It helps new nerve cell creation in your brain even in adulthood and helps your existing brain cells be healthy and happy.[1] It also seems to act as a moderator of neurotransmitters that would rev you up and those that calm you down. For anxiety relief, you want the calm-you-down neurotransmitters to win that battle. You need optimal levels of zinc so that can happen.

Anxiety-related zinc functions include:

- nerve cell growth and health[2] and

- balancing receptor operation for the lift-you-up and calm-you-down neurotransmitters glutamate and GABA.[3]

The zinc-copper interaction

Much like the balancing act performed by magnesium and calcium, zinc and copper play together. Too much copper gets in the way of zinc being available to do its job, and too much zinc gets in the way of copper doing its job. Of direct concern for anxiety is how each of these minerals impacts your use of the calming neurotransmitter GABA. Zinc and copper appear to have the opposite effect on GABA receptors: zinc helps GABA receptors and copper inhibits them.[4]

Typical sources of too much copper in the body are water that flows through copper pipes and multimineral/vitamin supplements. Too much zinc interferes with copper doing what it's supposed to do, so you have to be careful if you use supplements with zinc. Aim to hit the optimal amount of zinc but don't go overboard.[5]

What gets in the way of having zinc when you need it

There are many conditions, circumstances, and lifestyle choices that can cause you to burn through zinc, interfere with your body absorbing it, or flush zinc out of your body, including:[6]

- stress,
- gut problems like food intolerances or Irritable Bowel Syndrome that make it difficult to absorb the zinc you eat,
- alcohol overuse,
- kidney disease,
- chronic inflammatory disease,
- diets high in phytate (unsprouted legumes, whole grains, nuts, seeds), and
- too much copper in your system.

Encouraging research

Animal studies have revealed multiple negative mental and emotional effects from a **zinc-deficient diet**, including impaired learning and memory, and increased stress response, depression-like behavior, aggression, and anxiety.[7]

Several **animal studies** have demonstrated improvement in anxiety-related behaviors after **supplementation** with zinc.[8] At least one such project with mice showed that the improvement in a group given zinc was similar to the improvement in a group given the anti-anxiety drug diazepam, while another group given both zinc and diazepam had the most improvement.[9]

Zinc and copper levels of fifty **General Anxiety Disorder (GAD) patients** recruited from a hospital in Bangladesh in 2013 were compared to those in fifty healthy volunteers. The anxiety group had lower zinc and higher copper levels than the control group.[10]

Similarly, an American study demonstrated the presence of both decreased zinc and increased copper in **people with anxiety.** This study added an extra step in that they treated the anxiety patients with zinc and vitamins (C, E, and B6) for eight weeks. After treatment, zinc levels went up, the copper-to-zinc ratio improved, and anxiety went down.[11]

Zinc bonuses

Zinc may also help with:[12]

- autism,
- Attention Deficit Hyperactivity Disorder (ADHD),
- depression,
- schizophrenia,
- epilepsy,
- postpartum depression,
- testosterone synthesis, and
- traumatic brain injury and stroke recovery.

Alzheimer's Disease (AD) is a unique paradoxical situation in that "both increased and decreased zinc concentrations in the brain have been linked to AD."[13] Recent discoveries have pointed toward the potential that zinc supplementation may help Alzheimer's patients.[14]

Recommended amounts

Zinc RDA in mg/day:

- Men: 11
- Women: 8

Zinc UL in mg/day:

- Men and women: 40

To put the UL in perspective: six oysters can potentially put you over this limit. Oysters are considered by many to be a great anti-anxiety food, but it may be wise to not overdo eating them or you'll get into "too much of a good thing" territory.

Zinc food sources

Oysters are by far the most zinc-rich food, with 30–50 mg in a serving of six oysters. The next richest source is beef, but it falls far behind oysters: 4–6 mg per 3-ounce serving.

Top zinc foods for stress resilience

	FOOD	Approx. mg (per serving)
1	Oysters	30–50 (6 oysters)
2	Pasture-raised beef	4–6 (3 ounces)
3	Sea scallops or crab	5 (3 ounces)
4	Free-range turkey/chicken, dark meat*	3 (3 ounces)
5	Pasture-raised pork or lamb	2–4 (3 ounces)
6	Sprouted beans or lentils	2–3 (1 cup)
7	Yogurt	2 (1 cup)
8	Sprouted rice or quinoa	1–2 (1 cup)

*The light meat of turkey and chicken has much less zinc than the dark meat.

12 How B Vitamins Help

There are eight B vitamins, all of which are *cofactors* in your body's chemical reactions: they need to be present in order for certain reactions to happen. They are particularly important to your brain cells, adrenal glands, and nerves.

The connection between B vitamins and anxiety

B vitamins help you process omega fats to create your brain's nerve cell myelin sheath as well as the glucose needed to keep your brain running. They are also needed for the chemical reactions that create calming neurotransmitters.

> The B vitamins represent a group of eight essential dietary micronutrients that work closely in concert at a cellular level and which are absolutely essential for every aspect of brain function.[1]

B vitamins also assist your adrenal glands to deal with stress and relieve adrenal fatigue.

The B vitamins are involved in many anxiety-related biochemical reactions:[2]

- B1, Thiamine (serotonin, GABA, and glucose synthesis)
- B2, Riboflavin (helps other B vitamins)
- B3, Niacin (omega fat synthesis: nerve health; supports adrenals)
- B5, Pantothenic acid (supports adrenals; glucose and omega fat synthesis)
- B6, Pyridoxine (synthesis of serotonin, dopamine, GABA; supports adrenals)
- B7, Biotin (omega fat synthesis: nerve health; glucose)
- B9, Folate (synthesis of serotonin, dopamine; omega fat synthesis: nerve health)
- B12, Cobalamin (synthesis of serotonin, dopamine, and omega fat synthesis; B9 metabolism)

There are **gaps in the numbers for B vitamins** (there is no 4, 8, 10, or 11) because scientists have changed their minds about what should be included in this category. Some nutrients that were previously designated as B vitamins have lost that designation. For example: Inositol was called B8 but is no longer considered a B vitamin.

Folate is the natural active form of vitamin B9. **Folic acid** is a synthetic form of B9 often found in supplements and food additives, but it is not found in food naturally. (More on this in Part Five: Stress Resilience Supplements.)

B vitamins are **water soluble.** That means that you have to keep putting them into your body because you don't retain what you don't use.[3]

Alcohol abuse depletes B vitamins.

When taken as a supplement, it is most common to take **B-complex**, which includes a mix of all the Bs. "All the B vitamins work together in concert with each individual B vitamin while it does its 'job.'"[4]

Encouraging research

B vitamins have long been seen as the anti-stress vitamins, but much of the recent research has been done on vitamin B6 alone or high-dose B-complex combined with lower doses of other vitamins and minerals.

A **2013 review** of previous studies found that supplements containing high doses of B vitamins reduced levels of perceived stress and anxiety.[5]

Swedes with celiac disease who had been eating gluten free for at least eight years were given a B-complex supplement for six months. "Those with reduced psychological well-being at entry showed a significant improvement in psychological well-being, notably with Anxiety and Depressed mood and scored normal at six months."[6]

Blood tests performed on patients who presented at Japanese emergency rooms with **panic** attacks found that they had low levels of vitamin B6 compared to a control group.[7]

In an animal test, biochemical stress reactions in **milkfish** that were exposed to a stress-inducing condition returned to their pre-stress levels after they were given vitamin B6.[8]

Many research projects have demonstrated a reduction in stress when people are given a **multivitamin/mineral** containing vitamin C, calcium, magnesium, zinc, and high-dose B vitamins.[9] I detailed these projects and their results in the Encouraging Research section of Chapter 10: How Magnesium Helps.

Several studies have shown a B6 positive effect on psychological and physical **Premenstrual Syndrome (PMS)** symptoms.[10] In one such study, vitamin B6 supplementation over two months reduced PMS anxiety in patients referred to medical clinics, while a placebo had no effect.[11]

Vitamin B bonuses

B vitamins may help mood-enhancing pharmaceutical medications work better. Folate (B9) is often low in people with depression and supplementing with folic acid has been shown to improve outcomes when used in conjunction with the antidepressant fluoxetine.[12] Similar to those test results on human subjects, but somewhat contrary, mice given B6 along with clomipramine, fluoxetine, or venlafaxine medications had better outcomes for obsessive-compulsive behaviors and depression with the combination of B6 and either clomipramine or venlafaxine (but not with fluoxetine) compared to the medications alone.[13]

On another front, recent studies are showing positive brain cell protection for the elderly and reduced dementia when both omega-3 fats and B vitamins are supplemented together.[14]

Recommended amounts

A UL has been established for some, though not all, of the B vitamins. Amounts on the table below, are listed in mg (milligrams) or µg (micrograms) per day. ND = Not Determined

VITAMIN	RDA Men	RDA Women	UL Men & Women
B1, Thiamine	1.2 mg	1.1 mg	ND
B2, Riboflavin	1.3 mg	1.1 mg	ND
B3, Niacin	16 mg	14 mg	35 mg
B5, Pantothenic acid	5 mg	5 mg	ND
B6, Pyridoxine	1.3 mg (>50 yrs old: 1.7 mg)	1.3 mg (>50 yrs old: 1.5 mg)	100 mg
B7, Biotin	30 µg	30 µg	ND
B9, Folate	400 µg	400 µg	1000 µg*
B12, Cobalamin	2.4 µg	2.4 µg	ND

*The UL listed for folate is only for the synthetic alternative, folic acid, which is found in many supplements.[15]

B vitamin food sources

Meats are common sources of the full spectrum of B vitamins. Organ meats, like liver, are particularly rich in a wide range of Bs. Many vegetables are high in the B vitamins with the exception of B12. Vegetarians have to be especially attentive to getting enough vitamin B12 because it is often absent in their diets. VeganHealth.org has a great article about possible vegetable sources of vitamin B12 (veganhealth.org/b12/plant). The article says that most vegetable sources, such as tempeh, which have been thought to contain useable B12, don't demonstrate that in research.

Sprouted (aka germinated) beans and rice made it onto my B vitamins foods list even though they don't have B12 because they are good sources of the other B vitamins. Sprouting greatly increases their B values.[16]

Top B vitamin foods for stress resilience

	FOOD	NOTES
1	Pasture-raised beef liver (or liver from other pasture-raised animals)	Highest B vitamin levels
2	Pasture-raised beef, pork, lamb	
3	Wild-caught salmon, sardines or herring	
4	Sea scallops, crab, or oysters	
5	Free-range turkey or chicken, dark meat	
6	Pasture-raised eggs	
7	Yogurt	
8	Asparagus	Absent B12
9	Cruciferous vegetables (broccoli, cauliflower, cabbage . . .)	Absent B12
10	Sprouted beans and lentils	Absent B12
11	Sprouted rice or quinoa	Absent B12

How Vitamin C Helps

Two places in your body that are crucial to how you deal with stress and whether it becomes anxiety are your brain and your adrenal glands. They are also two of the places in your body with the highest concentration of vitamin C.

Vitamin C and your brain

Vitamin C (aka ascorbic acid, ascorbate) is an antioxidant. As I explained earlier when talking about nerve cells and your brain, antioxidants are your body's clean-up team. They swoop in and clean up junk molecules from harmful chemicals you breathe in, absorb, or eat, and also the biochemical remnants that are left over from normal metabolism. Since your brain has so much activity (remember it uses 20% of your body's energy because it is so busy), it creates a lot of leftovers that vitamin C can help clean up. Vitamin C reduces oxidative stress and helps keep the nerve cells in your brain functioning at their optimum.[1]

Vitamin C and your adrenal glands

We know that vitamin C is important for adrenal support because we know that the adrenal gland has relatively high concentrations of the vitamin.[2]

Vitamin C appears to be involved with:[3]

- the production of the stress hormone noradrenaline,

- cleaning up the metabolic remnants generated as the adrenal gland works to create stress-response hormones, and

- the stress hormone cortisol in some ways not yet clearly understood.

As for vitamin C and cortisol, their relationship status may best be described as "it's complicated."

All over the internet, vitamin C is touted as lowering cortisol. This is backed up by oldish animal studies such as a 1987 study using guinea pigs[4] and recent small, but repeatedly consistent, physical exertion studies using cyclists and runners.[5] On the other hand, a study testing the idea that vitamin C could *boost* cortisol production otherwise suppressed by anesthetic demonstrated that it *did* successfully increase cortisol in that condition.[6]

An interesting study in Germany in 2002 puts another twist on the connection between vitamin C and cortisol.[7] The German researchers subjected 120 healthy young adults to one of the most common stress-inducing situations—public speaking—so they could test how vitamin C impacted blood pressure, cortisol, and stress levels. Half were given vitamin C (3 x 1000 mg/day) for two weeks and half a placebo, then they were brought in for the Trier Social Stress Test (TSST).

The TSST starts by informing study participants that they have to give a five-minute speech to a panel on their suitability for a job in their field and then perform a challenging mental math task. They each prepare in isolation for their turn. When they enter the speech room, there is a microphone and video camera set up so that they have the extra pressure of being recorded. They are tested throughout the process and after to see how they are reacting physically and emotionally.

In the German TSST-based study, the vitamin C group had lower blood pressure and lower emotional stress scores compared to the placebo group. The two groups' cortisol levels were similar except that the vitamin C group had faster cortisol level recovery. In other words, their cortisol levels were the same with or without the supplementation, but the supplemented group's cortisol returned to normal faster than the non-C group. Cortisol returning to normal after stress is potentially a big plus for reducing anxiety.

Vitamin C appears to have a moderating effect on cortisol, but more details about exactly how they play together are yet to be discovered.

> Vitamin C appears to normalize cortisol, sometimes decreasing it for the good, sometimes increasing it for the good.

Encouraging research

Many **studies on animals** show decreased stress responses when vitamin C was given, for example:

- Mice supplemented with vitamin C prior to, and during, long-term exposure to noise were less stressed than non-supplemented mice.[8]

- Zebrafish pretreated with vitamin C before exposure to mercury were protected from the anxiety reaction seen in unsupplemented comparison fish.[9]

- Tests for the impact of differing levels of vitamin C supplementation showed that the vitamin decreased anxiety-related behaviors in standardized stress level tests and that the improvement maxed out at relatively low levels of supplementation.[10]

In another animal study, vitamin C reduced depression-like behavior in mice and also **improved the antidepressant effect of pharmaceuticals** fluoxetine, imipramine, and bupropion.[11]

Diabetic patients given 1000 mg/day of vitamin C showed better improvement in anxiety compared to groups given vitamin E or placebo.[12]

People hospitalized for a week for a variety of conditions had improved mood and less psychological distress when given vitamin C (500 mg twice a day).[13]

And, forty **high school students** given a modest dose of vitamin C (500 mg/day) for two weeks experienced a reduction in anxiety scores compared to a placebo group.[14] (An interesting aside: this article referenced a number of other studies showing how anxiety negatively impacts students' ability to retain information and their grades.)

Vitamin C bonuses

Vitamin C may help protect your brain from toxic assault (animals given vitamin C for three weeks prior to lead exposure were more resistant to cognitive loss)[15] and cognitive decline from aging.[16]

If you are a smoker, you may particularly benefit from upping your vitamin C. Smokers tested for levels of several nutrients were found to be relatively low in vitamin C. Their levels were brought up to normal after supplementation for three months.[17]

Vitamin C has the potential of improving your skin, waistline, and sex life:

- Vitamin C is required by collagen to do its thing to make your skin elastic and healthy.[18]

- A 2014 review of research found that increases in levels of vitamin C are associated with weight loss and fat-burning potential.[19]

- And, on the most-fun list of test results, a German study by Stuart Brody showed that vitamin C intake increased the number of times people had sex. Young healthy adults given 3000 mg of sustained-release vitamin C per day for two weeks, and a control group given placebos, tracked the number of times they had sex. The supplemented group had more intercourse (but not more of other forms of sexual activity). The increase was most profound for women. Brody anticipated this result because of vitamin C's reputation for increasing the love hormone oxytocin.[20]

Recommended amounts

Vitamin C stands out in that there are different RDA numbers for smokers compared to non-smokers.

RDA for vitamin C in mg/day:

- Men, non-smokers: 90, smokers: 125
- Women, non-smokers: 75, smokers: 110

UL for vitamin C in mg/day:

- Men and women: 2000

Vitamin C food sources

We're all pretty familiar with oranges and other citrus fruits, like grapefruit, being a good source of vitamin C. You may be more surprised by some of the vegetable sources for this vitamin.

Top vitamin C foods for stress resilience

	FOOD	Approx. mg (per serving)
1	Papaya	200 (1/2 of large fruit)
2	Cruciferous vegetables (broccoli, cauliflower . . .)	180 (1 cup raw) 100 (1 cup cooked)
3	Pineapple	100 (1 cup)
4	Sweet red pepper	100 (1/2 cup raw)
5	Kale	80 (1 cup raw) 50 (1 cup cooked)
6	Orange	70 (1 fruit)
7	Kiwi	60 (1 fruit)
8	Sweet green pepper	60 (1/2 cup raw)
9	Potato	40 (medium, baked)

How Vitamin D Helps

14

Vitamin D is the sunshine vitamin. It is a powerful antioxidant and anti-inflammatory nutrient. The main source of the vitamin is from direct exposure to UVB sun rays. There are only a few food sources, such as fatty fish.

The connection between vitamin D and anxiety

I have seen people have a 180-degree change from anxiety to calm when they raised their vitamin D up from unhealthy low levels.

Vitamin D is involved in many anxiety-related physical functions, including:[1]

- production of the calming neurotransmitter serotonin,
- use of GABA,
- movement of neurotransmitters, and
- optimum health of nerve cells.

Getting vitamin D from the sun

Your skin converts the sun's rays into vitamin D. Getting your vitamin D from the sun requires long enough exposure to bare skin. That's particularly challenging in cloudy climates like Seattle, WA where I live.

Tips for getting your vitamin D from the sun:

- The square footage of skin exposed determines the amount of vitamin produced.

- You have to be outdoors. The UVB rays don't make it through glass.

- The rays don't pass through clothes either. Your skin has to be bare.

How Vitamin D Helps   71

- Sunscreen can get in the way too. You may want to allow some exposure before putting on the sunscreen. (I'm not saying dump sunscreen entirely.)

- The UVB rays are strongest around 10 am to 2 pm.

- There is an optimal length of exposure for each person. That time is influenced by skin color. A fair-skinned person may only need 10 to 20 minutes. People with darker skin tones (because of a tan or genetics) require longer exposure times. After the optimum time is reached, your body stops producing the vitamin.

> **To Boost Vitamin D** get outside, especially midday, with your skin exposed without sunscreen, and wait a while before showering.

- How many UVB rays make their way to your body is influenced by where you are on the planet relative to the equator, how cloudy it is, and the level of air pollution.

- You can use the dminder app, created by an authority on vitamin D, Dr. Michael Holick, to help you track the potential for vitamin D exposure at different times of day wherever you are.

- The vitamin needs some time after production to pass into your bloodstream. If you shower (especially if you use soap) too soon after being in the sun, you may wash off your potential for vitamin D.

Encouraging research

More research has been done about vitamin D's connection to depression than anxiety, but the results may be relevant to many who are dealing with anxiety because people often have both together.

This is just a small sample of vitamin D **depression** research:

- Examination of data collected on 8,000 US residents between the ages of 15 and 39 showed that people with low vitamin D were much more likely to have depression than people with higher levels of the vitamin.[2]

- A couple thousand people in the Netherlands divided into three groups (current diagnosis of depression, past diagnosis of depression, and non-depression) were compared for vitamin D levels. The comparisons were controlled for lifestyle—including sunlight exposure—to eliminate confounding factors. Low vitamin D levels were associated with both the presence of depression and the severity of symptoms.[3]

- 600 young adults in New Zealand from the general population were tested for depression symptoms and vitamin D levels. Results—adjusted for time spent outdoors, etc.—showed that those whose vitamin D fell in the lowest quarter of the values had more depression symptoms than those whose values fell in the highest quarter of the values.[4]

- Many studies show that vitamin D supplementation may help alleviate depression. In his 2014 examination of previous studies regarding vitamin D and depression, Simon Spelding concluded that vitamin D had a similar effect to antidepressant medication.[5]

Data collected on 7,500 British people who were followed for fifty years found a strong correlation between low vitamin D and both **depression and panic**.[6]

A study by the Institute of Endocrinology and National Institute of Mental Health in the Czech Republic compared vitamin D levels in three groups: forty men and women with depression, forty with an anxiety disorder, and healthy matches. Those with **depression** and those with **anxiety** had similarly low vitamin D levels when compared to the healthy control subjects.[7]

Low vitamin D levels corresponded with both **depression and anxiety** in seventy-five **fibromyalgia** patients.[8]

When 200 stroke patients were followed for a month, low vitamin D levels were associated with the development of **post-stroke anxiety**.[9]

Studies with **rodents** have shown an increase in anxiety behaviors when the vitamin D receptor gene is absent,[10] and reduced anxiety-related behaviors with vitamin D supplementation.[11]

Vitamin D bonuses

Vitamin D is fundamentally involved in your use of calcium, so it helps every part of your body that needs calcium (including your bones).

Low levels of vitamin D appear to be common in people with a variety of emotional and mental challenges including Alzheimer's,[12] schizophrenia,[13] and ADHD.[14]

Vitamin D deficiency in pregnant moms and children may be a contributing factor for autism and the vitamin may help improve autism-related behaviors.[15]

Recommended amounts

Recommended Dietary Allowances for vitamin D are given in two ways.

Vitamin D RDA in IU (International Units)/day:

- Men and women under 70 years old: 600
- Men and women over 70 years old: 800

Vitamin D RDA in µg (micrograms)/day:

- Men and women under 70 years old: 15
- Men and women over 70 years old: 20

A Tolerable Upper Intake Level (UL) has been established for vitamin D. This upper limit only pertains to supplements because your body won't over-make vitamin D from the sun. The US Food and Nutrition Board suggests staying under the limit unless supervised by a doctor. (Doctors will often prescribe supplement levels that go way over this limit for a short period of time if your blood tests show a low result for vitamin D.)

UL for vitamin D:

- Men and women: 4000 IU/day or 100 µg/day

Vitamin D is fat soluble.
You store it in your fat cells. Your body won't make more than it needs from the sun, but if you take in excess with supplements, it will be stored in your body and can drive levels up to harmful amounts (unlike water soluble vitamins that are simply flushed out if you take too much). Because of this, you need to be careful not to overdo vitamin D supplementation.

Vitamin D food sources

The best source of vitamin D is sunlight. There are a few food sources, but even those get a little tricky because animal sources give you D_3 while plant sources, such as mushrooms, offer only D_2. Your body doesn't use D_2 itself. It must convert it to D_3 before plugging it into your body's vitamin D chemical reactions. (The D_2 to D_3 conversion is a questionable process which I'll get into more in a minute.) D_3 is found in the oil of fatty fish like wild-caught salmon, herring, or sardines, and in pasture-raised eggs.

Food sources of vitamin D

Animal sources = D_3
Plant sources = D_2

You may have noticed by now that when I mention salmon as a food source for nutrients I clarify that I'm talking about *wild-caught* salmon. I'll explain more about why in Part Four: Stress Resilience Foods, but a 2007 Boston University Medical Center study into the vitamin D levels of farm-raised and wild-caught salmon is a great example of research that delineates the nutritional differences. The study results showed that wild-caught salmon varied in D_3 content from between 500 IU and 1000 IU per 3.5 ounces, but farm-raised salmon had about 75% less than that: between 70 and 300 IU.[16] (This is just the tip of the iceberg of downsides with farm-raised fish.)

Like the vitamin D difference between farmed and wild salmon, eggs have different vitamin D levels depending on the way they are raised. The amount of D_3 in eggs varies with the amount of time the hens spend in daylight. A German study using three groups of hens, with thirty hens in each group, found that hens given at least some freedom to be outside created eggs with 3 to 4 times more D_3 than hens raised in the typical industrial farm method of being kept entirely indoors. More time outdoors resulted in more D_3.[17] The study determined that it wasn't the mere fact of hens being offered a door for potential outside access. Conditions, such as feeding location and size of roaming area, had to be correct to encourage the hens to spend time outside. In Part Four: Stress Resilience Foods, I'll explain egg jargon, including the difference between typical unlabeled eggs, cage-free, free-range, pasture-raised, and so on. Some of the terms had me fooled for quite a few years.

Now to the mushroom sources of vitamin D: two types of mushrooms, portabella and maitake, stand out as possible sources of D_2. The Beltsville Human Nutrition Research Center in Maryland studied the vitamin D content of mushrooms sampled from a variety of producers across the US. They included mushrooms that were and were not purposefully exposed to light to boost vitamin D.[18]

The Beltsville study demonstrated that mushroom sun exposure could increase vitamin D_2 from almost nothing without exposure to large numbers with exposure:

- **Portabella mushrooms**
    - not exposed to UV light: 2–30 IU vitamin D_2
    - exposed to UV light: 125–1000 IU vitamin D_2

- **Maitake mushrooms**
    - not exposed to UV light: about 4 IU vitamin D_2
    - exposed to UV light: about 2000 IU vitamin D_2

The study also showed that, in general, mushrooms not purposefully exposed to sun with the goal of boosting vitamin D have only small amounts to offer. Because commercially farmed mushrooms are typically grown indoors in the dark, most mushrooms you buy in the store will not be a good source of vitamin D. We also know that some mushrooms can become a good source of D_2 with light exposure. But that still leaves the issue of how well your body uses D_2 given that what it really needs is D_3.

The research on the usefulness of ingesting D_2 is complicated. Some research supports the idea that we can use D_2 to increase D_3 if we ingest it daily, but there is also evidence that it is not effective and even some evidence that supplementing with D_2 reduces D_3. (Notice that the concern is about supplementing with D_2, which isn't necessarily the same as eating foods with D_2.)[19]

Because the value of getting vitamin D from plant sources that can only offer it in the form of D_2 is doubtful, mushrooms didn't make it onto my food sources list. A few animal sources of D_3 are listed, but, for the most part, we need to get our vitamin D from the sun or supplements.

Top vitamin D foods for stress resilience

	FOOD	Approx. IU D_3 (per serving)
1	Wild-caught salmon	400 (3 ounces)
2	Sardines or herring	160 (3 ounces)
3	Pasture-raised eggs	140 (1 medium)[20]

How Omega-3 Fats Help

Your brain is 70% water. The remaining dry matter in your brain is 60% fat because your brain has a massive number of nerve cells and nerve cells are largely made up of fat. To make those cells in your brain work at their optimum and help you deal with stress, you don't want them to have just any fat. You want them to have the fats that make them work best: omega-3 fats.

The connection between omega-3 fats and anxiety

Omega-3 fats help you deal with stress and reduce anxiety in several ways, including helping:[1]

1. your nerve cells be healthy and happy,
2. increase the calming neurotransmitters serotonin and dopamine production and receptor function,
3. reduce inflammation and oxidative stress, and
4. possibly moderate cortisol levels.

The lowdown on fats

2 main types of polyunsaturated fats in your body: omega-3 and omega-6

3 main forms of omega-3 fats: Eicosapentaenoic Acid (EPA), Docosahexaenoic Acid (DHA), and Alpha-Linolenic Acid (ALA)

Omega-3s most needed by your body: EPA and DHA (ALA can be converted to EPA and DHA but not efficiently.)[2]

EPA is particularly anti-inflammatory and anti-oxidative.[3] DHA is particularly abundant in nerve cells.[4]

EPA and DHA come from animal sources (meat, fish, and eggs). ALA is more prevalent in plant sources such as seeds and nuts.

The ratio of omega-3 and omega-6 fats is important

How much omega-3 fat you have available when you need it is not just about taking in enough omega-3. It is also about not taking in too much omega-6. The two fats compete for attention in some reactions, but omega-3 gives a healthier result than omega-6 in many cases including in nerve cells.[5] You can think of omega-6 as creating dysfunctional rigid nerve cells that can't take in the neurotransmitters like they are supposed to.

The historic dietary ratio, seen by many as the ideal ratio, of omega-6 to omega-3 is between 1:1 and 2:1.[6]

Most people don't have to work at getting enough omega-6 fats. It's more likely that you get too much rather than too little. Estimates for the 6:3 ratio in the typical American diet fall around 15:1 (far from the desirable mark).[7]

Processed foods commonly contain high omega-6 oils like sunflower, corn, soybean, cottonseed, safflower, peanut, and canola oil. Hydrogenating or partially hydrogenating these oils adds insult to injury by turning them into trans fats. (Oil hydrogenation is a process created to increase the shelf life of oils. You may have heard about areas and even countries banning or limiting the use of trans fats in food because of their negative impact on health.)

Encouraging research

A 2011 American study tested levels of omega-3 fats in sixty people diagnosed with **Major Depression Disorder with or without co-occurring anxiety**, comparing them to a control group. The depression group had lower levels of EPA and DHA as well as higher ratios of 6:3 compared to the controls. Those who also had anxiety had the lowest levels of these omega-3 fats and the highest 6:3 ratios. And, the worse the numbers, the worse the anxiety.[8]

Similarly, researchers in Israel found relatively low levels of omega-3 fats in twenty-seven people with **social anxiety** compared to control subjects, and a significant relationship between lower levels and the severity of social anxiety.[9]

A couple of projects demonstrate that omega-3 fats appear to help people deal with **everyday stressors**:

- Thirty healthy Italians given 4 g of fish oil per day (EPA:DHA ratio 2:1) for thirty-five days were compared to control subjects using mood assessments, attention tests, and EEGs. Supplemented subjects showed a reduction in response time and a decrease in anger, anxiety, and depression.[10]

- Seventy American medical students randomly divided into an omega-3 supplement group (2000 mg/day EPA and 350 mg/day DHA) and a control group were followed for twelve weeks, including a period of high-stress exams. The omega group had less inflammation markers in blood tests and a 20% reduction in anxiety symptoms compared to the control group.[11]

Anger and anxiety levels were significantly and "robustly" reduced in eleven **substance abusers** supplemented with omega-3s for three months (2.25 g/day EPA, 500 mg DHA, and 250 mg other omega-3s) compared to eleven given a placebo.[12]

In 2016, an inpatient psychiatric facility published results of blood tests and omega-3 supplementation on patients with **mood and anxiety disorders**. They found that these patients had relatively low omega-3 levels on entry and significant symptom relief with supplementation.[13]

Spurred on by an established link between stress and urges to smoke, researchers gave twenty-four **smokers** omega-3 supplements (2710 mg/day EPA and 2040 mg/day DHA). Compared to twenty-four control subjects given a placebo, supplemented smokers craved cigarettes less and smoked less.[14]

A 2015 review of research concluded that: "accumulating evidence suggests a crucial role for membrane lipids [omega-3 fatty acids] in the pathogenesis of **depression and anxiety** disorders; these lipids could be exploited for improved prevention and treatment."[15]

Meta-analysis (analysis of research studies) projects in various parts of the world in the last several years have uncovered a reason why tests of omega-3's impact on **depression** have given mixed results. High-dose **EPA** appears to be the key. EPA shows a more consistent positive impact on depression than DHA.[16] Improvement in depressive symptoms has been seen in both mild and major depression with the use of mainly EPA in the EPA/DHA supplement mix.[17] EPA was also shown to improve depression reduction in people taking antidepressants.[18]

> **EPA** appears to be the most important omega-3 for mental health.

These meta-analysis projects are a great example of how new research builds on past research. A 2011 project concluded that an EPA content of 60% or greater in an EPA/DHA omega mix was important for a positive effect on depression.[19] Then, a 2016 project concluded that it was not the relative mix that determined the result, but rather a general emphasis on EPA over DHA.[20]

Omega-3 bonuses

Omega-3 fats may impact many mental health conditions, including:[21]

- ADD and ADHD,
- Depression (major and post-partum),
- Bipolar disorder,
- Schizophrenia, and
- Alzheimer's.

Besides helping your brain, optimizing omega-3 fat intake has been associated with reduced chronic illness, including:[22]

- decreased inflammation,
- boosted immune response, and
- reduced risk of heart disease.

Recommended amounts

Unlike minerals and vitamins, there is no Recommended Dietary Allowance for omegas. There is, however, a different recommendation value, *Adequate Intake (AI)*: "established when evidence is insufficient to develop an RDA; intake at this level is assumed to ensure nutritional adequacy."[23]

The AI for total omega-3s is:

- Men: 1600 mg/day
- Women: 1100 mg/day

I'll talk more about therapeutic levels specific to EPA and DHA in Chapter 50: Omega-3 Fats, EPA and DHA. For now, we can get a general idea of target levels from those used in the studies mentioned above in the Encouraging Research section (EPA: 2000 to 2700 mg/day; DHA: 350 to 2040 mg/day), and this American Psychiatric Association (APA) recommendation, which is quite a bit lower:

> The American Psychiatric Association has adopted the consensus recommendations of the American Heart Association for an EPA + DHA dose of 1 g/d [1000 mg/day] in patients with Major Depression Disorder.[24]

Omega-3 food sources

Our omega-3 anti-anxiety goals:[25]

lots of EPA

some DHA

omega-6:3 ratio no worse than approximately 2:1

Finding foods that are good sources of anti-anxiety omega-3s is a bit tricky. Most of the talk about foods rich in omega-3s clumps all the omega-3s together, but that can give a distorted picture.

If you only look at total omega-3 content of food, you're including ALA along with EPA and DHA. The idea that ALA can be converted to the other target omegas has long been the reason given for clumping them together, but there's a major problem with that thinking. While ALA omega-3 can be converted to EPA and DHA in your body, the conversion rate appears to be fairly low.

A report presented at the Fourth International Congress on Vegetarian Nutrition in 2002 describes it this way: "Conversion of ALA by the body to the more active longer-chain metabolites is inefficient: approximately 5–10% for EPA and 2–5% for DHA."[26] The report describes several factors that impact an individual's ability to turn ALA fats into EPA and DHA, including gender (women are better converters than men), amount of omega-6s consumed (high omega-6 interferes with conversion), and genetic presence of the enzymes required for conversion.

While nuts and seeds have some, or even lots, of ALA omega-3s and are therefore often touted as good sources of omega-3s, they are not on my recommended list for two reasons:

1. They don't have EPA or DHA.

2. Except for flaxseeds and chia seeds, they have a high to uber-high 6:3 ratio (walnuts 4:1, pecans 20:1, pumpkin seeds 100:1, sunflower seeds 300:1, almonds 2000:1).

Top omega-3 foods for stress resilience

FOOD 3 oz. serving	EPA (mg)	DHA (mg)	6:3 ratio
1 Wild-caught salmon*	860	620	1:12
2 Sardines	450	740	Depends on oil packed in
3 Oysters	750	430	1:25
4 Herring	1060	750	1:6
5 Crab	240	100	1:6
6 Sea scallops	60	90	1:10

*Farmed salmon often has higher EPA and DHA amounts than wild-caught salmon, but the farmed version has many other downsides including notoriously high quantities of toxins.[27] I'll get into more detail about farmed versus wild-caught fish in Chapter 32: Wild-Caught Salmon, Sardines, and Herring.

16   How Protein Amino Acids Help

When we think of amino acids, we usually think of those that are component parts of proteins. There are about 200 amino acids that are not part of proteins, but we'll start our discussion about amino acids' relationship to anxiety with the more familiar protein amino acids and talk about their non-protein cousins in the next chapter.

Proteins are the building blocks for your body, and amino acids are the building blocks for proteins. (You can think of amino acids as the beads on a protein necklace.) Proteins that you eat are broken down into individual amino acids. (You take the necklace apart.) Those amino acids are then used for biochemical reactions or put back together in amino acid sequences to make the particular proteins your body needs. (You repurpose the beads to make necklaces, bracelets, earrings, etc.)

Protein amino acids are divided into three categories: *essential, non-essential, and conditional.*

When *essential* is associated with a nutrient, it means that your body cannot produce it on its own. It has to be consumed. In other words, you must get it from your diet from food or supplements, or you don't have it available for the biochemical reactions that need it.

Non-essential means your body can make it from component parts you ingest.

You can also make *conditional* amino acids, but illness, stress, or some other less-than-optimal *conditions* can limit the amount you can create and you would benefit from eating more of the actual amino acid.

There are 21 protein amino acids:

- **The 9 essential amino acids are:** isoleucine, leucine, lysine, methionine, phenylalanine, threonine, tryptophan, valine, and one that is essential for children but not adults—histidine.

- **The 4 non-essential amino acids are:** alanine, asparagine, aspartate (aka aspartic acid), and glutamate (aka glutamic acid).

- **The 8 conditional amino acids are:** arginine, cysteine, glutamine, glycine, ornithine, proline, serine, and tyrosine.

To reduce anxiety, you need protein to give your body the raw material it needs to function by providing it with all the essential amino acids. You may also benefit from being attentive to which amino acids you are consuming in high or low proportions because they serve different functions in your body.

The connection between protein amino acids and anxiety

A large percentage of your body is made of amino acids. They are used to create and maintain cells, and they participate in biochemical reactions that keep you going. Of particular interest to our discussion about anxiety is the fact that protein amino acids are intimately involved with neurotransmitters.

Remember that neurotransmitters help you feel calm or revved up. They are inhibitory or excitatory. Some of the protein amino acids are actual neurotransmitters themselves, some are precursor component parts of neurotransmitters, and one is dual purpose: it is both an actual neurotransmitter and it is a precursor of a neurotransmitter.

Four protein amino acids' relationship to neurotransmitters:[1]

1. **Glycine** is an inhibitory neurotransmitter itself.

2. **Tryptophan**, famous for turkey dinner sleepiness, is a precursor for the calming neurotransmitter serotonin.

3. **Glutamate** is dual purpose: it is your body's major excitatory neurotransmitter as is and a precursor for your body's most common inhibitory neurotransmitter, GABA.

4. **Aspartate** is an excitatory neurotransmitter.

Neurotransmitter Production Sequences
(neurotransmitters are in bold)

- **Glycine**

- Tryptophan >>> 5-HTP >>> **Serotonin** >>> Melatonin

- **Glutamate** >>> **GABA**

- **Aspartate**

It may be helpful to maximize the intake of amino acids that provide calming neurotransmitters (glycine) or support their production (tryptophan), and reduce or monitor intake of those that are excitatory (glutamate and aspartate).

The artificial sweetener aspartame is of particular concern when dealing with anxiety. Aspartame is 50% phenylalanine, 40% aspartate, and 10% methanol. Aspartate is an excitatory neurotransmitter, and aspartame has been implicated in increasing anxiety.[2] (I'll talk more about this in Chapter 25: How Processed Foods Hurt.)

The rest of this chapter will focus on glycine and tryptophan as those are the main protein amino acids involved in calming neurotransmitter production. I'll talk about 5-HTP and GABA when we cover relevant non-protein amino acids in the next chapter.

Amino acid competition

One of the tricky parts of trying to get enough of the right protein amino acids into your brain so that you can optimize whether you are inhibiting or exciting your neurons is that they compete with each other to cross the blood-brain barrier (BBB). Your BBB acts like a bouncer deciding who gets into your brain and who is denied entry. Some elements are kept out entirely and some are prioritized.

Tryptophan is the amino acid starting point for the calming neurotransmitter serotonin, but it gets sent to the end of the amino acid brain entry line. If you are loaded with other amino acids, they will get through and tryptophan won't. In fact, a broadly accepted method for studying the effects of low serotonin is a technique called *Acute Tryptophan Depletion (ATD)*. ATD is achieved by feeding test subjects a drink that is high in a mix of protein amino acids but has no tryptophan. Within four to seven hours, tryptophan is typically reduced by 45–90% and serotonin levels go down drastically.[3]

Amino acid competition for passing the BBB is important to consider if you want to boost serotonin by taking tryptophan as a supplement or by eating foods that are high in tryptophan. Consuming the tryptophan without other amino acids, or in high amounts relative to other amino acids, may improve the amount of tryptophan that enters your brain.

Tryptophan controversy and concerns

Tryptophan in supplemental form was banned in the US and some other countries in 1990 because of an outbreak of a fatal disease, Eosinophilia-myalgia syndrome (EMS), in people who were taking the supplement. Though outbreak follow-up studies quickly discovered that the problem was contamination of product from a single source,[4] it took many years for the ban to be lifted completely. Now tryptophan is available again as a supplement in most countries including the US.[5]

A remaining concern is that tryptophan supplements may create an unhealthy doubling-down if combined with antidepressant, pain, or migraine pharmaceutical medications (especially SSRI or MAOI antidepressants like Celexa, Lexapro, Paxil, Prozac, Zoloft, Nardil, or Parnate) or other serotonin-increasing supplements like 5-HTP. (I'll talk more about 5-HTP in the next chapter.) Creating too much serotonin by combining tryptophan with these medications/supplements is theorized to possibly cause Serotonin Syndrome with symptoms of agitation, confusion, rapid heartrate, and blood pressure fluctuations.[6] Drugs.com has a more complete description of these potential interactions.[7]

> **Serotonin Syndrome** can be a negative side effect of taking tryptophan or 5-HTP while also taking some pharmaceuticals.

Encouraging research

Glycine's effect on sleep has been studied extensively by Japanese researchers. They found that glycine:

- passes through the blood-brain barrier,[8]

- decreases time to get to sleep, improves sleep quality, and decreases sleepiness the next day when 3 g is ingested an hour before bed,[9] and

- does not have negative side effects even at three times the dose that improved sleep.[10]

Tryptophan may also help with sleep. Dutch researcher Rob Markus tested the impact of a high-tryptophan evening meal on sleep. Healthy subjects with and without sleep complaints spent the night in a sleep lab after a meal including lactalbumin whey protein (6% tryptophan) or a control meal. The next morning, all the subjects that received the lactalbumin meal were less sleepy and did better on attention tests compared to control subjects.[11]

Markus also performed studies demonstrating **tryptophan's effect** on subjects' ability to deal with stress and cognitive performance, comparing reactions in people who are "high stress-vulnerable (HS)" to those that are "low stress-vulnerable (LS)." He found that people who have a tendency toward being more vulnerable to stress were helped by tryptophan:[12]

- His studies used a shake containing lactalbumin (6% tryptophan) from whey protein and solid foods as the test meal and a control meal with the same solid foods but a low-tryptophan protein powder in the shake. (The test meal had 12.3 g/kg tryptophan and the control had 9.51 g/kg, so this was not a tryptophan depletion situation.)

- All the subjects who received the lactalbumin shake had greatly increased blood level ratios of tryptophan compared to other amino acids when tested post-meal.

- HS subjects had significantly improved cognitive function on a memory test after tryptophan compared to those who received the control meal, but LS people did not have an effect from tryptophan.

- HS subjects exposed to a stress-inducing math test after receiving the tryptophan meal showed more coping ability compared to those that received the control meal, but LS people did not have an effect from tryptophan.

In a small Canadian study, seven subjects with **social anxiety** underwent two rounds of tests after ingesting food bars with (1) protein-sourced **tryptophan** along with carbohydrates and (2) only carbohydrates. The subjects started with either condition 1 or 2 and experienced the opposite condition a week later. An hour after eating the bar, they had to read a page of complex text while sitting in front of a video and believing that a panel of thirty people was going to score them for accuracy, speed, and quality of performance. (It wasn't really true: there was no tape in the video recorder.) Heart rate measures demonstrated that tryptophan plus carbohydrate significantly reduced the stress response to the reading test stressor compared to carbohydrate alone.[13]

On the tryptophan flip side, **tryptophan depletion** created by feeding subjects amino acid mixes with no tryptophan consistently:

- results in depression symptoms in people who have a tendency toward depression,[14] and

- increases anxiety and panic responses to standardized panic stimulators, like CO2 exposure, in people who have Panic Disorder or who have had the disorder in the past.[15]

Recommended amounts

The Recommended Dietary Allowance (RDA) for protein is calculated for individuals through an equation that takes into account weight, activity, age, and gender. The RDA for protein is considered to be a starting point for basic health.

On average, the protein RDA in g/day is:

- Men: 56
- Women: 46

Because tryptophan is considered an essential amino acid, it has an RDA value. The RDA for tryptophan is 5 mg/kg of body weight per day (1 kg = 2.2 pounds). The RDA translates into about 2.3 mg/pound. For a 140-pound person, that comes out to around 322 mg per day.

L and D forms of amino acids

If you've looked at taking amino acids as supplements you may have noticed that most have an L in front of the amino acid name (like L-tryptophan). Some amino acids occur in two forms that are mirror images of each other: L and D. Only the L forms can be used by your body's cells. Glycine is an exception. It just has one form.

Amino acid food sources

You need to be getting enough protein to supply the mix of amino acids required by your body. Foods that provide all the essential amino acids are known as *complete proteins*. Complete protein foods include meat, chicken, fish, dairy, and eggs. Beans and nuts offer *incomplete proteins*. They have some, but not all, of the essential amino acids. They are often mixed with whole grains to round out the rest of the amino acids needed.

Eating protein throughout the day is important for keeping your body going. It helps maintain a steady blood sugar level and evens out peaks and valleys of energy and mood that would potentially appear if your glucose goes through peaks and valleys.

Tryptophan and glycine food sources

It isn't just turkey that supplies tryptophan. Most protein foods are good sources of tryptophan.

Some high-glycine food sources didn't make the recommended list because they have other amino acid downsides. Collagen and gelatin protein powders have tremendous amounts of glycine but have *zero* tryptophan. If you use these powders, be sure to add other proteins (e.g., whey powder, eggs, or meat) to the same meal. Some collagen powder manufacturers add whey to their products to complete the protein profile. Collagen and gelatin also have high levels of glutamate, which might up your anxiety.

Bone broth is similar to collagen and gelatin in its amino acid mix. It is low in tryptophan unless meat is included in the creation of the broth or added when consumed. Long-cooked bone broth has concerningly high levels of glutamate. An alternative to bone broth is shorter-cooked meat stock that is created from a mix of chicken or beef bones and accompanying meat.

Top tryptophan and glycine foods for stress resilience

Foods in parentheses have similar tryptophan and glycine to the first food listed on that line. Levels are given in mg per serving. TRYP. = Tryptophan.

	FOOD	TRYP.	GLYCINE
1	Turkey or chicken (3.5 ounces)	400	1300
2	Beef (pork, lamb) (3.5 ounces)	300	800
3	Crab (3.5 ounces)	300	1300
4	Wild-caught salmon (herring, sardines) (3.5 ounces)	250	1200
5	Sprouted beans or lentils (1 cup)	100-200	600-700
6	Cheese (3.5 ounces)	300	400
7	Yogurt (3.5 ounces)	200	800
8	Eggs (1 egg)	85	200

17 How Non-Protein Amino Acids Help

There are amino acids other than protein amino acids that are important to consider for helping you deal with stress and reduce anxiety. Several non-protein amino acids are involved with neurotransmitter production and function.

There are 3 non-protein amino acids of particular interest:

1. Theanine,
2. 5-HTP, and
3. GABA.

1. Theanine

Theanine is a non-protein amino acid most commonly found in tea. Its relaxing effects have the potential of counterbalancing the caffeine in tea so that you have a lift in energy and alertness without a caffeinated amped-up anxious feeling.[1]

Theanine is able to cross the blood-brain barrier and has been shown to impact your neurotransmitters in several ways that can help you deal with stress and reduce anxiety, including:[2]

- increase GABA, serotonin, and dopamine, and

- reduce the impact of the excitatory neurotransmitter glutamate by blocking glutamate receptors.

2. 5-HTP

5-HTP is 5-hydroxytryptophan. Notice that *tryptophan* is in its name. 5-HTP is the biochemical in the middle of the production sequence between tryptophan and serotonin. You make 5-HTP from tryptophan, and then you can make serotonin from 5-HTP. As I mentioned earlier, the sequence looks like this:

Tryptophan > > > > 5-HTP > > >> **Serotonin**

Serotonin is not available as a supplement but 5-HTP is. Oral 5-HTP is known to be well absorbed into the bloodstream. Unlike tryptophan, it doesn't have to compete with other amino acids to get across the blood-brain barrier.[3]

You can get tryptophan from proteins in your food but you don't typically get 5-HTP from your diet; your body typically makes it. It is, however, available as a supplement created from the African plant *Griffonia simplicifoli*. Supplemental 5-HTP has been studied more in relation to depression than anxiety. It may help you if you are experiencing both of these (as many people do) or it may be useful for sleep.

> You don't get 5-HTP from diet.
> Your body makes it from tryptophan.
> 5-HTP for natural supplements is sourced in one African plant.

5-HTP got a bad rap at the time of the tryptophan controversy and subsequent ban of tryptophan. Just as the US tryptophan ban has been lifted, the related apprehensions about 5-HTP have faded as well (though some people haven't caught up with the whole story), but there are different lingering concerns with 5-HTP supplementation:

- Like tryptophan, taking too much 5-HTP or taking it with antidepressant meds may mess with the balance of other neurotransmitters and lead to Serotonin Syndrome.[4]

- A couple of studies have linked 5-HTP supplements with impaired decision-making, possibly because of competition with dopamine.[5] The study participants were not clinically anxious to begin with. It is possible that people who started off with lower-than-normal serotonin levels would have different results. Before using 5-HTP during the day, it may be a good idea to experiment with taking it when you won't be driving, such as in the evening. Because it is often used to help with sleep, this could be ideal timing anyway.

3. GABA

The calming neurotransmitter GABA is itself technically an amino acid, but it is not a protein amino acid. GABA is also used by your body for roles other than as a neurotransmitter (i.e., it lowers blood pressure, which might be useful if your anxiety has resulted in high blood pressure).[6]

GABA is being used by some as a natural remedy for anxiety, although its use is highly controversial. The belief that GABA can't cross the blood-brain barrier—based on animal studies dating back to the 1950s—all but shut down medical inquiry into its effectiveness as a supplement for anxiety, so there has been very limited research in this area. However, there is some newer research pointing toward the possibility that GABA can cross the BBB in small amounts, and even if it can't, there may be another route to success: increasing GABA in your gut may be able to reduce anxiety through nerves connecting your gut and brain.[7]

On the pro-GABA side of the controversy, practitioners working with patients attest to seeing improvement with GABA supplements. In *The Mood Cure*, Julia Ross, nutritional psychology pioneer, suggests the use of GABA for anxiety: "I've seen GABA supplements restore blessed biochemical calm in a matter of minutes."[8]

As I mentioned earlier, GABA in your body is made from the protein amino acid glutamate, which is an excitatory neurotransmitter, so trying to increase GABA by increasing glutamate may or may not be helpful. It might be helpful as long as you also supply your body with other nutrients, such as vitamin B6, needed to convert glutamate to GABA, but increasing glutamate might be excitatory.

Encouraging research

Regarding **theanine** and anxiety, several research projects, such as a 2016 study in the Netherlands,[9] have demonstrated that alpha brain wave levels (typical of a relaxed state) increase after ingesting a theanine supplement.

Japanese researchers, including Keiko Unno, studied the effect of **theanine** in socially stressed mice. They have developed an interesting model for exposing mice to a social confrontation by having males enter another male's established territory. The manipulated situation creates stress in both the dominant and subordinate mice but does not result in physical attack or harm. Very extensive study of the effects of theanine in this condition demonstrate that theanine supplementation results in better adaptability to the stress—as evidenced by a more normal corticosterone pattern, less adrenal gland enlargement, and complete elimination of depression-related behavioral markers compared to control mice.[10]

Dr. Timothy Birdsall, ND's review of **5-HTP** research details many relevant studies including:[11]

- several studies in the 1980s and '90s that found 5-HTP to be as good as pharmaceutical medications for reducing depression, and

- a placebo-controlled study of 50 fibromyalgia patients showing that those given 5-HTP had significantly better improvements in all parameters examined, including pain, sleep, and anxiety.

Twenty-four patients with Panic Disorder and twenty-four "healthy" people were tested for panic response an hour and a half after taking 200 mg of **5-HTP** or a placebo. (The panic stimulator was exposure to 35% CO2.) While the healthy people did not exhibit an effect from the supplement, the Panic Disorder patients had significantly less anxiety and panic symptoms if they received 5-HTP than the patients who received the placebo.[12]

Japanese researchers gave sixty adult subjects **GABA** (100 mg) or a placebo before a mentally stressful task on two different days: one day for the placebo and one for the GABA. EEG results and an anxiety assessment showed some improvement to their stress response on the GABA day.[13]

Non-protein amino acid bonuses

5-HTP may help reduce carbohydrate cravings while dieting because low serotonin levels are associated both with dieting and carbohydrate cravings.[14]

Theanine may be neuroprotective and improve learning and memory.[15]

Theanine food sources

The food source for theanine is tea.

Recent studies give different and conflicting results for the theanine content of various teas. One found more theanine in green tea compared to black tea.[16] Another study found the opposite.[17] A third found both to be about the same.[18] Averaging the results from these studies, the approximate amount of theanine is 4 to 30 mg per cup of brewed tea. For comparison, the 2016 Dutch study referenced above in the Encouraging Research section used 200 mg theanine supplement for subjects.[19]

GABA food sources

GABA is not typically found in food, but there are a couple of ways you can potentially increase your GABA levels with foods: fermented foods and GABA rice.

Some bacteria, particularly *Lactobacillus*, have the potential of creating GABA.[20] Those bacteria can be introduced or increased by eating fermented foods or taking probiotics.

There is a form of rice known as *GABA rice*. GABA rice is created by soaking and germinating (aka sprouting) brown rice. The GABA content of rice can be increased from 4 mg/3.5 ounces to 18 mg/3.5 ounces after twenty-four hours of soaking.[21] Note that the GABA research study mentioned in Encouraging Research above used 100 mg/day as its test amount. The amount of GABA created in soaked rice is fairly small, so it is unknown whether it can impact your mood. (There are other benefits of soaking/sprouting rice that I'll expound on in Chapter 30: Why Not Phytates and Oxalates? and Chapter 42: Sprouted Rice and Quinoa.)

How Probiotics Help

Probiotics are live helpful microorganisms: they are pro-health microorganisms. More specifically, what we are usually talking about when we are dealing with probiotics are pro-health bacteria.

Your digestive tract contains about as many microorganisms as there are human cells in your body. (The ratio used to be reported as about 10:1 microbes to human cells, but the number was revised recently to 1:1. Still—you've got lots of microbes.)[1] Gut microbes include yeasts, fungi, viruses, and other organisms, but it's mostly bacteria. And there's typically lots of diversity in there created by a mix of many different species.

Not all gut bacteria treat you nice. The specific species of bacteria in your gut and their relative numbers impact the health of your gastrointestinal tract, the rest of your body, and your mind.

The connection between probiotics and anxiety

Recent studies are indicating that the microbial content of your gut impacts stress-related intestinal conditions such as Inflammatory Bowel Disease (IBD) and Irritable Bowel Syndrome (IBS).[2] It also affects how you handle stress.

Exciting things are happening in the crossover between microbiology and psychology. Discoveries in the last decade have homed in on gut microbes that affect your mood and mental state. As I explained in Chapter 6: What's Gut Got to Do with It?, there is growing understanding that your gut and brain communicate, each impacting the other via what is being called the gut-brain axis.

Psychobiotics

Now, there is a designation for microbes that researchers believe specifically help you mentally and emotionally: *psychobiotics.*[3] Psychobiotics include some bacterial names you are probably pretty familiar with, like *Lactobacillus,* and some others you may not recognize such as *Bifidobacterium longum.*

Psychobiotics can help you deal with stress and reduce anxiety by helping you:[4]

Bacteria have two names. You can think of it as family name first and the equivalent of a given name second.

- use glucose,
- heal your gut wall,
- even out your cortisol,
- reduce inflammation, and
- help your brain in stress-reducing ways.

While the evidence of probiotics' positive impact on your stress resilience piles up, we don't understand all the mechanisms yet, especially when it comes to neurotransmitter production. One way we can see them help with neurotransmitters is that probiotic bacteria enhance tryptophan levels.[5] Tryptophan is an essential amino acid used in the production of serotonin, so the tryptophan in your gut has the potential of passing into your blood and making its way to your brain to be used to make serotonin there.

Mystery remains around the fact that some bacteria in your gut can be mega-producers of the calming neurotransmitters GABA and serotonin. In theory, those substances can't get past your blood-brain barrier, so it is unknown whether their existence in your gut and blood translates into their use in your brain.[6]

Even though we don't know yet how gut GABA and serotonin might play into the anxiety-reducing effect of psychobiotics, or if they have a role at all, we have lots of evidence that these beneficial bacteria do help reduce anxiety.

Good vs. evil

There can be an OK Corral fight going on in your gut to see who is going to dominate and survive: good microbes or bad microbes. The good microbes are going to help you feel better and function at your optimum. The bad microbes have the potential of pushing out the good ones and making you feel stressed, anxious, and crappy.

If bad microbes dominate in your gut, they have the potential of doing the opposite of everything that made it onto the psychobiotics benefits list above. An overabundance of bad gut microbes relative to good species can increase anxiety by messing with your glucose,[7] gut wall,[8] and cortisol.[9] It can create inflammation and get in the way of your brain's ability to deal with stress.[10]

Maintaining the good/evil bacteria balance

The balance of good/bad microbes in your gut can get hurt by many things you ingest or are exposed to, including:[11]

- antibiotics,
- previous intestinal infection,
- use of proton pump inhibitors (e.g., Nexium, Prevacid, Prilosec),
- the typical Western diet that is low in plant fiber and high in bad fats and sugars,
- alcohol abuse, and even
- stress.

How do you get good bacteria into your gut?

One way you get good bacteria into your gut is by eating fermented foods that still have live bacteria in them. For example, yogurt is a common fermented food that has had bacteria such as *Lactobacillus* added to milk to create the taste and texture of yogurt. If you buy yogurt that doesn't have live bacteria, you won't get the benefit of a bacterial boost. You just get a food that tastes like yogurt.

The same is true for all products that have the potential of containing probiotics. If they aren't alive there's limited, if any, benefit. The probiotics in canned sauerkraut or pickles sitting out on your grocery store's shelves are long dead. The store's fridge section is where you'll find the good live stuff.

Besides fermented foods, the other typical way to up your good gut bacteria count is with probiotic supplements. I'll give you the lowdown on those in Part Five: Stress Resilience Supplements.

There is another method of getting good bacteria into you that is drawing some attention: fecal transplants. Officially called *fecal microbiota transplant (FMT)*, it is performed by taking stool from a healthy person and putting it into the intestines of an unhealthy person. It is currently being used for one particular condition: intestinal infection caused by the bacteria *Clostridium difficile*. There is growing evidence that FMT beats out the percentage effectiveness of traditional methods of treatment for this illness.[12] John Hopkins Hospital even has info on its website about preparing for the procedure.[13] Fecal transplants may be common in the future for a wide range of conditions, but for now they aren't being used broadly.[14] (I'll tell you about an exciting study using human-to-mice fecal transplant coming up in the next section.)

Encouraging research

There has been a huge amount of interest in probiotics in the last decade spurred on by the US National Institutes of Health (NIH) Human Microbiome Project. The goal of the project is to map and catalogue the microorganisms of the human body. The info they unearthed led to increased research in probiotics and then psychobiotics.

As with other food-related substances, researchers often start by working with animals to figure out what helps and how it helps. Many **animal studies** have revealed promising results for the idea that altering the composition of bacteria in your gut can alleviate anxiety, for example:

- Adding *Lactobacillus plantarum* to the diet of mice made them more adventurous and reduced anxious behaviors.[15]

- Zebrafish given that same species of probiotics spent more time in the top portion of a test tank (compared to unsupplemented control fish), demonstrating a reduction in stress response.[16]

- *Lactobacillus rhamnosus* reduced cortisol and anxiety-related behavior in mice put through a stress test.[17]

In a study that looked at **both animals and people**, French researchers found that a combination of *Lactobacillus helveticus* and *Bifidobacterium longum* reduced anxiety in rats as measured by "defensive burying" behavior, and also reduced anxiety symptoms in humans. (The humans were given the probiotics for a month.)[18]

A Japanese study demonstrated that milk fermented with *Lactobacillus casei* probiotic consumed by twenty medical **students** daily for eight weeks prior to a major exam offered the students stress-protective advantages over a twenty-student control group. Leading up to the exam, cortisol levels, abdominal discomfort, and reports of emotional stress went up for the non-probiotic group, but not the probiotic group. Additionally, members of the probiotic group that started out with abdominal discomfort had their symptoms improve even though the exam got closer.[19]

Researchers in Ontario, Canada found that patients with **Chronic Fatigue Syndrome** showed anxiety reduction after two months of daily treatment with 24 billion colony forming units (CFU) of *Lactobacillus casei*.[20]

Encouragement that probiotics may help with **social anxiety** comes from an American study that examined information gathered on 700 adults. Questionnaire answers revealed a connection between increased fermented food intake and less social anxiety, even in those people who have traits that would put them at higher genetic risk for social anxiety.[21]

Healthy women given a **milk product fermented by four probiotics** (*Bifidobacterium animalis*, *Streptococcus thermophiles*, *Lactobacillus bulgaricus*, and *Lactococcus lactis*) twice daily had their brain activity examined for stress reactions at the end of a month. While being monitored by a functional MRI, they were shown pictures of emotional faces that are part of a "standardized emotional faces attention task which measures rapid, precocious, and conscious brain responses to emotional stimuli." Less reaction to the pictures is associated with less hypervigilance for threat and less anxiety. Compared to a group given a placebo, the twelve women who consumed the probiotics were less reactive.[22]

The study that had the biggest "Wow!" for me while I was doing research for this book is a project spread across three Canadian universities. Fecal matter from people was transplanted into mice and their psychological condition went with the transfer![23]

The people were either: (1) healthy, (2) had IBS with diarrhea and anxiety, or (3) had IBS with diarrhea but without anxiety. The mice were raised germ free until they received the human stool. The IBS candidates all had symptoms for at least two years and all of the humans involved tested negative for signs of infection. There were four different human donors in each category and stool from each person was transplanted into at least ten mice.

> Since **fecal transplants** aren't available for most of us, the take-home message from the human-to-mouse transplant study is that the bacteria in your gut can profoundly impact your response to stress and anxiety level.

Three weeks after the fecal microbiota transplant (FMT), the mice were given a battery of tests that revealed:

- The mix of bacteria in recipient mice paralleled that in the donor stool.

- The mice who received transplants from either of the IBS groups of donors got IBS diarrhea symptoms: their intestinal contents moved through more quickly and their colon walls became more permeable.

- And, the mice that received fecal matter from the anxious humans became anxious, but the other mice did not. (All were put through the typical testing for anxiety-related behaviors for mice.)

Probiotics bonuses

The microbes in your gut can impact just about everything in your body. At the most basic level of surviving and thriving, bacteria in your gut help you break down your food into useable parts. Some do a better job than others. Probiotics can help you heal gastrointestinal problems like peptic ulcers, diarrhea caused by antibiotics or infections, Inflammatory Bowel Disease (IBD), Irritable Bowel Syndrome (IBS), and lactose intolerance.[24]

Beyond having a direct impact on the health of your GI tract, good gut bacteria may protect against ill health throughout your body by helping to reduce:[25]

- diabetes,
- allergies,
- high blood pressure, and
- inflammation.

And, changing the bacteria in your gut might help you lose weight by decreasing insulin resistance and inflammation.[26]

Recommended amounts

Unlike nutrients, there are no Recommended Dietary Allowance (RDA) values for probiotics.

Bacteria in probiotic supplements are measured in *Colony Forming Units (CFU)*. A common guideline for probiotic supplements is that you should look for supplements with around 50 billion CFU. (Yes, that's *billion* with a *b*.) It can also be helpful to use a mixture of bacterial species.[27]

Psychobiotics most often mentioned in anti-anxiety and anti-depression studies include:[28]

- *Lactobacillus acidophilus*
- *Lactobacillus casei,*
- *Lactobacillus plantarum,*
- *Lactobacillus helveticus,*
- *Lactobacillus rhamnosus,*
- *Bifidobacterium breve,*
- *Bifidobacterium infantis,*
- *Bifidobacterium lactis,* and
- *Bifidobacterium longum.*

Probiotic food sources

Fermented foods contain probiotics. At least, they contain them when they are fermented. That's how they get fermented.

Foods that can be a good source of probiotics include:

- yogurt,
- kefir,
- sauerkraut,
- kimchi,
- pickles, and
- other pickled vegetables and foods.

As I mentioned earlier, a tricky thing about buying fermented foods, including pickles and sauerkraut, for their probiotics is that you need the bacteria to still be alive in order to reap the full benefits and get those bacteria to impact the bacterial mix in your gut. Most of the grocery store foods that aren't in the fridge aren't going to have live bacteria. Instead of picking up cans and jars of pickles and sauerkrauts from the shelves, look in the fridge section for versions with live probiotics.

How Adaptogens Help

Adaptogens are a category of plants that help you adapt to all forms of stress: noise, physical exertion, chemical toxins, cold, exhaustion, psychological stress, and so on. They simultaneously help you feel less jittery and more energetic. They can both bring you down and raise you up.

Adaptogens help you feel less anxious by moderating how your body deals with stress. They adapt and they help you adapt. They can serve as a general tonic that helps you feel better overall.

The first adaptogen I was introduced to was maca, which is native to South America. Over the years, I learned about many more adaptogens and I began to notice that it seems like every region around the world has an adaptogenic plant in their traditional medicine repertoire. This really brings home to me the importance of this category of plants for health and well-being.

> Use of adaptogens as feel-better tonics dates back thousands of years in many different parts of the world.

Botanicals versus individual nutrients

Before we talk about the specifics of adaptogens' impact on anxiety, I want to take a minute to point out a major difference between the use of botanicals (herbs and roots) such as adaptogens versus the nutrients we have been talking about so far.

With botanicals, we are taking in a combination of biochemicals as they coexist in a plant instead of focusing on individual biochemicals like a single isolated vitamin or mineral. This allows the combination of biochemicals present in nature to support each other and provide a combined benefit to your body. It is thought that the combination of chemicals in these plants may have a synergistic effect on each other so that their combined impact is greater than if individual chemicals were extracted.

While herbs and roots offer many benefits, we don't know everything about all their constituent chemical parts, so it is important to use caution when using them in combination with pharmaceutical drugs and it is typically advised that their use during pregnancy or nursing only be under a doctor's care.

The connection between adaptogens and anxiety

In their 2012 journal article "A Current Status of Adaptogens: Natural Remedy to Stress," Indian pharmacology scholars Vinod Pawar and Hugar Shivakumar tout the use of adaptogens to counter stress:

> One of the best and most powerful ways to lower excess cortisol levels, bring the body into a state of metabolic harmony and reduce the damaging effects of stress is to use adaptogens. Adaptogens positively change our stress response and help prevent many health problems.[1]

Adaptogens may help you deal with stress by:[2]

- reducing oxidative stress and inflammation,
- supporting your adrenal glands, and
- moderating cortisol, blood sugar, and your immune response.

Ginseng

Ginseng is an adaptogen that you may be familiar with. When you think of ginseng, the Asian variety is probably what comes to mind, but many of the adaptogens from other parts of the world are commonly referred to as ginseng also. It's not surprising given that they have similar effects.

Adaptogens that may help your body and your mind feel less stressed include these plants from around the world:

- **Asian ginseng** *(Panax ginseng)*, possibly the most widely known adaptogen, is from China and Korea.[3]

- **American ginseng** *(Panax quinquefolius)* is a North American plant that has been used medicinally by many Native American tribes for hundreds of years.[4]

- **Eleuthero** *(Eleutherococcus senticosus)* is also known as Siberian ginseng, but it is not in the same plant genus as Asian and American ginseng. (Notice that American and Asian ginseng have the same plant genus name, *Panax*, but eleuthero's plant genus name is different.) Eleuthero was heavily studied by Dr. Nicholai Lazerev, Dr. Israel Brekhman, and a large group of researchers in the communist Soviet Union because of its purported ability to improve endurance and performance, and to reduce the impact of all types of stress: physical, mental, and emotional. Dr. Lazerev was the first to use the term "adaptogen." The Soviet studies resulted in a directive that all USSR athletes take eleuthero during training.[5]

- **Maca** (*Lepidium meyenii*), sometimes called Peruvian ginseng, is from the Andes Mountains of Peru.[6]

- **Ashwagandha** *(Withania somnifera)* from northern Africa, the Middle East, and India is an important botanical in Ayurvedic medicine. Sometimes called Indian ginseng, it has been in use for more than 2,500 years.[7]

- **Holy basil** *(Ocimum sanctum, O. tenuiflorum)* from Southern Asia is also known as tulsi. Holy basil most likely comes by its name because it was held in high regard in Hindu traditions. It is sometimes used in Thai cuisine, but so are other types of Thai basil that do not have the same adaptogenic qualities as holy basil.[8]

- **Licorice root (*Glycyrrhiza glabra, G. uralensis*)** has been used medicinally since ancient times in many parts of the world including the Middle East, Europe, Asia, and North America. The root is used to flavor black licorice candy, but don't eat a bunch of the candy to get the adaptogenic benefits because you'll be consuming a lot of sugar too. There are other plants, such as anise and fennel, which have a licorice flavor but are not related to licorice root and are not adaptogens.[9] (Note: I've included licorice on this list because it is used in small doses in some adaptogen mixtures, but it should not be taken in high doses for extended periods.[10] More on this in Part Five: Stress Resilience Supplements.)

- **Rhodiola *(Rhodiola rosea)***, also known as Arctic root, is from the far north and is said to have been used by the Vikings to increase physical stamina.[11]

- **Schisandra** *(Schisandra chinensis)*, popular in Traditional Chinese Medicine as a yin tonic, is among the adaptogens widely studied by the Soviet researchers.[12]

Adaptogens versus stimulants

Both stimulants (caffeine, nicotine, amphetamines, etc.) and adaptogens can help you feel more energetic, alert, and focused, but they have major differences in how they achieve those results. Adaptogens don't create the negative side effects of stimulants.

> Adaptogens give you a lift without the negative side effects of stimulants like caffeine.

Caffeine and other stimulants can make anxiety worse. They can make you jittery, irritable, and on edge. They can stress your body and interfere with sleep. The lift from adaptogens is adaptive in that they are helping your body systems do their work and improve your physical health. They increase your potential for dealing with stressors in a mentally and physically healthy way.

Stimulants create an energy spike and dive. The lift from adaptogens does not create a shadow energy dip. Stimulants contribute to insomnia. Adaptogens may relieve insomnia. Stimulants are addictive. Adaptogens are not.[13]

Having said all that, some adaptogens are more stimulating than others. If you are experiencing adrenal fatigue symptoms, you may do better with adaptogens on the more stimulating end of the continuum, such as Asian ginseng. If your symptoms are more in the high cortisol wound-up range, you may do better with adaptogens on the more calming end of the continuum, such as American ginseng and ashwagandha.[14]

Encouraging research

In their book *Adaptogens: Herbs for Strength, Stamina, and Stress Relief*, David Winston and Steven Maimes describe the diverse ways that adaptogens can help lower anxiety and the specifics of individual adaptogens.[15] Swedish researcher Alexander Panossian gets more detailed in his analysis of adaptogen biochemistry and how their component parts impact your component parts in his many journal articles about these helpful plants.[16] Other researchers explain the action of ginsenosides, unique biochemicals found in members of the *Panax* family (e.g., American and Asian ginseng).[17] I won't go into the biochemical explanations of exactly how adaptogens affect your body, but you can check out those resources if you would like to know more.

For some adaptogens, there seems to be more high-quality research using animals than humans. Here's a sampling of **animal results**:

- A 2015 review of twenty-eight studies recounted evidence that **ashwagandha** reduced anxiety behaviors and brain oxidative stress markers in rodents.[18]

- A control group of rabbits exposed to acute stress had increased levels of the oxidative stress marker nitrogen oxide and increased cortisol, but rabbits pretreated with either **eleuthero**, **schizandra**, **rhodiola**, or **Asian ginseng** all had nitrogen oxide and cortisol levels that remained nearly unchanged from pre-stress levels, demonstrating that each of these adaptogens rendered the rabbits more stress-resistant.[19]

- **Asian ginseng** significantly reduced corticosterone (the animal equivalent of cortisol), stomach ulcers, adrenal gland weight, and blood glucose in mice exposed to chronic stress.[20]

- Mice given **American ginseng** were studied in tests that provoked anxiety and depression. They were compared to mice given pharmaceutical anti-anxiety medication (diazepam) and antidepressant medication (Imipramine) and also to an untreated control group of mice. The mice given ginseng were significantly less stressed and depressed than the controls and were close in their reactions/symptoms to the medicated mice.[21]

A clinical study published in 2012 demonstrated almost 40% better overall improvement in stress-related symptoms in seventy-nine adults who received **holy basil** (1200 mg per day) for six weeks compared to a control group that received a placebo. Also, compared to the placebo group, the holy basil group had significant improvement in many individual symptoms, including forgetfulness, sexual problems of recent origin, exhaustion, and sleep problems.[22]

Fourteen postmenopausal women were given 3.5 grams/day of **maca** for six weeks preceded by or followed by six weeks of placebo (some starting with maca and some ending with maca). When they received the maca, their anxiety and depression scores went down significantly and their sexual function went up.[23]

Ashwagandha reduced stress and cortisol levels in people with a history of chronic stress significantly better than the performance of a placebo in a control group.[24]

Students given **rhodiola** for twenty days during an examination period were less physically and mentally tired and scored higher for mental well-being than their placebo counterparts.[25]

A hundred and sixty Russian cadets were broken into four groups (untreated control, placebo, 370 mg rhodiola, and 555 mg rhodiola) to test the effect of a single dose of **rhodiola** on fatigue and mental ability during the stress event of working a twenty-four-hour shift. There was highly significant anti-fatigue protection seen in the groups receiving the adaptogen compared to the others. Pre- and post-shift, the control and placebo groups showed a decline in ability on three mental capacity assessment tests, but the scores for the groups receiving rhodiola were kept constant or improved. (Both dosage groups had similar results.) The researchers noted that the effects were different than what would be expected from a stimulant, such as caffeine, in that the quality of answers on the mental ability tests, but not the speed of completion, were better in the treated groups.[26]

Adaptogens bonuses

Adaptogens are general feel-good tonics so they potentially help with many health issues. They can increase energy, vitality, and a sense of virility.

Adaptogens may impact sexual function. For example, studies show that:

- ginseng may help alleviate erectile dysfunction[27] and also improve sexual arousal in menopausal women,[28] and
- maca may improve sexual desire in men and women,[29] while
- holy basil may reduce fertility.[30]

There is considerable evidence that maca,[31] rhodiola,[32] ashwagandha,[33] Asian ginseng,[34] and schisandra[35] help decrease the likelihood of osteoporosis.

Recommended amounts

Because adaptogens are plants rather than individual nutrients, there are no Recommended Dietary Allowance (RDA) values for adaptogens.

Adaptogen food sources

Adaptogens are plants themselves, but they are rarely eaten as a whole food. Traditionally, they have been ingested in medicinal teas, tonics, and broths. Now, in many parts of the world, they are most often taken as supplements in capsule, tincture, or powder form. Winston and Maimes offer traditional adaptogen recipes in their book *Adaptogens: Herbs for Strength, Stamina, and Stress Relief.*[36]

20 How Nervine Herbs Help

Nervine herbs are a group of herbs that help support your nervous system. They potentially help you relax physically and mentally and may be particularly helpful for sleep.

As with adaptogenic herbs, it is important to use caution when using nervine herbs in combination with pharmaceutical drugs and it is typically advised that their use during pregnancy or nursing only be under a doctor's care.

The connection between nervine herbs and anxiety

Difficulty sleeping is a common problem with anxiety. Stress can keep your brain whirling around, making it challenging to fall asleep, and restlessness can disturb sleep. Even when you do sleep, you may wake up anxious or worn out.

It seems like every major herbal tea company offers a mix of nervine herbs as a sleep aid. While each has some components unique to their formula, some herbs repeatedly appear across formulas. I'll focus on the most common.

Common herbs to help you relax include:

- Passionflower *(Passiflora incarnata)*,
- Chamomile *(Matricaria recutita)*,
- Lemongrass *(Cymbopogon citratus)*,
- Kava* *(Piper methysticum)* aka kava kava,
- Valerian *(Valeriana officinalis)*, and
- Hops *(Humulus lupulus)*, which you might recognize as an ingredient in beer.

Research supports the idea that these herbs help you deal with stress by assisting the receptors and uptake of your calming neurotransmitter GABA.[1] Valerian seems to positively impact serotonin use as well.[2]

*Kava controversy

Kava has been used as a relaxant in the South Pacific for a thousand years. Its use spread around the globe until it was banned in several countries in 2002 because of its connection to cases of liver disease in 1999 and 2000, including the death of a German woman.

Some of the national bans have recently been lifted or reduced, while some remain in place. Germany lifted its ban in 2014. Kava is now available in stores in the US, Australia, and New Zealand. In Canada, it is available from select government-approved sources online.

A 2011 article in the journal for the Royal Australian and New Zealand College of Psychiatrists made the following observations and recommendations:[3]

- Current evidence supports the potential of kava for anxiety reduction.

- Kava should not be used with alcohol or other liver-challenging drugs.

- The World Health Organization (WHO) recommended that water-based kava solutions, rather than acetone or ethanol extractions, are preferable.

- Plant parts used and particular strains of plant may be important for safety. Use kava produced from roots and processed using good manufacturing practices from a reputable source.

- Beware of overuse. If you use kava long term, your liver should be assessed through liver enzyme blood tests.

Encouraging research

Several **passionflower** studies have compared the herb to pharmaceutical medications for anxiety relief or light anesthesia:

- In Iran, thirty-six outpatients with generalized anxiety disorder (GAD) were randomly placed into one of two groups. For four weeks, one group received the benzodiazepine drug oxazepam plus a placebo and the other group received passionflower (45 drops PassipayTM/day) plus a placebo. At the end of the study, tests showed that passionflower was as effective as oxazepam in anxiety reduction. There were two major differences: (1) oxazepam showed an anti-anxiety effect earlier in the test period than passionflower did, and (2) oxazepam interfered with job performance, but passionflower did not.[4]

- People undergoing dental extraction were given passionflower (260 mg *P. incarnata*) or a pill of the mild anesthetic drug midazolam thirty minutes before a local anesthetic injection and tooth removal. The passionflower worked equally well as midazolam to reduce pre-operative anxiety. A major difference was that there was some amnesia effect with the drug but not with the herb.[5]

- In a similar study, sixty pre-operative patients were administered either a placebo or passionflower a half hour before they were to be given a spinal anesthetic. There was a significantly better reduction in anxiety with passionflower compared to the placebo, but no change in motor function.[6]

Dr. Jay Amsterdam, MD and others at the University of Pennsylvania have studied **chamomile's effect** on anxiety and depression. Two research projects they performed tested capsules of chamomile extract compared to placebo. Each study used approximately sixty subjects and spanned eight weeks. The results: depression and anxiety were significantly reduced by chamomile consumption compared to placebo. (An unusual twist in their procedure was that they started everyone on one capsule, upped it to two the next week, and then continued to increase the dosage several more times weekly if the participant had less than a 50% improvement. Maximum dosage was five capsules of 220 mg chamomile each.)[7]

In another study, nurses in Iran monitored stress levels in chronic heart failure patients who drank **chamomile tea** three times a day for a month, comparing them to a non-chamomile control group. The patients in the chamomile group showed a significant reduction in anxiety throughout the test period, while the control group showed an increase in anxiety.[8]

Studies on mice in Nigeria[9] and Brazil[10] have demonstrated **lemongrass's ability** to reduce anxiety.

Another Brazilian study examined the impact of **lemongrass aroma** exposure on men's stress levels:[11]

Essential Oils

The smell of many nervine herbs is enough to give a relaxing effect. Their oils are often used in aroma therapy.

- Forty men were divided into groups. The men inhaled "essential oil" from a tissue for three deep breaths and then the scent was immediately removed. The lemongrass group experienced a drop in anxiety markers compared to groups exposed to either tea tree oil or water. All the participants were then put through an anxiety-provoking scenario known as the Stroop Color-Word Test (SCWT).

- The SCWT: While being videotaped and believing that they are being observed and evaluated by "professionals" in another room, study participants have to name as quickly as possible (with a two-minute maximum) colors presented to them. The trick is that they have to name the color of ink used to print the color name, and it is different than the color name (e.g., BLUE printed with pink ink has to be named as "pink"). To add to the stress, if they hesitate or make an error, a bell rings.

- The quick exposure to lemongrass aroma prior to the SCWT did not reduce the anxiety of the participants compared to the control groups *during* the color word test, but within five minutes *after* the tricky color naming test, anxiety levels in the lemongrass group returned to their baseline while the other groups' anxiety remained elevated.

Australians Shanah Salter and Sonya Brownie reviewed research articles for use of **valerian** to help with sleep. While they found flaws in some of the research projects, there still remained reliable evidence that valerian can potentially help you get to sleep and have improved sleep quality, on its own and in combination with **hops**.[12]

The effect of **hops** was tested by giving **non-alcoholic beer** to highly stressed nurses. One non-alcoholic beer at dinner resulted in improved sleep. The nurses wore wristbands that recorded sleep activity, etc. The results showed that they got to sleep quicker and sleep was less restless than without the beer. (This test is particularly interesting because alcohol was removed from the beer.)[13]

The sleep-assisting effect of a supplement pill containing a **combination of passionflower, valerian, and hops** was compared to the sleep medication zolpidem (Ambien is zolpidem tartrate) in people suffering from primary insomnia. Eighty people completed sleep diaries recording nightly total sleep time, how long it took to get to sleep, and the number of times they woke up during the night. Results after two weeks of treatment were the same for both the medication and herbal supplement groups: more than half of the people in each group no longer had insomnia, time getting to sleep decreased, and quality of life increased. About a quarter of the people in each group still had insomnia at the end of the study (slightly fewer in the herbal remedy group than the medication group).[14]

An eight-week study of 129 outpatients diagnosed with generalized anxiety disorder found that 400 mg/day of **kava** extract (LI 150) was as effective in reducing anxiety symptoms as either of the anti-anxiety meds buspirone or opipramol.[15]

A 2010 Cochrane Review of studies examining the use of **kava** to treat anxiety concluded that kava significantly reduced anxiety better than a placebo in seven studies representing a total of 380 subjects. (To meet the Cochrane Review standards for inclusion, studies must exhibit a high level of reliability.)[16]

Nervine herbs bonuses

For the most part, the predominant benefit and use of these herbs is for relaxation, but chamomile is well known for its ability to soothe the digestive tract.[17]

Recommended amounts

Like adaptogens, nervine herbs are plants rather than individual nutrients and have no Recommended Dietary Allowance (RDA) values. Most sources will include recommendations for usage. Consult with your doctor for more information about dosage and also any potential interactions with medications.

Nervine herb food sources

As a food, nervine herbs are often used in teas, either individually or in mixtures. (I'll talk more about specific brands in Part Five: Stress Resilience Supplements.)

Just the smell of some of these herbs (particularly chamomile, lemongrass, and valerian) may be enough to reduce anxiety, help you deal with stress, and improve sleep.[18] Drinking tea made from these botanicals gives you the double benefit of the herb itself and its aroma.

21

Here's a summary of the stress-related physical processes each identified anti-anxiety element is involved with.

	ELEMENT	WHAT IT IS INVOLVED IN
1	**Magnesium**	cortisol and glucose levels, nerves, gut, neurotransmitter synthesis, muscle relaxation, sleep
2	**Zinc**	nerve cell growth and health, balancing glutamate and GABA
3	**B vitamins**	neurotransmitter synthesis, adrenal glands, nerve cells, glucose
4	**Vitamin C**	oxidative stress reduction, nerve cell health, adrenals
5	**Vitamin D$_3$**	serotonin, GABA, nerve health
6	**Omega-3s (EPA and DHA)**	nerve cells, serotonin and dopamine; reduction of inflammation, oxidative stress, and possibly cortisol
7	**Probiotics**	gut health, cortisol, glucose, nerve cells, inflammation reduction
8	**Amino Acids (protein amino acids plus theanine, 5-HTP, GABA)**	neurotransmitter building blocks and support
9	**Adaptogens**	nerve cell health, adrenal gland adaptation to stress, glucose balance
10	**Nervine Herbs**	relaxation

Before I introduce you to my lists of favorite foods and supplements to help you boost the stress-relieving minerals, vitamins, fats, bacteria, herbs, and amino acids, let's talk about what you might be taking in that is adding to your body's stress load and contributing to your anxiety.

Part Three

What Hurts Your Calm

You are what you eat,
so don't be fast, cheap, easy, or fake.

– Unknown

Introduction to What Hurts

22

When thinking about optimizing your ability to cope with stress and reducing your anxiety, it's important to consider increasing what can help and also decreasing what can hurt. You may be spinning your wheels if you go to a lot of work and expense to add helpful nutrients to your food and supplement intake to feed your calm but undermine those positives with foods that are boosting your anxiety and interfering with your ability to handle stress.

Before you take a look at the What Hurts list, keep in mind that I'm not saying that you have to suddenly, or even ever, remove these entirely from your life. Pull yourself back from looking at the list in terms of absolutes: *all or nothing, always, never, none, all.* People react differently to different foods and substances. How negative something on the list is for you is very individual.

I encourage you to approach the list with the idea of "What is one change I want to start with?" so that you don't get overwhelmed. Changing one thing at a time also allows you to see whether that change was helpful. You may decide to eliminate some of these things cold turkey or through a process of weaning, cut back on something but not forgo it completely, or not adjust your consumption at all. It's up to you.

Some foods and groups of food to watch out for:

1. Caffeine
2. Alcohol
3. Processed foods
4. GMO foods
5. Foods you are sensitive to

Introduction to What Hurts 131

Notes for Bringing It All Together

As you read the chapters of Part Three, keep a lookout for mention of any symptoms or conditions that you experience. Note those and the related foods. Also note any food changes that might be of particular help to you. What would be a relatively easy change to make? What change might not be easy but worth the effort? What might help you let go of a food that isn't serving you well?

You may want to note your insights on the pages set aside in Part Six: Bringing It All Together.

How Caffeine Hurts

Caffeine can jack up your reaction to stress and increase nervousness, anxiety, and panic. It can make you feel on edge and wired. And, it can interfere with sleep.

Caffeine is a stimulant. It can stimulate your fight-or-flight adrenal response creating the physical cascade of symptoms related to anxiety, including increased heart rate and a spike in blood sugar. (I've seen people end up in the emergency room from a panic attack brought on by a high-caffeine energy drink.)

Different people can be more or less sensitive to caffeine and an individual may be more sensitive at different times in their life and under different circumstances. Stress may up your reaction to caffeine.

I was having dinner one night with a friend who was going through a dramatic divorce. She topped off her meal with an espresso and mega-chocolate cake. When her heart started racing and she got very anxious, she totally discounted the possibility that it was brought on by the caffeine she had just inundated her body with. She poo-pooed my efforts to point to the caffeine as the cause, even though she said the same thing had happened to her a couple of nights earlier when she had coffee with another friend. It appears that she was accustomed to dealing better with caffeine when she wasn't under so much stress and that her previous experiences of being OK with it blinded her to what was clearly happening to her now.

Caffeine, the sleep buster

One of the worst potential problems with anxiety is not being able to quiet your mind so you can sleep. It is painful to be lying there having your mind go round in circles. And worry about not being able to sleep compounds whatever other worries are cycling through your mind, adding anxiety about not sleeping to your other anxiety.

Even if you get to sleep without trouble, caffeine can still ruin your sleep.

Caffeine can:

- make it difficult to fall asleep,
- make you restless during sleep,
- keep you stuck in a light stage of sleep,
- interrupt your sleep, and/or
- shorten the length of sleep by waking you up early.

The half-life for caffeine is around five hours. That means that it takes five hours for half of the caffeine consumed to be eliminated. Notice that it's only half gone in five hours. Caffeine that you consumed ten hours ago can be wrecking your sleep. It's also noteworthy that some things can extend caffeine's half-life, such as: older age, smoking, pregnancy, and particular illnesses and medications. So—you might react differently to caffeine at different times in your life.

Caffeine can be part of a vicious anxiety cycle:

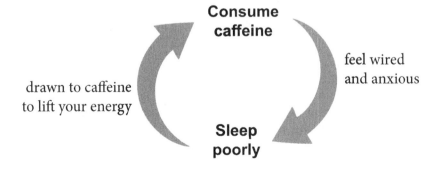

The only way to break the cycle is to change something about your caffeine consumption. The change may be eliminating caffeine altogether, but that's not the only option. It may be enough to cut back on the caffeine or change the times of day that you consume it. (I'll give you some ideas for cutting back in a minute.)

Many people say that stopping caffeine by 3 pm provides a cut-off point for protecting sleep. That rule seems to fit well with caffeine's half-life under the majority of circumstances, but for some people and/or under some circumstances, the rule doesn't create a big enough caffeine-free time period for undisturbed sleep. Naturopath Dr. Anne Procyk says that "even one cup of coffee or tea, even in the morning, can affect sleep for 48 hours."[1] If you have trouble getting to sleep or tend to wake up during the night, experiment with pushing back your caffeine consumption window.

Caffeine can also contribute to you waking up with anxiety. One of my clients, who was going through a bout of waking up in the middle of the night with a panic attack, eliminated those attacks when he eliminated his morning coffee.

Caffeine sources

The most obvious sources of caffeine are coffee, tea, and cola, but they aren't the only sources. Some foods that have caffeine, like orange soda, may sneak up on you.

When I was attending college, I worked as the newspaper editor for a couple of quarters. Every two weeks, I'd go through a cycle of less and less sleep in order to get the paper out. I was amazed at my ability to stay up all night the night before each deadline. Finally, I thought to take a look at the orange soda I was inexplicably drawn to and was uncharacteristically drinking on those nights, and I realized it had caffeine! That was eye-opening! (Pun intended.)

There is caffeine in:

- coffee;
- black, white, and green tea;
- chai tea;
- iced tea;
- kombucha;
- yerba mate;
- guarana;
- cola;
- other sodas like Sunkist Orange Soda, Mountain Dew, Barq's Root Beer, and A&W Cream Soda;
- chocolate;
- "energy" drinks like Red Bull, Monster, and Crystal Light Energy;
- some nootropic supplements and many workout supplements;
- some pain medications and diet pills;
- just about any processed food, from granola bars to beef jerky, that has "Bang," "Boost," "Energy," or similar words in their name; and even
- decaffeinated coffee and tea.

If you want to monitor your caffeine intake, start checking food and beverage labels to see if there are caffeine or caffeine sources on the ingredients list. Sometimes the list won't include the word *caffeine*, but will say something like *green tea extract* or *guarana*.

There are some great websites to help you figure out how much caffeine is in particular foods, such as Caffeine Informer (caffeineinformer.com).

Caf, decaf, no caf

Decaffeinated is not the same thing as *caffeine free.*

Caffeine free has no caffeine. *Decaffeinated* coffee and tea still have caffeine in them. They have way less caffeine than their normal counterparts, but they still have caffeine. I know for myself that I can't handle a decaffeinated latte from Starbucks any time of day and I have to avoid even decaffeinated tea late in the day so that my sleep isn't disturbed.

Products that are *caffeine free*, like caffeine-free herbal teas, don't start out with caffeine and they don't have caffeine added.

Decaffeinated products have to go through a process of caffeine removal because they contain caffeine in their natural state. There are several different ways to remove caffeine from coffee and tea, but none of the methods remove all of the caffeine. By law, at least 97% of the caffeine must be removed before something can be called decaffeinated, but that still leaves around 3% of the caffeine. How much caffeine still remains in a particular product depends on how much it started with and the decaffeinating process used.

Caffeine Free = no caffeine

Decaffeinated = up to 3% of the original caffeine is still present

The most common decaffeination methods involve a solvent: either methylene chloride or ethyl acetate. Ethyl acetate is found naturally in small amounts in fruit, so coffee or tea decaffeinated with ethyl acetate may be labeled *naturally decaffeinated.*

There are two other decaffeination methods that do not use solvents. There is a water process, the most common of which is the Swiss Water Method. And there is a relatively new solvent-free decaffeinating process that uses CO_2. The Swiss Water Method is usually used for organic coffee. The CO_2 method is often used for very large quantities such as decaf for grocery store chains.

Ways to cut back on caffeine

Research has linked anxiety to caffeine consumption and also to caffeine withdrawal, so if you have a big caffeine habit, quitting abruptly may not be the way to go.

There are many potential ways of cutting down on caffeine, including:

- quit entirely;
- abruptly or gradually move back the time of day you stop consuming caffeine;
- eliminate some, but not all, of your sources of caffeine;
- consume smaller portions;
- change all or some of your drinks to decaffeinated versions;
- mix in decaffeinated portions (half caf, half decaf);
- replace caffeine beverages with naturally caffeine-free alternatives, like herbal teas instead of black tea, or chicory root "coffee" or dandelion root tea instead of coffee; or
- drink water instead (your body will thank you).

How Alcohol Hurts

There is a huge overlap between people who have anxiety and people who either abuse alcohol or are addicted to it. Dr. Joshua Smith and Dr. Carrie Randall of the Charleston Alcohol Research Center expressed it this way:

> Across different large-scale studies, at different times, and both in the United States and abroad, anxiety and AUDs [Alcohol Use Disorders] co-occur at rates greater than would be expected by chance alone. The odds ratios (ORs) characterizing the comorbidity between an AUD and any anxiety disorder in these studies ranged between 2.1 and 3.3—in other words, the two conditions co-occurred about two to three times as often as would be expected by chance alone.[1]

People with anxiety can be drawn to self-medicate with alcohol. You may be drawn to overuse alcohol as a relaxation aid or to reduce anxiety in social or performance settings. And on the anxiety flip side, overdoing alcohol can lead to anxiety because it stresses your body and/or mind.

There are many possible negative side effects from using alcohol to relax and "forget" about your stress.

Some people can keep their alcohol use under control and it doesn't have negative consequences. But, for others, it's a trap waiting to be sprung (or already sprung). Self-medicating with alcohol can set up a vicious anxiety-alcohol cycle, begin a downward spiral to addiction, or keep you stuck at the alcoholic end of that spiral.

There are several potential versions of an anxiety-alcohol cycle. For example:

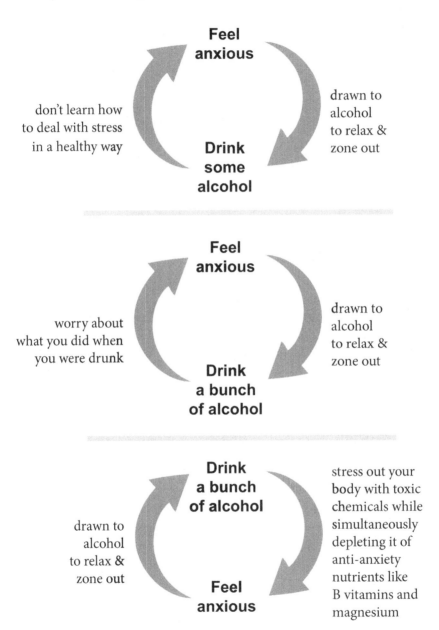

The draw to zone out with alcohol may become more and more intense when the alcohol consumption within any of these cycles creates negative consequences such as damaged relationships, decreased job performance, a DUI charge (or even driving while under the influence that you haven't yet been caught at), negative health effects, and so on.

The anxiety-alcohol cycle can make it difficult to stop drinking because anxiety swells when you quit and you are pulled back to alcohol to temporarily drown the feeling.

Alcohol disturbs sleep

It's counterintuitive, but drinking alcohol late in the day disturbs sleep. While alcohol consumed before bed acts as a sedative initially thereby helping you fall asleep, it disturbs sleep and interferes with getting a restful rejuvenating sleep.[2]

A particularly harmful cycle is found in people who use alcohol at night to fall asleep, caffeine during the day to counteract the poor sleep the alcohol created, then alcohol at night again to counteract the caffeine's stimulating effects.

Other ways to relax

If you are using alcohol to relax after work, before bedtime, or in social situations, that might not be all that bad for you if you are able to keep the amount in a safe usage zone. If you wander into unhealthy territory or you're already deep into it, or you want to preemptively protect yourself from going there, you might consider addressing your anxiety with a therapist and trying some other ways to relax.

Healthy ways to relax

Here are some ideas for relaxing:

- go for a walk or get some exercise
- replace the alcohol drink with some other drink like herbal tea or juice with bubbly water
- replace an alcoholic beverage that you use to mark the transition from work to not-work times of day with some other marker of the transition
- do something creative like coloring or wood working
- play with your kids or pet
- talk to your partner
- take a hot shower or bath
- listen to music
- do a relaxing meditation or guided visualization
- write in a journal
- read something inspiring
- play a video game (not in an addictive way)
- do a deep breathing exercise
- watch something that makes you laugh or smile (videos of cats doing silly things, giggling babies, sitcoms, funny movies . . .)
- smile for a minute even if you don't feel like it (fake it 'til you make it)
- check out my website, annsilvers.com, for the five relaxation skills I teach to clients and incorporate in my *Discover Calm, Anti-Anxiety Hypnosis* downloadable mp3

How Processed Foods Hurt

Anything that stresses your body can stretch your ability to cope with other stressors and tip your inner scales toward anxiety. Processed foods have the potential of stressing your body and adding to your anxiety by making your organs work hard to counter the assault on your system.

Processed foods tend to be produced in a way that focuses on taste, appearance, long shelf life, and reducing production costs rather than the health of the consumer. Natural foods are often stripped of their nutrition while being processed. Unnatural chemicals are added and ingredients that would be relatively safe in small amounts are included in hazardous proportions. Maybe you can handle one product with the questionable chemicals, but what about the entire load from multiple sources you consume?

Opportunity cost is also a consideration when it comes to eating processed foods. There is an opportunity cost associated with consuming junk-ingredient foods. If you're eating the negative stuff, you aren't eating the positive stuff. That can double down on backwards motion. Your body has to deal with the stressors you're eating while at the same time the nutrients it would use to deal with stress are in short supply.

Dr. Felice Jacka, an Australian university professor and President of the International Society for Nutritional Psychiatry Research (ISNPR), has done a lot of research into the connection between mental health and eating processed foods. Studies she, along with many colleagues, performed and reviewed on large groups of adolescents and adults followed for long periods of time showed a strong correlation between the degree to which someone stuck to a healthy non-processed diet and their mental health. The more they ate a diet of natural foods, the better their mental health.

Conversely, the more processed foods they ate, the worse their depression and anxiety became.[1]

At least one of their studies also demonstrated that the poor food quality in the typical Western processed-foods diet created the reduction in mental health rather than the other way around: it was not that depression or anxiety made them make bad food choices. Their work also showed that if people made different choices and switched their diet toward or away from processed foods, their mental health followed suit.[2]

Six common ingredients of processed foods that may add to your anxiety include:

1. Too much sugar
2. Aspartame
3. Bad fats
4. MSG
5. Dyes (aka food coloring)
6. Preservatives

These ingredients can cause all kinds of bad in your body and contribute to anxiety by:[3]

- adding to your stress load,
- feeding bad gut bacteria overgrowth,
- creating leaky gut by hurting your intestinal wall,
- causing inflammation and brain cell oxidative stress,
- replacing healthy brain fats with trans fats,
- producing insulin resistance, and
- contributing excess excitatory neurotransmitters.

Having said all that, just because a food product is manufactured doesn't make it automatically bad for you. To limit the potentially harmful ingredients you ingest, you need to know what to look for on ingredient labels so you can make an educated decision about what you're putting in your body.

It is a bit of a numbers game. If you eat well most of the time, you may be able to afford some less-than-ideal foods part of the time. On the other hand, it depends on your individual reaction to food additives and ingredients. For example, if you react badly to MSG, food preservatives, or coloring, even a small amount may stress your body and stimulate anxiety.

1. Too much sugar

Sweet sells! Many processed foods are loaded with sugar, even in unexpected places like "health" food bars, granola, yogurt, fruit juice, ketchup, iced tea, sports drinks, and frozen French fries.

Sugar is found naturally in fruits and some vegetables. In those whole foods, your body is getting the sweetness and sugar energy mixed in with other helpful nutrients as well as fibers that slow down the absorption of the sugar. However, the sugar added to processed foods tends to hit your system quickly, creating a spike in your blood glucose. That glucose spike can make you feel wired and stimulate an increase in insulin to deal with all that sugar, followed by a shadow blood glucose deep dive, potentially followed by an increase in cortisol to stimulate release of glucose from your reserves. The cortisol increase can jack up your heart rate and blood pressure giving you the fight-or-flight feeling of anxiety. The sugar overdo gets you comin' and goin'.

Excess sugar also feeds bad bacteria in your gut, potentially contributing to anxiety by throwing off your balance of good and bad bacteria.[4]

The worst of the worst when it comes to sugars added to processed foods is high-fructose corn syrup. The natural sugar found in corn is uber-processed to turn it into an uber-sugar: high-fructose corn syrup. This sugar additive has been associated with inflammation and insulin resistance, both of which can contribute to anxiety.[5]

High-fructose corn syrup is the worst sugar offender.

An extra danger to your health and well-being that lies in high-fructose corn syrup is that it does not give your body cues that you have consumed enough calories. The same number of calories in natural sugar would tell you to stop eating, but the fructose does not. It is possible that this is one of the reasons for the increase in obesity that has accompanied the increase in consumption of processed food.

There are dozens of sugar sources and aliases that might show up on an ingredient list. Here are just some of them:

- corn syrup, corn sweetener, high-fructose corn syrup
- rice syrup
- evaporated cane juice
- molasses
- fructose, lactose, maltose, dextrose, galactose
- malts, malted barley, rice malt, maltodextrin
- sorbitol, hexitol, xylitol

Ingredients are listed on packaging by relative weight, so the earlier on a package's ingredient list an item appears, the higher the percentage of the product it represents. Sugar might appear under many different names on a single package. The misleading label spreads out the sugar bad news, potentially making it look less overwhelming than reality.

To give you a guidepost, the American Heart Association recommends limiting the amount of *added sugars* you consume to no more than 100 calories per day for women and no more than 150 calories per day for men. *Added sugars* would exclude those found naturally in foods, but include anything you add to your food yourself or that is added to processed foods you consume. For example, one typical can of soda would put you right at the limit, or over the limit, because the 150 calories it contains is all sugar (usually, BTW, from high-fructose corn syrup).

2. Aspartame

It isn't just an overdose of refined sugar that can contribute to your anxiety; the artificial version may also be zinging you.

Aspartame is an artificial sweetener that contains 50% phenylalanine, 40% aspartate, and 10% methanol. It can jack up your anxiety because aspartate is an excitatory neurotransmitter.[6]

You're probably aware that aspartame is commonly found in diet foods and beverages. It may be a surprise, though, that it is also in most chewing gum and some toothpaste and medications. Aspartame brand names include NutraSweet®, Equal®, Sinosweet®, Vitasweet®, Pal Sweet®, Aminosweet®, Canderel®, and Spoonful®.

3. Bad fats

In order to increase the shelf life of oils in processed foods, North American manufacturers sometimes use a hydrogenation process that starts with natural oils and turns those relatively healthy fats into the big bad wolves of fats: trans fats. Trans fats (aka hydrogenated oils) are also often used for deep frying in restaurants.

Trans fats are most notorious for causing heart problems, but they have the potential of harming your body in all kinds of ways.

In a 2015 policy brief, the World Health Organization (WHO) cautions that the intake of trans fats "should be as low as possible." The brief also points out that as an individual's consumption of trans fats increases, their chance of dying of heart problems increases rapidly and dramatically: a "2% increase in total energy derived from trans fats is shown to be associated with an increase in risk of death from Chronic Heart Disease or myocardial infarction of 23%."[7]

Many countries have set caps on the amount of trans fat that can be in processed foods or banned it completely. Some American cities and counties have banned their use in restaurants. The American FDA gave manufacturers until June 2018 to eliminate hydrogenated oils from processed foods, but extended that deadline for a year and is also allowing time for manufactured products to work their way through the food delivery chain.

Animal studies in Brazil have shown that trans fats:[8]

- increase brain oxidative stress,

- invade the outer membranes of brain cells, replacing omega-3 fats that those cells need to function well with dysfunctional trans fats,

- increase anxiety, and

- increase the draw to psychostimulant drugs.

farm-raised Atlantic salmon. The fact that they have to add red dye to it in order to make it look appealing attests to just how unnatural farm-raised salmon is.

Wellness osteopathic doctor Dr. Joseph Mercola has this to say in a blog post warning against the many dangers of food dyes:

> If you need further incentive to ditch artificially colored foods from your diet, remember the reason they're added to processed foods in the first place: to make a food that would otherwise be an off-colored mess look appealing.[11]

Much of the research on the negative health effects of food dyes has been focused on the possibility that it sparks hyperactivity in children. And that research is pointing towards "yes."[12] Anything that revs you up can potentially add to an anxious feeling, so the research results are of interest for anxiety as well as hyperactivity.

Studies by researchers at the University of Southampton in 2007 found that food dyes were associated with increased behavior and concentration problems even for kids that were not diagnosed with ADHD.[13] These studies led to a voluntary ban in the UK and mandatory warning labels in Europe for all six of the food dyes they tested. These dyes are known as the Southampton Six. The US and Canada have banned some food dyes in the past, but have lagged behind with adding to the no-fly list.

It appears that many companies in the UK, including international biggies like McDonald's, are complying with the voluntary ban. That means that a McDonald's strawberry milkshake in the UK has beet juice for color,[14] while an American McDonald's shake has bright red artificial color— Red #40.[15]

The table below shows the Southampton Six with their common names, international numbers, and US names and status. (If a US name is listed, then it is permitted in the US.) INTERNA. NUMBER = International Number.

The Southampton Six food dyes		
COMMON NAME	INTERNA. NUMBER	U.S. NAME/STATUS
Tartrazine	102	Yellow #5
Sunset Yellow	110	Yellow #6
Allura Red	129	Red #40
Quinoline Yellow	104	Yellow #10 (used in US drugs and cosmetics, but not food)
Carmoisine	122	not used in US food
Ponceau 4R	124	banned in the US

In 2008, the Center for Science in the Public Interest asked the FDA to ban all of the artificial colors that are currently being added to food in the US. The only food dye they left off their wish-to-ban list is Citrus Red #2, which is used to dye orange peel in states other than Arizona and California where this practice is banned. (You maybe didn't know that early-season oranges are dyed to make them look better. That's how far we've come—cosmetics for food!) The FDA talked about it, but didn't pull the trigger.[16]

Given that all six of the dyes in the Southampton study are now seen in many parts of the world as unhealthy, it may be wise to avoid all artificial color in your foods. Focus on foods with natural color additives, no color additives, or even better, unprocessed, real food. (And don't eat the peel from non-organic citrus fruits.)

6. Preservatives

A chemical that makes a food last a long time in the captivity of a package may not be helpful to *your* longevity. It may stress out your inner workings like an invader who has made its way into your fort.

Many of the preservative chemicals used in foods, food packaging (some of the chemicals are sprayed onto food packaging material, such as cereal box liners), cosmetics, shampoo, toothpaste, and skin creams in the US are banned in other countries. Some of these chemicals are allowed in the US in strictly limited amounts out of concern that they are extremely dangerous when consumed in higher amounts. But what happens if you eat a lot of different foods and use other products that contain the chemical? What happens when you use them at the allowable amounts but they are just part of the total chemical load your body has to deal with? What happens if you have a sensitivity to them?

Anything that assaults your body and stresses your body's systems can make it harder to deal with other stressors. Getting these chemicals out of your diet may do your body good (and your mind too).

Processed food preservatives of possible concern include:

- butylated hydroxyanisole (BHA),
- butylated hydroxytoluene (BHT), and
- tertiary butylhydroquinone (TBHQ, tBHQ).

BHA

In its 2016 *Report on Carcinogens*, the US Department of Health and Human Services described BHA as "reasonably anticipated to be a human carcinogen."[17] A university study in Spain using primate kidney cells found that "low doses of BHA exerted a significant cytotoxic effect, associated with loss of mitochondrial function."[18] *Cytotoxic* means that it is destructive to your body's cells.

Multiple animal studies suggest that BHA alters production of hormones including testosterone and estrogen.[19] The European Commission of Endocrine Disruption classified this food additive as being of "High Concern."[20]

BHA accumulates in the body, so taking in the chemical from multiple sources over time may cause problems even if single doses would be tolerated.[21] Besides showing up in processed foods, BHT is used in cosmetics including shampoos and lipstick.

BHT

A 2002 review of the safety of BHT reported that it had toxic effects on liver, kidney, and lung tissue. The negative impact increased when BHT and BHA were present in combination, as they often are in processed foods.[22]

TBHQ

Dr. Cheryl Rockwell, assistant professor of pharmacology and toxicology at the College of Human Medicine at Michigan State University, is in the forefront of research connecting TBHQ to increased food allergies and impaired immune response. She has been awarded a grant from the National Institutes of Health to fund further research in this area.

This excerpt from a research paper detailing Dr. Rockwell's work explains one of TBHQ's potential negative impacts on your body:

> Activation of T cells is an important event for the initiation of a variety of adaptive immune responses. Such responses are critical for host defense against a number of bacterial and viral pathogens as well as fungi and parasites. The current studies are the first to demonstrate that the food preservative tBHQ impairs primary human T cell activation.[23]

How GMO Foods Hurt

So, what's all the fuss about GMO foods?

GMO stands for *Genetically Modified Organisms*. The World Health Organization defines GMOs as "organisms in which the genetic material (DNA) has been altered in such a way that does not occur naturally."[1]

Genetically modifying seeds is a relatively new thing. Since the first GMO seeds were field tested in the late 1980s, their use has taken over some crops to the point where 90% of corn, soybean, and canola grown in the US is genetically modified.[2]

This statement on the WHO website gives you a window into one of the glaring things that is wrong with GMO foods: "Most existing genetically modified crops have been developed to improve yield, through the introduction of resistance to plant diseases or of increased tolerance of herbicides."[3]

Herb, the root of the word *herbicides*, represents plants. *Cides* means killer. Herbicides kill plants. Why would you want to create plants with increased "tolerance to herbicides"?

If you are Monsanto, the producer of the herbicide Roundup, you would financially benefit from genetically engineered crop seeds that are resistant to your herbicide so that you can cash in on both ends: sell the seeds for food crops and sell the herbicide that now will selectively kill the weeds around the crop. That is exactly what Monsanto has done.

The poison in Roundup is glyphosate. And, as it turns out, one of the main reasons for the existence of GMO foods is so they won't die from being sprayed with glyphosate. (In fact, many of the GMO seeds proudly display the registered trademark Roundup Ready®.) The weeds are natural plants, so they die from exposure to the herbicides. The GMO crops absorb the poison but don't die.

Another creator of GMO frankenseeds is Dow. Dow has their own herbicide to promote: 2,4-D. Their GMO seeds won't die when sprayed with 2,4-D.

What about us humans? We haven't been genetically modified for resistance to glyphosate or 2,4-D.

If you eat herbicide-tolerant GMO foods, chances are most of them have absorbed the poison. It isn't something you can wash off of vegetables or other foods. It is *in* the food. Thus, when you eat the food, you are eating the poison.

There are other reasons for creating GMO seeds, such as resistance to certain insects, or the alteration of fat composition, and they have their own pros and cons, but herbicide tolerance is the stated goal of the most common GMO seeds.

The American crops with the most herbicide-tolerant GMOs are:[4]

- corn,
- soybean,
- cotton,
- canola,
- alfalfa, and
- sugar beets.

In 2009, the American Academy of Environmental Medicine (AAEM), an international association of medical doctors and other professionals founded in 1965, presented accumulated evidence of GMO health risks and called on all doctors to educate their patients against eating GMO foods and to consider the role these foods might be playing in the health problems patients are displaying. They also called for a moratorium on the use of GMO seeds until long-term independent studies are performed.[5]

The same AAEM GMO position paper[6] cites studies showing a connection between consumption of GMO foods and:

- changes in kidney, pancreas, spleen, and liver in animals,
- infertility, accelerated aging, and insulin resistance in animals, as well as
- immunity problems, inflammation, asthma, and allergies in humans.

All of it adds up to the potential of GMO foods creating inflammation, stressing out your body, and taxing your ability to deal with other stressors.

While the governments of Canada and the US are not requiring foods to be labeled if they contain GMOs, the Non-GMO Project offers verification for foods. If the organization verifies that a food is GMO free, it can display the "Non-GMO Project Verified" badge on its package.

To reduce anxiety, you may want to limit your intake of non-organic foods or those that are not labeled as non-GMO, particularly for the foods on the list of herbicide-tolerant GMO crops above, including sugar from sugar beets and high-fructose corn syrup.

You may find you feel less anxious after reducing your GMO intake.

How Foods You Are Sensitive to Hurt

We are hearing lots about gluten intolerance these days. That awareness is important and welcome. When you are looking at potential contributors to your anxiety, gluten is one potential source of sensitivity and negative physical and mental reactions. But, it's not the only one. Just about any food can have a negative impact on any one individual.

A food that is beneficial to one person might be toxic to another, setting up a cascade of physical problems ultimately leading to anxiety. While there are some common food intolerance culprits like gluten and dairy, I have seen people's allergy reports come up with positive results for surprising foods, like carrots.

Two groups of foods could cause you problems: (1) those that you are allergic to, and (2) those you are sensitive to. Allergy testing can tell you what foods you are allergic to, but not necessarily those you are sensitive to. So, something can show up negative on an allergy test and still cause you problems.

Your food sensitivities can change

Some food sensitivities develop because you have over-consumed a particular food. On the flip side, sometimes food sensitivities can disappear after a period of abstaining from that food. One woman I know developed a reaction to all things dairy after an extended trip to Europe during which she ate *a lot* of delicious European cheese. After a few years of being dairy-free, she was able to slowly reintroduce dairy products without a negative reaction.

If you have food sensitivities and you are eating those foods you are sensitive to, they can contribute to a wide array of problems including many that you'll recognize for their connection to anxiety:

- rashes
- heart palpitations
- breathing difficulties, asthma
- sinus symptoms, post-nasal drip, plugged ears
- headaches, migraines
- diarrhea, constipation, gas, bloating
- Irritable Bowel Syndrome (IBS)
- leaky gut
- poor absorption of nutrients from food because of intestinal disturbance
- increased cortisol because of allergic reactions
- inflammation
- depression
- anxiety

When you are trying to figure out if you are sensitive to a certain food, it is important to take into account that it could take hours or days before symptoms show up after you have eaten the triggering food.

The Big 8

While just about any food can cause problems for an individual depending on their biology and situation, eight foods have been identified as being the source of 90% of food allergies and must be identified on processed food labels in many countries around the world.

These foods are known as the Big 8:[1]

1. milk (from cow, goat, and sheep)
2. eggs
3. fish
4. crustacean shellfish (shrimp, crab, lobster . . .)
5. tree nuts (walnut, almond, coconut . . .)
6. peanuts
7. wheat
8. soybean

Gluten

Gluten intolerance has become so common in the US that it warrants special mention.

It is represented on the Big 8 by wheat, but other grains besides wheat contain gluten, and they need to be avoided if you are gluten intolerant or have celiac disease.

You can think of celiac disease as a subset of gluten intolerance. If you have celiac disease, you have an immune reaction to gluten. That immune reaction stimulates an attack on the wall of your small intestine and tell-tale antibodies can show up on blood tests if you are currently eating gluten products. Some people do not have this immune reaction, but they are sensitive to gluten in some other way.

Here are some of the major sources of gluten:

- wheat
- rye
- barley
- malt
- wheat starch
- beer
- brewer's yeast (beer by-product)

Depending on your level of sensitivity to gluten you may react to even small amounts that could be present in foods like soy sauce, corn flakes that contain malt extract, and oats that are exposed to wheat, barley, or rye contamination during transportation from farms or processing in factories. Oats that are labeled *gluten-free* guarantee non-contamination.

A 2015 article in *The Annals of Nutrition and Metabolism* offers this list of the most common symptoms for gluten sensitivity[2] (you would not likely get all of these symptoms if you are sensitive to gluten):

- bloating
- abdominal pain
- lack of well-being
- tiredness
- diarrhea or constipation or alternating between the two
- acid reflux
- nausea
- headache
- anxiety
- foggy mind
- joint/muscle pain
- skin rash

If you are gluten intolerant, take heart. Living gluten free isn't as difficult as it used to be. There's lots of info out there. Many foods are clearly labeled as gluten-free, and restaurants often include gluten-free options on their menu.

You do have to be attentive in restaurants and ask what is gluten-free. I was mistaking French fries and Mexican rice as safe until I was told that I needed to ask. Turns out restaurants I frequented were adding wheat flour to these items or cooking them in oil that is contaminated with wheat from other foods. Uncovering this information explained why I was getting intestinal disturbance or feeling lethargic after eating at those restaurants.

Food elimination experiment

To figure out whether a particular food, or a certain amount of that food, is adding to your anxiety and getting in the way of you dealing with stress, you can try eliminating or cutting down on it while you monitor for the effects of that change.

There are different options for how to approach your food elimination experiment. It's not a one-size-fits-all thing. Start where you are with the goal of progress toward figuring out what will help you feel less anxious and better able to deal with stress. One change might reap huge rewards for you. That one change might just require cutting back on a food. It may also be that you would do well to change your diet more drastically.

When I was working on this section of the book, I searched for an elimination diet journal I could refer you to so that you could get additional guidance on the process and an easy way to track how food affects you. Since I couldn't find such a journal, I created one. Check out my *Discovering How Foods Affect Me: Silver Lining Elimination Diet Journal.*

What Hurts Cheat Sheet

Here's a cheat sheet summary of potential stress-adding foods:

FOOD	WHAT TO WATCH OUT FOR
1 **Caffeine**	coffee, tea, kombucha, yerba mate, guarana, cola and other sodas, chocolate, decaffeinated coffee and tea, some pain medications and diet pills, "energy" drinks, processed foods, and supplements
2 **Alcohol**	
3 **Processed food hazards**	aspartame, bad fats, MSG, dyes (Yellow #5, #6, and #10; Red #40), preservatives (BHA, BHT, TBHQ), too much sugar
4 **GMO foods**	**most common herbicide-tolerant GMO foods:** corn, soybean, cotton, canola, alfalfa, and sugar beets
5 **Foods you are sensitive to**	**the Big 8:** milk (all dairy from cow, sheep, and goat), wheat, eggs, fish, crustacean shellfish (shrimp, crab, lobster...), tree nuts (walnut, almond, coconut...), peanuts, soybean **gluten sources other than wheat:** rye, barley, malt, brewer's yeast, and soy sauce

We've talked about what's going on in your body while you deal with stress and the target nutrients that can help. We've also talked about foods and food ingredients that can possibly contribute to anxiety. Now we get to focus on my top 12 foods for feeding your calm and boosting your stress resilience.

Part Four

Stress Resilience Foods

Those who think they have no time for healthy eating
will sooner or later have to find time for illness.

– Edward Stanley

Before we dive into my list of 12 stress resilience foods, let's talk generally about a good anti-anxiety diet.

My general advice for anti-stress eating is the same basic advice given for healthy eating:

- focus on real food
- eat protein throughout the day
- eat your vegetables
- have some fruit but don't overdo it
- eat a variety of foods
- eat organic and pasture-raised if and when you can
- reduce regular salt but include sea salt or Real Salt™

Focus on real food

As we discussed in Part Three: What Hurts Your Calm, processed foods come with lots of baggage that can tax your physical processes and muck up your inner workings.

Eat whole foods. Have fun learning how to cook. Add spices and herbs to please your taste buds and add bonus nutrients. Even if you have limited time for meal prep, some healthy foods are more about planning than prepping: it doesn't take much time to make a hard-boiled egg and it takes no time to make an apple.

Eat protein throughout the day

In a conversation with Mental Health Integrative Medicine specialist and pioneer Dr. Kristen Allott, she told me that when working with anxiety patients, her first area of focus is getting them to eat protein regularly throughout the day. Protein provides sustained energy rather than the spikes and dips of sugary or high-carb foods.

I include many protein-rich foods such as eggs, beef, pork, poultry, and fish on my recommended list. If you are vegetarian, you can look at other listed foods such as sprouted lentils, beans, and rice for your protein. Vegetarians need to make a concerted effort to get a mix of foods that create complete protein because, unlike animal sources, single plants do not typically possess all the essential amino acids.

USDA dietary guidelines for protein
(grams/day)

women: 46 men: 56

Protein examples
(in grams)

3 oz meat or fish: 15
1 lg egg: 6
1/2 cup beans: 8
1/2 cup quinoa: 4

Dr. Allott suggests you eat every three hours. If you aren't fueling your body, you are stressing it out and you'll feel stressed out. You don't expect your car to get you where you want to go without gas. Don't ask yourself to run on fumes either.

That doesn't mean you need 16-ounce steaks. Moderation is good. Rather than gorging on a large protein-heavy meal, aim for consuming protein throughout the day so that you are steadily fueling your body.

Eat your vegetables

Vegetables are a major source of a variety of vitamins, minerals, and bonus nutrients that help your body and brain do what they need to do.

I've heard different recommendations about the target number of vegetables per day, from five to nine. If you don't eat many vegetables now, don't focus on the higher number.

Consider adding one daily serving. Add more when you are ready. Aim for at least five servings a day and then consider increasing it.

A serving is about one cup of fluffy raw salad greens or half a cup of other vegetables; some say to use your fist size as a serving. It doesn't have to be five different vegetables. If you have two cups of one non-fluffy vegetable, that is four servings.

> **Fruit & vegetable**
> **serving sizes**
> (in cups)
>
> fluffy salad greens: 1
> other veggies: 1/2
> berries: 1/2

Have some fruit but don't overdo it

Like vegetables, fruits offer many valuable nutrients, but be careful about overdoing it because they also contain sugar. It's a natural sugar and provides a healthy way to soothe a sweet tooth when taken in moderation, but that sugar adds up if you overdo fruit. Aim for about two servings a day, no more than four. A serving is a small apple or a half cup of berries.

Eat fruit, but eat more vegetables.

Eat a variety of foods

While there are benefits to individual foods that make them stand out for their anti-anxiety qualities, variety is important so that you get a mix of what you need. If you get too narrow of a food focus, even with relatively healthy foods, you can suffer from too much of a good thing. You need vegetables, fruits, proteins, and starches. And you need variety within those food groups.

Mental health nutrition specialist Dr. Leslie Korn coined the phrase *brainbow* to accentuate her belief that your brain needs elements from fruits and vegetables that represent the colors of the rainbow: red, orange, yellow, green, blue, and purple. (I'll be talking more about bonus nutrients that are found in different-colored vegetables and fruits in Chapter 38: Sweet Peppers and Chapter 41: Berries and Cherries.)

Understandably, there may be times that you must drastically limit your choices, such as when you are on an elimination diet or dealing with a restrictive condition. Hopefully those times are short term.

Eat organic and pasture-raised if and when you can

My Top 12 list mentions organic and pasture-raised often when describing target foods. Organic foods are beneficial for what they don't have: GMOs, pesticides, chemicals . . . all the things we talked about in Part Three: What Hurts Your Calm. The eggs and meat from pasture-raised animals also possess nutrients that their factory-farm-raised brethren don't have. I'll point out those pluses in the upcoming individual food chapters.

I understand that organic and pasture-raised foods are relatively expensive and may be challenging to find in some areas. Do what you can with what you've got. Get creative about how you can adjust your food budget to make room for better quality.

Some areas have stores like Trader Joe's that specialize in clean food at bulk-purchased prices. Some big-box stores, such as Costco, have a surprising number of organic foods at great prices.

Here are some ideas for doing organic on a budget:

- focus on cheaper cuts of organic meat (e.g., hamburger instead of steak)
- check for frozen organic fruits and vegetables
- use the EWG's Dirty Dozen and Clean Fifteen lists to learn which fruits and vegetables are more important to buy organic (www.ewg.org)
- buy in bulk
- focus on what's in season and local
- eat out less
- skip that latte, soda, or bottle of wine
- plan your menus to minimize waste

Reduce regular salt but include sea salt or Real Salt™

Regular table salt is a stripped down, adulterated version of its original self. Minerals are removed as it is processed and anti-clumping chemicals are added.

Redmond's Real Salt™ or unrefined sea salt from a clean source such as the Himalayas has 60–80 minerals that support your body in general and your adrenal glands in particular. It is important to look for *unrefined* sea salt without additives as products can be labeled *sea salt* but still be processed like regular table salt.

A Dozen Stress Resilience Foods

Here's my list of foods to feed your calm and boost your tolerance for stress. The foods are not listed in order of recommendation. They are listed in a way that let me group together types of foods: protein sources, vegetables, fruit, and so on.

1. Water
2. Wild-caught salmon, sardines, and herring
3. Oysters
4. Pasture-raised eggs
5. Pasture-raised meat
6. Sprouted lentils and beans
7. Cruciferous vegetables
8. Sweet peppers
9. Fermented foods
10. Seaweed
11. Berries and cherries
12. Sprouted rice and quinoa

In upcoming chapters, I'll give you more information on each of these foods and why each made it onto the list. Before we address each food, I'll talk about why phytates and oxalates bumped some foods off the recommended list.

Notes for Bringing It All Together

As you read the chapters of Part Four, note any general eating advice that you would like to adopt, and keep a lookout for foods that contain elements that piqued your interest when you read Parts Two and Three. Note which foods fit your lifestyle and foods that you would be willing to change your lifestyle to accommodate.

You may want to write your insights on the pages set aside in Part Six: Bringing It All Together.

Why Not Phytates and Oxalates?

As I was creating recommendations for anxiety-relieving foods, I eliminated those with high phytate and oxalate levels. Here's why.

Phytates (aka phytic acid) and oxalates (aka oxalic acid) are classified by many as *antinutrients*. In their source plants, these biochemicals have jobs to do such as warding off insects that might harm the mature plant or destroy seeds before they have a chance to germinate and reproduce themselves. While they protect the plants and seeds they are found in, they may not be so great for us humans.

A major concern with antinutrients is that they may interfere with your ability to use nutrients found in food and throughout your body (thus *anti*-nutrient). Research supports the theory that phytates and oxalates combine with minerals and may interfere with absorption and utilization of the minerals from the foods you eat.[1] In their 2016 *Review of Dietary Zinc Recommendations*, researchers from New Zealand, the UK, and the US declared: "phytate has been identified as the most important inhibitor of zinc absorption in adult human diets."[2]

Because magnesium and zinc are so important for helping your body deal with stress, I don't want to be recommending foods that contain elements that may interfere with absorption of these vital minerals. An additional negative for oxalates is that there is considerable evidence that high oxalate levels can contribute to oxidative stress,[3] which in turn can contribute to anxiety.

The state of your gut may have a lot to do with how well you deal with oxalate and phytate. Healthy gut bacteria may be able to break them down and use them up. On the flip side, if you have leaky gut, these antinutrients that would be kept out of your body by a healthy gatekeeping intestinal wall sneak in and mess with your body's cells.[4]

Phytates are found in high concentrations in seeds, nuts, legumes (beans and lentils), and whole grains including brown rice. Soaking, fermenting, and sprouting (aka germinating) change the phytate picture. These processes activate the enzyme phytase, which breaks down phytate. Milling of whole grains removes the phytate along with the bran and the nutrients found in the bran.

Foods with the highest amounts of oxalate include these greens: spinach, beet greens, and Swiss chard. To give you a feel for relative oxalate amounts in some greens: raw spinach has a whopping 650 mg/cup (cooked spinach has 750 mg in a half cup) and chopped raw kale has a minuscule 2 mg/cup.[5]

> Soaking, fermenting, and sprouting reduces **phytates** in seeds, nuts, legumes, and whole grains.
>
> Long boiling and discarding the water reduces **oxylates** in spinach, beet greens, Swiss chard, etc.

Boiling foods can result in some of the oxalate moving from the food into the water. That can be a way of reducing your consumption of oxalate, but only if you boil the sources for extended periods and throw away all the water.[6] For example, one study showed a loss of half of the oxalate in spinach that was boiled for fifteen minutes.[7] (The oxalate content for cooked spinach in the preceding paragraph is higher than that for raw spinach because cooking shrinks spinach so much that to end up with half a cup of cooked spinach you have to start with a much larger amount of the raw vegetable. If you eat a half cup of cooked spinach, even if you boil it and throw away the water, you're going to be consuming a hefty amount of oxalate.)

Not everyone takes concerns about phytates and oxalates seriously, but those who do have quite a bit of research to back up those concerns. I'm not saying that you have to shun all foods with high phytate and oxalate, but I am avoiding recommending them as anxiety relievers because of their potential downsides. Instead, I've focused on greens that make the low end of the oxalate list like kale, collard, bok choy, and arugula, and included sprouted grains and beans but not their whole grain or unsprouted versions.

31

Water

It may come as a surprise that the first thing on my suggested foods list is something I haven't mentioned earlier in the book, but I'm thinking that water doesn't need a lot of explanation. That doesn't mean it's not important, though.

Your body is 50–60% water. All your organs and glands need water. Water is the vehicle that transports biochemicals throughout your body. It moves nutrients to the spots they are needed and moves toxins and reaction leftovers out of your body. If you don't take in enough water throughout the day, you hamper cellular function and stifle your body's ability to create neurotransmitters and hormones required to deal with stress. Dehydration also stresses out your body and, as I've mentioned before, that adds to your stressor load and can lead to anxiety symptoms.

Research has shown that even mild dehydration can cause negative changes in mood and energy, increased confusion and anxiety, and poorer sleep quality.[1]

You get about 20% of your water requirement from food. That percentage goes up if you consume more fruits and vegetables. The rest comes more directly from liquids. Beverages that contain caffeine don't count towards your water intake because caffeine is a diuretic (it pulls water out through your kidneys). Broths in soups and non-diuretic herbal teas do count.

How much water is enough? The answer to that question varies with your activity level, heat exposure, and body size. A common guideline is the number of ounces that equals half your body weight measured in pounds.

Body weight in pounds ÷ 2 = number of ounces water
For example: 150 lbs ÷ 2 = 75 oz.

Wild-Caught Salmon, Sardines, and Herring

32

Wild-caught salmon, sardines, and herring are good to great sources of:

- EPA and DHA omega-3 fats,
- magnesium,
- Vitamin D_3,
- B vitamins, and
- a mix of amino acids (including tryptophan and glycine).

A major problem with our current fish supply is that many species are highly contaminated with mercury. (Coal burning is a primary source of the oceans' and lakes' mercury contamination.) Among a multitude of other health problems, mercury has the potential of creating anxiety symptoms.[1]

The longer the fish has lived and the higher up it is on the food chain (big fish eat little fish), the greater its potential for high levels of mercury. I recommend wild-caught salmon, sardines, and herring because they have relatively high levels of omega-3s while they also have relatively low levels of mercury. There are several online resources for checking the mercury contamination of different breeds of fish. The Natural Resources Defense Council (NRDC) has a reference card infographic about the relative healthiness of different fish species.[2]

Even though the fish I've listed are low in mercury compared to other fish, everyone should be mindful not to overdo fish consumption. Some is good, but more is not necessarily better because of the mercury. I think that we would all do well to adhere to the advice for pregnant women. The 2017 guidelines of the EPA (US Environmental Protection Agency) suggest pregnant women consume 8 to 12 ounces of low-mercury seafood per week.

When buying salmon and other fish, you should check that it is wild-caught because there are many potential problems with farm-raised fish. Farm-raised fish are often:

- fed GMO grains (so they are potentially ingesting herbicides like Roundup),

- given antibiotics because their unnaturally dense living conditions give rise to increased exposure and vulnerability to infection, and

- contaminated by PCBs, dioxins, and other toxic chemicals.[3]

Nearly all Atlantic salmon is farm-raised. Most Pacific salmon is wild-caught.

> The fact that farmed salmon commonly
> have **red dye added**
> to their diet,
> or to their meat after they are harvested
> —so that it looks like salmon—
> attests to the unnaturalness of their life.

Oysters

Oysters are a good to great source of:

- zinc,
- magnesium,
- EPA and DHA omega-3 fats,
- B vitamins, and
- a mix of amino acids (including tryptophan and glycine).

As far as seafood goes, oysters are relatively low in mercury contamination.

Oysters are so high in zinc that you should not overdo them. The Upper Limit (UL) for zinc is 40 mg. There is 30–50 mg in a serving of six oysters. That doesn't mean that it's awful to have more than six oysters at a sitting; just be mindful not to be doing that day after day. As with salmon, some is good, more is not necessarily better. Remember that too much zinc can throw off your copper levels.

Most oysters sold in the US are "farmed," but farming methods are much different than for shrimp and fish. Farmed oysters aren't fed a concoction like farmed fish are. Farmed oysters eat plankton and nutrients from the seawater around them just as their wild counterparts do. They also aren't living in high concentrations of waste material (poop) like captive crowded farmed fish, so there isn't the need to deal with managing the negative effects of those wastes and thwarting the spread of infection throughout the colony with antibiotics. In general, farmed oysters are exposed to much the same eating, chemical, and living conditions as if they were wild.

> Unlike farmed salmon, farmed oysters are raised in natural conditions.

Pasture-Raised Eggs

Eggs are a good source of:

- B vitamins and
- a mix of amino acids (including glycine and some tryptophan).

Pasture-raised eggs—but not eggs from indoor factory farms—are one of the few food sources of:

- Vitamin D_3[1]

Pasture-raised eggs are better than typical eggs from factory farms in many ways, including:[2]

- more vitamin A,
- more DHA and EPA omega-3s, and
- a better omega 6:3 ratio.

Eating eggs can help you make sure that you get sufficient complete protein throughout your day and get other nutrients to deal with stress, but eggs vary in their costs (not just financial) and benefits depending on the conditions of their creation.

How poultry are raised impacts the birds and their eggs. It can be confusing to understand the many different designators for how chickens are raised. I thought I understood it all, but was shocked to find out a couple of years ago (in a class about nutrition and mood) that the cage-free eggs I was buying were not from chickens romping outdoors. Turns out, *cage-free* is different from *free-range* which is different from *pasture-raised*.

The typical way that hens are handled in the US has them housed in "battery cages" inside large buildings and fed GMO foods and "animal byproducts." The close quarters they are packed into leads to common practices such as vaccination and prophylactic administration of antibiotics to counteract the spread of diseases. They also have their beaks trimmed as chicks to minimize the harm inflicted between birds that become aggressive because they are stressed out.

Producers of eggs that are not created under these typical mass production conditions can proclaim one of several designations to set their eggs apart.

Here are the different ways eggs are described in the US and the conditions to warrant the designation:

1. *No added hormones* really doesn't give eggs any stand-apart quality because US poultry are not allowed to be given hormones.

2. *Omega-3 Enriched* eggs are from hens given ALA-rich flaxseeds and/or fish oil in their diet. Producers of these eggs tout increased omega-3 but don't usually tell you what the eggs' breakdown is for ALA versus our target omega-3s, EPA and DHA.

3. *Raised without antibiotics* only means exactly that. It doesn't directly speak to any other living or feed conditions. It may be a good sign that the birds are treated more humanely because the overcrowding in typical factory farms leads to antibiotics being given to chicks in order to stave off infectious outbreaks in flocks.

4. *Cage-free* means not housed in battery cages. This is a designation that has a great deal of significance for eggs in the US because typical factory farms

confine hens to overcrowded battery cages. The cages don't allow room for natural chicken behaviors like spreading their wings and preening. Battery cages have been banned in some countries and in some American states but are currently the norm for US-produced eggs. However, cage-free hens are still kept in overcrowded indoor high-density conditions.

Free-range chickens may or may not be getting outside and might not be having the life the designation alludes to. The living conditions in this category vary greatly between farms.

5. *Free-range* means they are cage-free and have access to the outdoors. This would seem to be a glorious jump up in living conditions, but outdoor access might be very limited and not conducive to them using the opportunity to get outside.

The outdoor access could be a small obscure opening that is generally unnoticed by the birds.

The outdoor area could be anything from cement to pasture and there are no size requirements.

6. *Free-range + Certified Humane Raised and Handled* means higher standards for outdoor access and conditions are met.

7. *Organic* eggs are from hens given non-GMO organic food that hasn't been exposed to pesticides or synthetic fertilizers, not fed animal by-products, not given antibiotics or vaccinations, and having access to the outdoors as in the free-range designation.

(The USDA had new rules for organic poultry—ensuring more indoor and outdoor space and access to pasture or soil—which were to be phased in by 2023. However, a change in administration changed all that and rolled back the organic standards. Unlike the US, Canadian organic standards include minimum space and living requirements beyond non-organic standards.)

8. *Pasture-raised* means that the hens spend most of their time in a pasture where they get natural sunlight (leading to increased vitamin D in these hens' eggs) and primarily eat grasses, plants, seeds, insects, and worms. They can be supplemented with non-organic feed. In theory they could be given antibiotics and vaccines but the need for them is reduced because of their improved living conditions.

9. *Pasture-raised + Organic* tells you that any supplemental feed that the pasture-raised birds are given is organic and they conform to all other organic regulations.

As you move to higher numbers on the list above, you also move up in price. Pasture-raised organic eggs may be difficult to find and are expensive relative to other eggs (though even this quality of egg may be less costly than other sources of protein, eating in restaurants, and luxury foods like a Starbucks coffee).

I can't in good conscience recommend eggs from caged hens, but there are many other options. You may take a look at what's available around you and consider researching different brands online to see if you can find out whether they meet standards in a minimal way or are above the minimum.

In summary

The typical egg from a factory farm has lots of baggage that comes with it.

The next steps up in humane treatment are cage-free, free-range, Certified Humane Raised & Handled, and pasture-raised.

Buying eggs that are organic will get you away from the potential chemical contaminants from the hens' feed and the downsides of the use of antibiotics and cages, but the time the hens spend outdoors varies.

Time in pasture can up the nutritional value of the eggs including improving the omega-3s and vitamin content.

Pasture-Raised Meat

In this category I'm including poultry, beef, pork, lamb, and game meats such as deer and elk. These are all good protein (and therefore amino acid) sources no matter how the animals are raised, but natural grazing has additional anti-anxiety benefits. Organic animals are ideal because any feed used to supplement grazing will be free of GMOs and additives.

Poultry

Chicken and turkey are good to great sources of:

- a mix of amino acids (especially high in tryptophan and glycine),
- B vitamins, and
- zinc (dark meat).

As I explained when talking about eggs, how poultry are raised impacts their meat and eggs. For the most part, the designations I described for eggs also fit for poultry raised for meat, but there is at least one exception.

Factory farms that raise chickens for meat don't use cages, so the designation *cage-free* doesn't indicate any improvement from the standard procedure. They typically house chickens in buildings packed so tight with birds that they don't have space to move around. As with egg-laying hens, the chickens are fed GMO foods and "animal byproducts," vaccinated, given prophylactic antibiotics, and have their beaks trimmed to minimize the harm

> Unlike with hens raised for their eggs, factory farms that raise chickens for meat don't use cages, so the designation *cage-free* on whole chickens or their parts doesn't indicate any improvement from standard mass production treatment.

they can inflict on the other birds because they are stressed out by the overcrowding and unnatural conditions.

While I found some research on the nutrient differences in eggs depending on how chickens are raised, I didn't find similar information about nutrients in the meat. No matter how they are raised, poultry meat will have the basic nutritional elements of amino acids, zinc, and B vitamins.

We can assume that the zinc and vitamins may vary somewhat depending on their living conditions and feed, but the biggest difference in the bird's meat quality as you move from the lower to higher numbers on the list given in the eggs section may be about what isn't there: GMOs, antibiotics, vaccinations, and stressed-out birds.

As with eggs, consider your budget and how high of a quality you want to go for.

Beef, pork, lamb, and game

Beef, pork, lamb, and game meats are good sources of:

- a mix of amino acids (including tryptophan and glycine),
- B vitamins, and
- zinc.

Any grocery store meats will give you the helpful nutrients listed, but there are bonuses with meat from animals that are allowed to graze. The more natural life of a grazed animal leads to a better omega 6:3 ratio. Though these meats don't have high enough omega-3 numbers to make it onto the list of top omega-3 foods I talked about in Chapter 15: How Omega-3 Fats Help, research shows that *pasture-raised or grass-fed* animals have much healthier omega-3 content than their grain-fed counterparts raised on most factory farms. For example:[1]

- Grass-fed beef has about twice the amount of EPA and DHA compared to grain-fed beef and a more beneficial 6:3 ratio.

- In 3.5 ounces of grass-fed beef there is approximately 25 mg EPA and 4 mg DHA.

- The 6:3 ratio for grass-fed beef is around 2:1 (which is right in the healthy target zone).

- The 6:3 ratio for grain-fed is around 8:1.

Eating meat from animals raised on pasture may not bump up your EPA and DHA omegas by much but it will not contribute to you going backwards by adding disproportionately to your omega-6 level as grain-fed meat can. (If you eat leaner cuts of meat, the omega ratios will matter less because you are getting less of any type of fat.)

Organ meats

The organs from poultry, beef, and other animals are particularly nutrient rich. We are coming back around to appreciate the benefits of our ancestral traditions of using the whole animal. Liver is a very potent source of B vitamins.

36 Sprouted Lentils and Beans

Legumes, such as lentils and beans, are a vegetable source of protein. For vegetarians and others, sprouted lentils and beans are good to great sources of:

- magnesium,
- zinc,
- B vitamins, and
- amino acids (including tryptophan and glycine).

As I mentioned earlier, a potential downside of typical unsprouted lentils and beans is that they contain phytate: an antinutrient that can bind magnesium and zinc, getting in the way of your body's ability to absorb and use these important minerals.[1] Phytate may also irritate your gastrointestinal tract, possibly contributing to leaky gut and other intestinal problems.

Besides phytates, lentils and beans contain lectin, a biochemical that may irritate your intestinal wall, cause inflammation, and contribute to autoimmune disease.[2] Like with phytates, sprouting reduces lectins.

Sprouting lentils and beans prior to cooking:

- greatly reduces phytates,
- increases nutrients like B vitamins,
- allows them to cook much faster, and
- makes them more digestible, thus reducing gas formation.

You can buy sprouted lentils and beans from stores or online sources like Amazon.com, or you can make your own. There is some concern about bacteria growth during the sprouting process because of the warm moist conditions, so wash your seeds before sprouting, take care throughout the sprouting process, and wash sprouts before cooking.

Cruciferous Vegetables

Cruciferous vegetables are also known as *brassica* and the *cabbage family*. Family members include broccoli, cauliflower, Brussels sprouts, cabbage, kale, collard, bok choy, and arugula.

Cruciferous vegetables are good to great sources of:

- magnesium,
- B vitamins (except B12), and
- vitamin C.

The cabbage family of vegetables also have an anti-anxiety bonus component: sulphuraphane. Sulphuraphane includes sulphur in its makeup and is believed to be anti-inflammatory[1] and anti-oxidative.[2] Both of these qualities could help you deal with stress. One study in 2016 showed that the form of sulphur found in cruciferous foods reduced anxiety in mice.[3]

A bonus with this group of plants is that study after study associates their consumption with decreased risk in a wide range of cancers including lung,[4] breast,[5] and prostate.[6]

The delicate subject of gas

The elephant in the room when dealing with cruciferous vegetables is that they can be gas forming, and their sulphur can make that gas smelly. To mitigate this, you may want to start off slow when adding them to your diet so your body can adjust. Taking probiotics or eating fermented foods can help ensure you have a healthy

Cruciferous Vegetables

broccoli
broccolini
cauliflower
Brussels sprouts
cabbage
kale
collard greens
bok choy
arugula
kohlrabi
turnip
radish
wasabi

mix of bacteria in your gut for digestion. Digestive enzymes like Beano may be helpful for breaking down elements that create the gas. Another approach is taking activated charcoal to absorb the gas.

Activated charcoal, which can be purchased as capsules, is very effective at reducing gas for many people. Organic forms are available, so choose those if you can. Activated charcoal is a good basic binder for toxic substances and is often suggested as a hangover remedy because it binds the alcohol metabolites. It is important to note that it should *not* be taken close in time to pharmaceuticals or supplements as it will sop those up too. Charcoal could also attach to vitamins and minerals in your foods if taken too close to meals. It is advisable to create a window of at least one hour before food or medication, or two hours after. Drink plenty of water with it and during the day. Don't take it daily for more than two weeks, but up to two to three times a week is typically OK.

Your thyroid and cruciferous veggies

There is a concern about cruciferous vegetables and thyroid problems. *Raw* members of this family can release goitrogens that *might* tax your thyroid. Specifically, goitrogens may interfere with your thyroid's ability to absorb iodine.

Cruciferous vegetables are not the only foods that contain goitrogens but they are the group that has taken the brunt of the bad press about the issue. Other sources of goitrogens include strawberries, pears, maca, canola oil, sweet potato, and soy. Different foods, even different subspecies of plants, have different levels of the suspect biochemical.[7]

When you dig beyond the "Stop Eating Kale" headlines, research shows that the goitrogens are a potential problem when combined with iodine deficiency[8] and that fermentation or cooking, even light steaming, drastically reduces the goitrogens in foods. (Seaweed, which is #10 on my list of stress resilience foods, is a potent source of iodine.)

If you have a thyroid condition such as hypothyroidism, Graves' disease, or Hashimoto's disease, you should consider having your iodine levels checked before upping your cruciferous intake and talk to your doctor about how these vegetables might impact your particular body.

Don't overdo raw cruciferous

The bottom line message about cruciferous vegetables is that they have many benefits, including anti-anxiety benefits, but don't overdo them in raw form. Don't make this family the only vegetables you eat, but enjoy adding them—especially in cooked versions—to your menu. And, if you have a thyroid condition, check in with your doctor for specific advice.

38 Sweet Peppers

Sweet peppers are good to great sources of:

- vitamin C and
- B vitamins (except B12).

Sweet peppers (aka bell peppers) are green, red, orange, and yellow bell peppers. They make the list because of their very high vitamin C content and their anti-anxiety bonus component: carotenoids.

Carotenoids (i.e., beta-carotene, lutein, and zeaxanthin) are associated with brightly and darkly pigmented foods. Research has demonstrated that they are very helpful for reducing oxidative stress and inflammation,[1] both of which could help you deal with stress. Though there isn't a lot of research into a direct link to an anti-anxiety effect, a 2017 American study of sixty young adults showed a correlation between increased carotenoid consumption and reduced stress and cortisol.[2]

Vitamin C in foods can be destroyed by heat or light, and it deteriorates over time with exposure to air. Don't overprocess or overcook peppers and other vitamin C foods. Eating them raw and fresh will maximize their benefit. You can cook them lightly, but don't overdo the exposure to heat.

One downside of peppers is that they are part of the nightshades family of foods. Some people are sensitive to this group, which includes tomatoes, potatoes, eggplant, and bell peppers. Joint pain is the most common complaint that is associated with nightshades. If you start eating more peppers and find you suddenly get more joint pain, intestinal problems, or allergy symptoms, then this may not be a good vegetable for you.

Fermented Foods

Fermented foods are a great source of:

- probiotic bacteria.

In addition to the probiotics, each fermented food has the benefits of the actual food that is fermented.

Foods that can be a good source of probiotics include:

- yogurt,
- kefir,
- sauerkraut,
- kimchi (aka kimchee),
- fermented pickles, and
- other fermented pickled vegetables and foods.

The bacteria have to be alive

Not all "pickled" foods are fermented. There are different pickling processes; some involve bacterial fermentation and some do not. I was frustrated to see a plethora of headlines like "Eat Pickles to Ease Social Anxiety" for articles that go on to report the results of research demonstrating that probiotics can help social anxiety. These articles commonly suggest anti-anxiety interventions like eating a pickle before a date to reduce your stress response. Eating a typical pickle from a jar that came off a grocery store shelf is not going to help you feel less anxious on a date or at any other social event!

To get the full benefit out of a fermented food, the bacteria have to be alive when you eat the food. Some fermented products have had their bacteria killed off or removed via heating or filtration in order to extend their shelf life. These products will be sitting on grocery store shelves, not in the refrigerator section. That doesn't mean that all refrigerated fermented foods have live cultures; you still need to check the label for the magic words: "live cultures."

Be particularly attentive when buying yogurt. It is a great example of a health food turned junk food. Most yogurt brands are dead and full of artificial color and sweetener or sugary ingredients like high-fructose corn syrup. Read the label and go for yogurts with live cultures and no sweetener of any kind. (You can add your own sugar-free fruits and a bit of honey or other natural sweetener.)

Even if the yogurt is free of negative additives, compared to other foods on the list above it is likely to have fewer species and fewer CFUs (Colony Forming Units) of helpful bacteria.

To get the probiotic benefits from foods you purchase, look in the refrigerator section of the grocery store and check for words like **"live cultures"** on labels.

Seaweed

Seaweed (aka sea vegetables) is a good to great source of:[1]

- magnesium,
- zinc, and
- B vitamins (except B12)*.

*Some types of seaweed might have B12, but it is disputed whether it is an active form.[2]

Seaweed is a great low-calorie food because of the nutrients listed and because of its bonus nutrient: iodine. The best natural sources of iodine live in the sea. According to Dr. David Brownstein, author of *Iodine: Why You Need It, Why You Can't Live Without It*:

> All the glands of the body depend on adequate iodine levels to function optimally. Animal studies have shown problems with the adrenal gland...as well as the entire endocrine system, when there is an iodine deficient state.[3]

Common in many coastal cultures, seaweed's use as a food has been introduced to other cultures as sushi has become more popular. There are many different varieties of edible seaweed including nori, arame, kombu, wakame, dulce, and kelp. Hijiki is another seaweed eaten in many parts of the world, but it should be avoided because of notoriously high arsenic levels.

Nori may be the seaweed that is most familiar to you. It is used to make sushi and is dried and roasted to make a snack food. When eating sushi, avoid large fish such as swordfish, shark, and tuna (ahi) because of the mercury. As I mentioned when talking about fish-sourced mercury earlier, mercury has lots of downsides for your body including the potential of creating anxiety symptoms. Also avoid farm-raised fish because it is fed GMO grain rather than a natural fish diet and may be dyed.

Next to nori, arame is my personal favorite. It is low on the fishy-smell scale and has a nice mild flavor. One way I make it is in a salad: soak dried arame according to the package, add cucumber, carrot, and onion, and toss with a balsamic vinegar, lemon juice, and olive oil dressing. Let it marinate in the fridge for a couple of hours or a couple of days. It's an easy make-ahead side dish.

A note of caution: Because seaweed is such a great source of iodine, consuming very large amounts of it could over-elevate your iodine level. Some iodine is good, too much could cause problems. While iodine is needed for your glands, and very helpful in particular if your thyroid is underactive, it may cause problems if your thyroid is overactive, or improve the potency of thyroid medications (if you are on them) to the point where your medications need to be adjusted. For an in-depth discussion about thyroid and iodine, check out Dr. Brownstein's book *Iodine: Why You Need It, Why You Can't Live Without It*.[4]

Berries and Cherries

Berries and cherries are good sources of:

- magnesium,
- zinc, and
- vitamin C.

Red, blue, purple, and black berries, along with cherries, have the anti-anxiety bonus of anthocyanins. Anthocyanins are flavonoids associated with red, blue, and purple/black fruits and vegetables. They fight oxidative stress, are anti-inflammatory, and protect nerve cells.[1] A study with stressed mice showed that anthocyanins helped mitigate stress by improving dopamine levels and reducing oxidative stress in brain tissue.[2]

There are many types of berries:

- acai berries
- raspberries
- blueberries
- blackberries
- elderberries
- cranberries
- strawberries*
- and more

*According to the Environmental Working Group (EWG), which examines results from the USDA's annual crop tests, strawberries are notorious for extreme levels of pesticides and the use of poisonous gas injected into the soil before planting.[3] The EWG recommends that you either eat other berries instead or buy your strawberries from reliable organic sources.

42 Sprouted Rice and Quinoa

Rice and quinoa are good to great sources of:

- magnesium,
- zinc, and
- B vitamins.

Sprouting (aka germinating) rice and quinoa:[1]

- increases their vitamins and minerals including magnesium and zinc, and

- diminishes antinutrient phytates that could interfere with mineral absorption.

Sprouted rice is sometimes called *GABA rice* because soaking and germinating rice can increase its GABA content. The GABA in 3.5 ounces of rice can be increased from 4 mg in ordinary brown rice to 18 mg after twenty-four hours of soaking.[2] While this is the only direct food source for GABA, the amount per serving after sprouting is still very small.

Even though it is questionable whether you would get a benefit from the GABA in sprouted rice, the boosts in nutrients and the reduction in phytate are clear pluses for sprouting. You can sprout rice and quinoa yourself or purchase them already sprouted.

Quinoa is used similarly to rice in meal planning but whereas rice is a grain, quinoa is a seed. Sprouted brown rice has some amino acids; it is not a complete protein on its own, but it can be combined with sprouted lentils and beans to create a complete protein meal. Quinoa, on the other hand, is a good vegetarian source of complete protein as it houses all of the essential amino acids.

Stress Resilience Foods Cheat Sheet

As a reminder, my advice about healthy eating is that you:

- focus on real food,
- eat protein throughout the day,
- eat your vegetables,
- have some fruit but don't overdo it,
- eat a variety of foods,
- eat organic and pasture-raised if and when you can,
- reduce regular salt but include sea salt or Real Salt™.

My Top Dozen foods for stress resilience:

1. Water
2. Wild-caught salmon, sardines, and herring
3. Oysters
4. Pasture-raised eggs
5. Pasture-raised meat
6. Sprouted lentils and beans
7. Cruciferous vegetables
8. Sweet peppers
9. Fermented foods
10. Seaweed
11. Berries and cherries
12. Sprouted rice and quinoa

There's a summary of the dozen foods and stress-managing elements each contain on the next two pages.

	FOOD	WHAT IT HELPS WITH
1	**Water**	hydration
2	**Wild-caught salmon, sardines, herring**	• EPA and DHA omega-3 fats • magnesium • Vitamin D3 • B vitamins • AAs (incl. tryp. & glycine)
3	**Oysters**	• zinc • magnesium • EPA and DHA omega-3 fats • B vitamins • AAs (incl. tryp. & glycine)
4	**Pasture-raised eggs**	**All eggs:** • B vitamins • AAs (incl. tryp. & glycine) **Pasture-raised:** • Vitamin D3 • more vitamin A • more DHA and EPA omega-3s • a better omega 6:3 ratio
5	**Pasture-raised meat** (poultry, beef, pork, lamb, game)	**Poultry** • AAs (esp. high in tryp. & glycine) • B vitamins • zinc (dark meat) **Beef, pork, lamb, and game** • AAs (incl. tryp. & glycine) • B vitamins • zinc
6	**Sprouted lentils and beans**	• magnesium • zinc • B vitamins • AAs (incl. tryp. & glycine, but not complete)

	FOOD	WHAT IT HELPS WITH
7	**Cruciferous vegetables** (broccoli, cauliflower, Brussels sprouts, cabbage, kale, collard greens, bok choy, arugula . . .)	• magnesium • B vitamins (except B12) • vitamin C • sulphuraphane
8	**Sweet peppers**	• vitamin C • B vitamins (except B12) • carotenoids
9	**Fermented foods**	probiotic bacteria
10	**Seaweed**	• magnesium • zinc • B vitamins (except B12) • iodine
11	**Berries and cherries**	• magnesium • zinc • vitamin C • anthocyanins
12	**Sprouted rice or quinoa**	• magnesium • zinc • B vitamins • rice: complements AAs in lentils and beans • quinoa: has complete AAs

Notes: AAs = mix of protein amino acids; tryp. = tryptophan; incl. = including; esp. = especially.

Now let's take a look at some supplements that can feed your calm and add to your stress management anti-anxiety arsenal.

Part Five

Stress Resilience Supplements

Your health is an investment,
not an expense.

– Unknown

Supplement Tips & My Top 10 List

Supplements offer a way to boost particular nutrients individually or in mixes of several together. They also give you an opportunity to consume some herbs or plants not readily available as a food that you would prepare and eat.

Even natural substances can cause problems for some people some of the time. Be thoughtful about taking supplements. You can be allergic to particular herbs or have other negative reactions. (I discovered that I am allergic to barberry when I tried taking it for an illness. It took me a couple of days to realize that the bumps I developed near my mouth were a reaction to the supplement. It seems pretty random what a person can react to.)

If you are on pharmaceutical drugs, check with your doctor to make sure there aren't any negative interactions between supplements you are considering and your medications. There are some online sources with lists of interactions between pharmaceuticals and supplements. The Medscape and WebMD websites, for example, have drug/supplement interaction checkers.[1]

If you are pregnant or breastfeeding, you should also check with your doctor about supplements, especially herbs or other botanicals.

Tips for taking supplements:

- Quality is important. Buy supplements that are from organic or non-GMO sources whenever you can.

- Look at the back of supplement bottles to see the full list of ingredients.

- Avoid supplements with added artificial color and preservatives.

- Start new supplements one at a time in small doses. Work your way up to a full dose over a few days so you get a chance to catch any negative reaction.

- You may want to get lab tests before starting supplements so you establish a baseline of where you are without them. (See Appendix: Lab Tests.)

Your body is different than everyone else's (unless you have an identical twin) and you have a unique set of circumstances and exposure to physical and emotional stressors. Which supplements are best for you and in what amount is very individual. Start with what stands out to you as potentially helpful. If you have co-occurring conditions, check the Bonuses and Encouraging Research sections throughout Part Two: What Helps Your Calm to review some of the other conditions each supplement helps with beyond anxiety relief.

My Top 10 Stress Resilience Supplements

1. Magnesium
2. Zinc
3. B vitamins
4. Vitamin C
5. Vitamin D_3
6. Omega-3 Fats, EPA and DHA
7. Theanine
8. Probiotics
9. Adaptogens
10. Nervine herbs

This is not an exhaustive list of supplements that may help feed your calm; these are the ones that percolated up to the top of the options during my research. GABA may be helpful, but didn't make the cut because of conflicting reports about its effectiveness. 5-HTP might be something you want to consider, but I didn't include it on the list because it tends to be used more for depression than anxiety. There are other supplements that we haven't discussed but your doctor may suggest.

As reference points, I will give you the Recommended Daily Allowance (RDA), Tolerable Upper Intake Level (UL), and commonly recognized supplement dosage recommendations for maintaining healthy levels of nutrients in adults. You should also check supplement labels for suggested serving sizes and doses. Note that I only list nutrient levels for adults. If you are supplementing children, seek other sources for recommended dosage.

If you have a deficiency for a particular nutrient, you may benefit from higher therapeutic doses of supplements. Consult a doctor to get up-to-date customized recommendations for therapeutic doses that fit your body and situation. Naturopathic doctors and Functional Medicine doctors are particularly well educated on the topic of supplements and experienced with supplement prescription.

Notes for Bringing It All Together

As you read the chapters of Part Five, keep a lookout for supplements that contain elements you noted being of particular interest to you when you read Parts Two and Three. Also note which supplements would be helpful in covering nutrients that you aren't getting in food. Consider how your food and supplements can work together to maximize your stress resilience.

You may want to note your insights on the pages set aside in Part Six: Bringing It All Together.

45   Magnesium

> **Reminder of magnesium's stress resilience benefits**
> Magnesium helps maintain healthy adrenal function
> and stable blood glucose, and it assists in muscle
> relaxation, gut and nerve health, sleep, and the creation
> and use of calming neurotransmitters.

Supplementing magnesium is both easy and complicated. It is easy because oral magnesium supplements are readily available and magnesium can be absorbed through the skin.

Magnesium can be taken orally or transdermally (through your skin.)

It is complicated because magnesium has to be compounded with some other ingredient to create a stable substance and there are many different compounds with a variety of results. Many of the magnesium compounds available in oral supplements are not absorbed well and/or cause diarrhea.

My personal experience with magnesium supplements is that I tend to feel slightly nauseous when I take them orally. I do much better with transdermal magnesium (magnesium oil and footbaths). I had chronic neck pain for a decade after a roll-over car accident. After I started using transdermal magnesium, I noticed my neck pain went away, which makes sense because magnesium is a muscle relaxer. If I slack off on using magnesium oil or footbaths, my neck pain returns after about three days. When I start using them again, the neck pain goes away within a few hours.

Some doctors suggest using both oral and transdermal magnesium initially to get your blood level up.[1]

Transdermal magnesium

One way to get magnesium is through your skin.[2]

Skin absorption methods for supplementation are called *transdermal*: through the dermis (skin). Transdermal magnesium application gets around the need to search through various oral compounds to find one that works for you and it lets you take in more magnesium without hitting laxative overload.

Magnesium can be administered transdermally using a solution that you spray on your skin, lotions, or as flakes/salts added to a twenty-minute foot or body bath.

Because magnesium helps relax your body and your mind, soaking in a magnesium-enriched foot or body bath before bed can be a great way to wind down and improve your sleep. A full-body bath gives you more skin exposure so it has the potential of increasing the amount you absorb, but also requires more of your magnesium source than you need for a foot bath because of the greater water volume. For even more relaxing effect, you can add lavender or other calming essential oils to your bath along with the magnesium flakes or salts.

To double the relaxing effect of a magnesium bath or footbath, add calming essential oils such as lavender, chamomile, holy basil, bergamot, valerian, rose, or frankincense.

There are 2 compounds of magnesium for transdermal use:

1. Magnesium sulfate
2. Magnesium chloride

1. Magnesium sulfate

Magnesium sulfate is also known as *Epsom salts*. The name Epsom comes from the British town where it was first created in the 1600s by boiling down spring water. Epsom salts are quite inexpensive and easy to find in grocery stores, drug stores, and online. This is the salt used in most of the floatation tanks that have become popular for relaxing and relieving tension. It can be used in foot and body baths.

If you are using Epsom salts, try to find a brand that talks about its purity. You don't want to be absorbing toxic stuff when you're trying to do your body good.

2. Magnesium chloride

Dr. Mark Sircus, author of *Transdermal Magnesium Therapy*, prefers magnesium chloride over magnesium sulfate:

> Epsom Salts are wonderful for many applications and one can put hundreds of pounds of it in isolation chambers so you can float easily in them . . .. For some reason magnesium chloride is hugely more absorbable through transdermal means than magnesium sulfate (Epsom Salt).[3]

Magnesium chloride can be applied to the skin as magnesium oil, gel, or lotion. Magnesium chloride flakes can be used in foot or body baths. (One cup per foot bath.)

Magnesium oil is not really an oil. It is a water solution of magnesium chloride but it feels slippery like an oil. You simply spray it on your body. There is one catch: some of the solutions available can make you itchy until you build up your magnesium level and they may leave a residue that you have to wipe off. Don't apply it right after shaving, or you'll definitely feel an itchy burn. I spray it on my abdomen, arms, and legs morning and night, and gently rub it in. I've never had any residue problems.

Like with Epsom salts, purity can be an issue with magnesium chloride. Dr. Sircus and others raise concerns about environmental contamination of sea and lake sources. The purest source appears to be a deep ancient mine in Northern Europe known as the Zechstein Seabed. The Ancient Minerals brand of magnesium chloride supplements uses the Zechstein mine as their source and is the brand recommended by Dr. Sircus and Dr. Dean, author of *The Magnesium Miracle*.

> **Magnesium Oil Tips**
>
> Don't spray it on newly shaved skin. If you get itchy from it, try diluting it 1:1 for a while. If it leaves a residue, try using less at one time or spray it over a larger area.

Oral supplements

Magnesium can't be offered as a supplement all by itself. It has to be combined with some other mineral ion. There are more than a dozen different magnesium compounds offered in oral supplements. Oral magnesium can be more or less absorbable and diarrhea-causing depending on what it is bound to.

There is a school of thought that oral magnesium only causes diarrhea when you hit your maximum useable intake, but that theory doesn't really hold up in practical use. Many magnesium oral supplements cause diarrhea in many people even when they are magnesium deficient.[4]

Oral magnesium supplement compounding partners

Here is a sample of magnesium supplement combinations:[5]

Magnesium oxide is the cheapest form and widely used for supplements, but it is also the worst. It is poorly absorbed by your body, and it tends to cause diarrhea.

Magnesium aspartate is more absorbable than the oxide form but it is *not* good for people with anxiety because aspartate is an excitatory amino acid.

Magnesium carbonate is less soluble and absorbable than the compounds listed below.

Magnesium citrate is one of the most common forms for oral supplementation but it is quite laxative. It may be good for people with a combination of anxiety and constipation. Natural CALM is a powder drink by Natural Vitality that is commonly used for anxiety relief and improved sleep. It is effective, but you have to be careful with dosage so you don't get diarrhea. Follow the bottle's directions to start off with a small dose and gradually increase it to find your optimum intake. (Other powder formulations may be better because they don't have this side effect, but this product is readily available and relatively inexpensive.)

Magnesium malate, taurate, lactate, succinate, fumarate, and gluconate are some middle-of-the-road oral magnesium supplements for people with anxiety.

Magnesium L-threonate is a new kid on the block. Research on rats shows promising evidence that this form of magnesium has superior ability to enter the brain and improve learning and memory.[6] Its ability to enter the brain might mean that it is particularly helpful for anxiety as well. But, it is very expensive and may be more hype than extra benefit.

Magnesium glycinate has the advantage of including the calming neurotransmitter glycine. It is fairly well absorbed and less laxative than some other forms. (Watch out for supplements that say magnesium glycinate on the front but then reveal on the back that they have some other magnesium compounds, like oxide, as well. I got burnt on this myself.)

Magnesium bisglycinate is a slightly different glycine formulation that is promising. Thorne makes a powder version that can be used to make an evening drink to help with sleep. It is more expensive than Natural CALM but less likely to cause diarrhea. Many companies produce it in capsule form.

If you use oral magnesium, it is recommended that you *not* take it with a meal that is phytate-heavy (unsprouted whole grains, legumes, nuts, or seeds) or oxalate-heavy (spinach, Swiss chard, almonds, rhubarb, or beets) because these antinutrients may grab the minerals before they get a chance to enter your bloodstream.

Contraindications

Dr. Dean mentions four contraindications to magnesium therapy in *The Magnesium Miracle*:[7]

- kidney failure,
- myasthenia gravis (a chronic autoimmune neuromuscular disease),
- excessively slow heart rate, and
- bowel obstruction.

Recommended amounts for magnesium

The chart below includes a range of supplementation recommendations from different sources.

WHO	RDA mg/day	SUPPLEMENTATION DOSAGE mg/day	
		PDR for Nutritional Supplements[8]	*Nutrition Essentials for Mental Health*[9]
Men			
19–30 yrs old	400		
over 30	420		
Women		100–350	100–400
19–30 yrs old	310		
over 30	320		

Zinc

> **Reminder of zinc's stress resilience benefits**
> Zinc assists with nerve cell growth and health,
> and balances receptor operation for the excitatory
> neurotransmitter glutamate
> and inhibitory neurotransmitter GABA.

Supplementing with zinc is a bit challenging because the Recommended Daily Allowance is quite low and there is a fairly small ideal zone between the RDA and the Upper Limit that has been established to ensure that you don't take in so much zinc that you interfere with your use of copper. Remember that one of your aims is a healthy copper-zinc ratio. Too much copper throws off your zinc and vice versa.

It may be helpful to your stress resistance to take a zinc supplement, but take your food sources into consideration when you're calculating your daily dose and don't go over 40 mg/day for extended periods without doctor supervision.

Zinc is available in lozenge, liquid, powder, and capsule forms. Lozenges seem to target cold symptoms and include other ingredients that are immune boosters.

Like magnesium, zinc has to be compounded with another biochemical for supplemental delivery. And, like magnesium, there are many different combinations on the market, some with better absorption track records than others and varying physical impacts.

Zinc supplement compounding partners

Here is a sample of zinc supplement combinations:[1]

Zinc oxide is the cheapest form and poorly absorbed by your body. Cream forms may work as a sunblock, but avoid it in oral supplements.

Zinc aspartate isn't the best choice for stress relief because aspartate is an excitatory neurotransmitter.

Zinc sulphonate may be harder on intestinal tissue than other forms of zinc supplements.

Zinc citrate or gluconate do not appear to be as absorbable as the following formulations.

Zinc picolinate has been demonstrated as highly absorbable in research studies.

Zinc bisglycinate includes the calming neurotransmitter glycine and is relatively well absorbed.

Zinc carnosine has the added benefit of healing gastrointestinal tract tissue so it seems like a good choice for countering leaky gut as well as other stomach and intestinal-lining issues.

As with magnesium, taking your zinc supplements at the same time as you eat high-phytate foods such as unsprouted whole grains, nuts, seeds, and legumes could reduce the availability of the zinc because phytate can bind with the mineral.[2]

Recommended amounts for zinc

WHO	RDA mg/day	UL mg/day	SUPPLEMENTATION DOSAGE mg/day *PDR for Nutritional Supplements*[3]
Men	11	40	15
Women	8		

B Vitamins

> **Reminder of B vitamins' stress resilience benefits**
> B vitamins help with your calming
> neurotransmitter synthesis, adrenal glands,
> nerve cells, and stabilization of blood glucose.

There are eight water-soluble B vitamins. All eight are often available together in *B-complex* supplements. It may be particularly helpful to get them together because they support and assist each other.

> *B-complex* supplements contain all eight B vitamins.

One strategy is to start by taking a high-quality B-complex and then add individual B vitamins if it seems appropriate for your circumstances and body. You might also consider a high-quality multivitamin as a way to get all your Bs and your vitamin C at the same time.

I provide more detail below on supplements for a couple of the B vitamins that need more explanation than the others: B9 (folate) and B12. These are available in different chemical configurations that are not all created equal. Even if you are looking for a B-complex, it is important to check that B9 and B12 are found in useable forms.

B9 (folate)

Vitamin B9 shows up in supplements in two different forms. One is natural. One is unnatural.

B9 occurs naturally in foods as folate. Folic acid is the synthetic form of the vitamin used in many supplements and as an additive to fortify food. Folic acid does not have the same chemical makeup as folate, and folic acid does not occur naturally in food. Folic acid is basically a B9 knock-off. (To make this vitamin even trickier to understand, many people use the terms *folate* and *folic acid* interchangeably when talking about B9.)

Natural vitamin B9 appears on supplement labels designated by several different terms such as:

- folate,
- L-methylfolate,
- L 5 methyl-tetrahydrofolate (5-MTHF),
- Metafolin (a folate patented by Merck), or
- Deplin (a prescription form of L-methylfolate).

If the label says *folic acid* you're getting the synthetic B9, not the natural. Folic acid as a supplement for B9 was introduced in the 1940s, but there are growing concerns about ingesting large amounts of this unnatural substance. If you take folic acid supplements, your body needs to use four different biochemical reactions to convert the folic acid to useable folate.[1] Some people's genetics allow them to do this more easily than others. There is recent research to suggest that folic acid at high doses may cause cancer or make cancer worse.[2] Sticking to folate instead seems like a better way to go.

I found a number of brands that use the preferred folate instead of folic acid in their supplements:

- Pure Synergy (organic whole food sourced)
- Garden of Life (non-GMO, mostly organic whole food sourced)
- Integrative Therapeutics
- Seeking Health
- Designs for Health
- Thorne

B12

Vitamin B12 (AKA cobalamin) has some complicating formulation and absorption factors that the other Bs don't have to contend with. And, like B9, B12 has natural and synthetic forms.

Some authors online call B12 "cyanocobalamin." That is a misrepresentation of the vitamin. The mix-up happens because cyanocobalamin is the most common synthetic supplemental form of B12, but it is not correct to equate them. It is more correct to call B12 *cobalamin* and recognize that there are different biochemicals compounded with cobalamin in nature and in the lab.

B12 (cobalamin) is found in two *active forms* in your body:

1. methylcobalamin
2. adenosylcobalamin

In supplements, the most common and cheapest cobalamin is cyanocobalamin (aka Cyano B12). It is not found in notable amounts naturally in humans or foods. It is very heat resistant and stable so it has been attractive to manufacturers as a supplement and food fortifier. However, cyanocobalamin can't be used directly by your body. It needs to go through a number of chemical reactions to be changed into something you can use. On top of taxing your body, in the process of converting cyanocobalamin into a form you can use small amounts of cyanide are split off and have to be detoxed, further straining your systems.

There are three forms of supplemental B12 that are bioavailable. Which one is best for you is an individual body thing.

Methylcobalamin (Methyl B12) is fairly easy to find and is used well by your body. It may be too stimulating for some people, however.

Hydroxocobalamin (Hydroxo B12) is another form of B12 found naturally in food and added to supplements. It is not as common as the methyl form but has the advantage of having more of a time-release quality so might give you sustained energy rather than a surge. It may be particularly helpful for reducing gut inflammation.

Bottom line for taking B12

Avoid cyanocobalamin. Choose one of the other forms or a combination of them that works best for your budget and body.

Adenosylcobalamin (Adeno B12) is a natural form of B12 that your body readily uses. It is less stable and more expensive than other forms of B12, making it not very common. It is one of the most bioavailable forms of B12, though, as it directly supports energy production inside your cells.

Seeking Health offers many different B12 options including the rarer Hydroxo and Adeno forms.

A couple of groups of people are particularly vulnerable to B12 deficiency:

1. Vegetarians tend to be low on B12 because it is predominantly sourced in animal products. The B12 vegetable sources some vegetarians rely on for this vitamin have been found to have mostly an inactive form.

2. People with low stomach acid have a problem getting the B12 from their food into their system because

stomach acid is needed to break the bond between the vitamin and the protein it is attached to. So, if you take antacids or have low stomach acid for other reasons, you should pay particular attention to supplementing this vitamin. Sublingual (under the tongue) vitamin B12 supplements or versions that you spray into your mouth get around the stomach acid issue. You may also get B12 injections from your doctor.

When to take B vitamins

Take your B vitamins in the morning and early afternoon because they can be energizing and could interfere with sleep if taken late in the day. Some people feel nauseous after taking B vitamins. This can typically be alleviated by taking B supplements at the same time as eating a meal. If you take too much B3 (niacin), you could experience flushing hot flashes. If that happens, reduce your intake or take niacin in the form of niacinamide.

Recommended amounts for B vitamins

David Kennedy, author of the 2016 journal article "B Vitamins and the Brain, Dose and Efficacy—A Review," recommends that we each get much more than the B vitamin RDAs:

> The optimum level of any micronutrient must lie well above the RDA, and the B vitamins can generally be consumed at many times the RDA.[11]

Doctors often recommend therapeutic doses higher than those listed in the table on the next page.

In the table below, amounts are listed in mg (milligrams) or µg (micrograms) per day. N/A = Not Available because no value has been set.

B VITAMIN	RDA Men	RDA Women	UL Men/ Women	SUPPLEMENTATION DOSAGE PDR for Nutritional Supplements
B1, Thiamine	1.2 mg	1.1 mg	N/A	1.5–10 mg[3]
B2, Riboflavin	1.3 mg	1.1 mg	N/A	1.7–10 mg[4]
B3, Niacin	16 mg	14 mg	35 mg	20–100 mg[5]
B5, Pantothenic acid	5 mg	5 mg	N/A	10–50 mg[6]
B6, Pyridoxine	1.3 mg > 50 yrs old: 1.7	1.3 mg > 50 yrs old: 1.5	100 mg	2–20 mg[7]
B7, Biotin	30 µg	30 µg	N/A	30–60 µg[8]
B9, Folate	400 µg	400 µg	1000 µg* (1 mg)	400 µg[9]
B12, Cobalamin	2.4 µg	2.4 µg	N/A	3–30 µg[10]

*The UL listed for folate is only for the synthetic folic acid, which is found in many lower-quality supplements.

Vitamin C

> **Reminder of vitamin C's stress resilience benefits**
> Vitamin C assists with nerve cell
> and adrenal gland health.

Vitamin C supplements have been around a long time, and I used to think that they were straightforward, all good. I was wrong. There is a big difference between lab-created vitamin C and food-sourced vitamin C. The typical vitamin C supplement contains ascorbic acid, which is a synthetic ingredient made in a lab from corn syrup (probably from GMO corn unless clearly marked non-GMO). In nature, ascorbic acid is found with other nutrients, not as a stand-alone.

Dr. Leslie Korn writes in *Nutrition Essentials for Mental Health: A Complete Guide to the Food-Mood Connection*, "A good vitamin C is a complex (not just ascorbic acid) and contains bioflavonoids and rutin."[1] Some natural vitamin C supplements contain citrus bioflavonoids or buckwheat berry sprouts, both of which include rutin.

Here are examples of food-sourced vitamin C supplements that include bioflavonoids and rutin and are non-GMO:

- Pure Synergy, Pure Radiance C
- Garden of Life, Living Vitamin C
- Naturelo, Vitamin C Organic Acerola Cherry with Citrus Bioflavonoids

The best way to get a high-quality C may be in a food-sourced multivitamin such as that made by Garden of Life where you can take it in with the B complex of vitamins also.

Recommended amounts for vitamin C

In the table below, note that there are higher RDA values for smokers.

WHO	RDA mg/day	UL mg/day	SUPPLEMENTATION DOSAGE mg/day PDR for Nutritional Supplements[2]
Men			
non-smokers	90		
smokers	125	2000	
Women			200–2000
non-smokers	75		
smokers	110	2000	

Vitamin D$_3$

> **Reminder of vitamin D's stress resilience benefits**
> Vitamin D helps with calming neurotransmitter
> synthesis and nerve health.

The best way to get vitamin D is from the sun, but if cloudy weather or other conditions get in the way of you achieving enough sun exposure, you may benefit from supplementing with vitamin D$_3$ because food sources of the vitamin are not thought to be adequate to get you to optimal levels.[1] Your need to supplement may change throughout the year as your sun exposure changes.

Vitamin D supplements are available in two forms: D$_2$ and D$_3$. D$_3$ is more useable by your body.[2]

Vitamin D is fat soluble so it can build up in your body. Water-soluble vitamins like the Bs or C will get flushed out through your urine if you take too much, but the fat-soluble vitamins are retained if you overdo the supplements. Too much vitamin D can have a negative impact on your body systems, including interfering with calcium getting laid down in your bones. You can't get too much D from the sun as your body will just stop making it when you've hit ideal levels. You can, however, overdo intake from supplements.

It can be particularly beneficial to do blood tests to check your baseline vitamin D amount before supplementing and then monitor levels with testing while you supplement so you can hit ideal levels. If your vitamin D levels are low, a doctor will typically prescribe short-term high doses above the UL to get your levels up to normal, but you should only megadose with a doctor's supervision. (See Appendix: Lab Tests for info about an online source for vitamin D tests.)

Recommended amounts for vitamin D$_3$

The recommended levels for supplementing vitamin D are the same for both men and women but the RDA increases with age. RDA and UL numbers are given in both IU (International Units) and µg (micrograms) per day.

WHO	RDA /day	UL /day	SUPPLEMENTATION DOSAGE IU/day PDR for Nutritional Supplements[3]
< 70 years old	600 IU 15 µg	4000 IU 100 µg	2000–4000 IU
> 70 years old	800 IU 20 µg		

> **Reminder of EPA and DHA's stress resilience benefits**
> These omega-3 fats help with nerve cell health,
> feel-good neurotransmitter production and reception,
> inflammation and oxidative stress reduction, and
> possibly moderation of cortisol levels.

Fish oil is the most common supplement source for EPA and DHA omega-3s. Fish supplements vary in the amount of omega-3s present. Choose supplements that have particularly high values for EPA.[1] Look for promises that the source fish are wild caught and tested for toxins such as heavy metals, and inclusion of natural-sourced antioxidant preservatives.

Keep your fish oil capsules in the fridge. You absolutely don't want to consume rancid fish oil. Don't use it past its expiration date. Ideally, spread the dosage consumed throughout the day.

Omega-3 supplementation goals

Look for supplements that have lots of DHA and EPA (especially EPA).

Krill oil is an alternative that is supposed to have the advantage of being more stable because it naturally contains antioxidants. Some doctors say that you require less EPA and DHA when it is coming from krill oil versus fish oil. I tried it myself for quite a while, but honestly, I didn't find it as helpful as fish oil for mental sharpness, so I went back to fish oil.

Nordic Naturals' Ultimate Omega with 650 mg EPA and 450 mg DHA per two capsules is the product that I personally use and recommend to my clients. It is made from deep sea anchovies and sardines, and includes rosemary extract as a preservative.

Several manufacturers produce a vegetarian EPA/DHA supplement from algae oil, but they offer less of the omegas we are targeting than the fish oil I mentioned above (that has 650 mg EPA and 450 mg DHA). For example, Nordic Naturals Algae Omega has 195 mg of EPA and 390 of DHA.

Fish oil is a mild anti-coagulant. Use with caution if you are on "blood-thinning" medication.

Recommended amounts for EPA and DHA

Instead of an RDA, omega-3s have a different recommendation value, *Adequate Intake (AI)*, which indicates a level assumed to provide nutritional adequacy. This value is for all omega-3s as a group. There are no daily requirement numbers for our target omegas, EPA and DHA.

The chart below includes supplementation dosage recommendations from different sources.

WHO	TOTAL OMEGA-3s AI mg/day	SUPPLEMENTATION DOSAGE mg/day	
		American Psychiatric Association[2]	*PDR for Nutritional Supplements*[3]
Men	1600	1000 EPA+DHA	3000 EPA+DHA
Women	1100		

Theanine

> **Reminder of theanine's stress resilience benefits**
> Theanine promotes relaxation without having a
> sedative effect.

L-theanine is an anti-anxiety amino acid that is readily available as a supplement in liquid, powder, capsule, softgel, chewable, or gummy form.

While L-theanine, not D-theanine, is the target anti-anxiety nutrient, many supplements contain a combination of the D and L forms. Look for supplements that only contain the L-form. *Suntheanine* is a patented type of theanine that is entirely L-theanine. Many different companies have Suntheanine-based products (e.g., Doctor's Best, Sport's Research, and Integrative Therapeutics).

As I mentioned in the previous section, when speaking of nervine herbs, Garden of Life Mykind Organics' Sleep Well combines several nervine herbs and L-theanine and is available as a mouth spray or capsules.

Jarrow makes a 100 mg gummy that could be handy for stressful situations. You may need to take two at a time to reach the common recommended adult dosage.

Theanine can lower blood pressure, so don't take it if you already have low blood pressure or if you are on medication for high blood pressure.

There are no RDA amounts for theanine. In *Prescription for Natural Cures*, doctors Mark Stengler, James Balch, and Robin Young Balch recommend 200 to 250 mg of L-theanine twice a day for anxiety.[1] They recommend 200 to 500 mg in one dose a half hour before bed if you suffer from insomnia.[2]

52

Probiotics

> **Reminder of probiotics' stress resilience benefits**
> Psychobiotics are a group of probiotic bacteria that
> have been found to improve mental health. Probiotics
> for anxiety help you use glucose, heal your gut wall,
> even out cortisol, reduce inflammation; they also help
> your brain in stress-reducing ways.

Probiotic supplements are a quick way to get large amounts of desirable bacteria into your gut. You want the bacteria to be alive and delivered in a way that will keep them alive so they can make it past your stomach acids into your intestine.

Recommendations typically talk about probiotic numbers in the range of 50 billion CFUs (Colony Forming Units) of a mix of bacterial species. You may need to start off at lower numbers to get your intestines used to the changes. If you get gassy or have intestinal upset with a brand of probiotics, consider trying a different brand or bacterial mix, or possibly reduce the number of CFUs and work your way back up.

These are the target probiotics most often mentioned in anti-anxiety and anti-depression studies:[1]

- *Lactobacillus acidophilus*
- *Lactobacillus casei*
- *Lactobacillus plantarum*
- *Lactobacillus helveticus*
- *Lactobacillus rhamnosus*
- *Bifidobacterium breve*
- *Bifidobacterium infantis*
- *Bifidobacterium lactis*
- *Bifidobacterium longum*

Besides looking at the mix of bacteria and the CFUs, also look for these quality markers:

- a guarantee that the potency is valid until the expiration date

- prebiotics included in the capsules (these foodstuffs will help the bacteria survive and thrive in your gut)

- resistance to stomach acids

- promises of being non-GMO and free of anything that would irritate your gut (e.g., gluten, soy, dairy, artificial preservatives)

I found UP4's Probiotics Ultra has a good number of the listed desirable bacterial species and fulfills the quality markers I mentioned.

High-quality probiotics are kind of expensive. To make them go further, you might only take them on days you don't eat fermented foods, especially after you have been on them for a while and have had a chance to change the bacterial mix in your gut.

Tip for when you take antibiotics

Because antibiotics can kill off healthy gut bacteria, boost use of probiotics during and after taking a round of antibiotics. During the course of treatment, stagger your probiotics in between antibiotic doses so that the antibiotics don't just immediately kill off the healthy bacteria in your supplement.

53   Adaptogens

Adaptogen supplements are created from the adaptogenic part of their respective plants. They are available as dried powders, capsules, extracts, or teas. As with all herbal products and supplements, adaptogens can interact with your pharmaceutical medications or be contraindicated during pregnancy or nursing. Consult with your doctor before taking them if any of these conditions apply to you.

Some adaptogens are more stimulating than others. Asian ginseng is the most stimulating so is not typically used for anxiety. (It might, however, be a good choice for you if you are worn down from adrenal fatigue.) If your symptoms are more in the high cortisol wound-up range, you may do better avoiding Asian ginseng and choosing one of the other more calming adaptogens instead. Ashwagandha may be the most calming. The other adaptogens land somewhere in between Asian ginseng and Ashwagandha. Whatever adaptogen you use, it is probably best to take it in the morning and early afternoon, avoiding ingesting it later in the day when it might interfere with sleep.

There are many adaptogens, including:

- Asian ginseng (*Panax ginseng*),
- American ginseng (*Panax quinquefolius*),
- Schisandra (*Schisandra chinenis*),
- Rhodiola (*Rhodiola rosea*, Arctic root),
- Eleuthero (*Eleutherococcus senticosus*, Siberian ginseng),
- Maca (*Lepidium meyenii*, Peruvian ginseng),

- Licorice Root (*Glycyrrhiza glabra, G. uralensis*),*
- Holy basil *(Ocimum sanctum, O. tenuifloru, tulsi)*, and
- Ashwagandha (*Withania somnifera*, Indian ginseng).

*Licorice can be toxic and cause an increase in blood pressure when consumed at high levels. Upper limits of the active ingredient glycyrrhizin have been set in some parts of the world; 100 mg per day is the lowest of the upper limits for glycyrrhizin. Note that this is not 100 mg per day of licorice root but rather 100 mg per day of glycyrrhizin. Glycyrrhizin varies from 2 to 5% of licorice root and can be as much as 15%,[1] so the limit would be 660 mg licorice root per day if the percentage is at its maximum. I include licorice root on the list of adaptogens because I see it appear in small amounts in anti-anxiety adaptogen mixes, but it isn't advised as a stand-alone high-dose adaptogen taken for extended periods.[2]

Many companies have produced adaptogen supplement mixes that include supporting nutrients. One example is Adrenotone by Designs for Health. Adrenotone has eleuthero, American ginseng, ashwagandha, rhodiola, a little licorice (20 mg), vitamin C, and some B vitamins.

Some people add maca powder to their morning shakes or other foods. I initially tried one brand of powder that had a very smoky flavor and I absolutely hated the taste of it. After many years of occasionally using maca capsules, I decided to give the powder a try again. The new brand I'm using, Raw Organic Maca Magic, doesn't have the offensive overwhelming flavor. Take-home message: it may take a couple of tries to find a powder that has a taste you like.

I also found some adaptogens in tea form:

- Traditional Medicinals (organic): Tulsi with Ginger
- Buddha Teas (organic): Ashwagandha Tea, Holy Basil Tea, Maca Tea

54 Nervine Herbs

> **Reminder of nervine herbs' stress resilience benefits**
> Nervine herbs are calming
> and potentially promote sleep.

Like with adaptogens, nervine herbs can have negative interactions with some pharmaceutical drugs and may have unknown or concerning effects for pregnant women or nursing mothers, so check with your doctor if these conditions apply. Be careful about using these herbs while driving. It would be best to test your reaction to them late in the day in case they cause drowsiness.

Herbs that may help you feel calm and help you sleep include:

- Passionflower (*Passiflora incarnata*),
- Chamomile (*Matricaria recutita*),
- Lemongrass (*Cymbopogon citratus*),
- Kava* (*Piper methysticum*, aka kava kava),
- Valerian (*Valeriana officinalis*), and
- Hops (*Humulus lupulus*).

*See Chapter 20: How Nervine Herbs Help in Part Two for a discussion about the kava controversy.

Nervine herbs are available in capsule form, liquid extracts, and teas. There are plenty of options with these teas so you may experiment with what you like in terms of relaxation effect and taste.

Garden of Life Mykind Organics has an interesting product called Sleep Well that includes several nervine herbs and L-theanine. It comes in capsule and mouth spray forms.

Many companies make teas of individual nervine herbs. Chamomile is probably the most common of these herbs available as a tea, but I easily found teas for other nervines:

- Yogi: Kava Stress Relief
- Alvita (organic): Passionflower and Lemongrass
- Buddha Teas: has an organic tea for each of the listed nervine herbs

Many tea companies have created mixes using a variety of nervines:

- Traditional Medicinals, Nighty Night (organic): passionflower, chamomile, hops, lemongrass . . .
- Celestial Seasonings, Sleepytime: chamomile, lemongrass . . .
- Yogi, Calming (organic): chamomile, lemongrass . . .

There are also some anti-anxiety and sleep-aid teas that combine nervine herbs and adaptogenic herbs or biochemicals:

- Traditional Medicinals, Cup of Calm (organic): passionflower, chamomile, the adaptogen licorice root . . .
- Yogi, Bedtime: passionflower, valerian, chamomile, the adaptogen licorice root . . .
- Yogi, Soothing Caramel Bedtime: chamomile, the amino acid L-Theanine . . .
- Organic India, Tulsi Sleep: chamomile, the adaptogens ashwagandha and tulsi (holy basil) . . .

There are no Recommended Daily Amounts for herbs. Each supplement or tea will have instructions about amounts to take. Be cautious about using them before driving until you figure out how they affect you.

Stress Resilience Supplements Cheat Sheet

This table is a summary of recommended amounts for stress resilience supplements discussed. For more details about supplementation levels, see each nutrient's individual chapter.

	NUTRIENT	RDA	UL	SUPPLEMENT DOSAGE
1	**Magnesium** mg/day	**Men:** 19–30 yrs old: 400 > 30 yrs: 420 **Women:** 19–30 yrs old: 310 > 30 yrs: 320	N/A	100–400
2	**Zinc** mg/day	**Men:** 11 **Women:** 8	40	15
3	**B1, Thiamine** mg/day	**Men:** 1.2 **Women:** 1.1	N/A	1.5–10
	B2, Riboflavin mg/day	**Men:** 1.3 **Women:** 1.1	N/A	1.7–10
	B3, Niacin mg/day	**Men:** 16 **Women:** 14	35	20–100
	B5, Pantothenic mg/day	**Men/Women:** 5	N/A	10–50
	B6, Pyridoxine mg/day	**Men:** 1.3 > 50 yrs old: 1.7 **Women:** 1.3 > 50 yrs old: 1.5	100	2–20
	B7, Biotin µg/day	**Men/Women:** 30	N/A	30–60
	B9, Folate µg/day	**Men/Women:** 400	1000*	400
	B12, Cobalamin µg/day	**Men/Women:** 2.4	N/A	3–30

* The UL listed for folate is only for the synthetic folic acid, which is found in many lower-quality supplements.

	NUTRIENT	RDA	UL	SUPPLEMENT DOSAGE
4	**Vitamin C** mg/day	**Men:** non-smokers: 90 smokers: 125 **Women:** non-smokers: 75 smokers: 110	2000	200–2000
5	**Vitamin D$_3$** IU/day	**Men/Women:** < 70 yrs old: 600 > 70 yrs old: 800	4000	2000–4000
	Vitamin D$_3$ μg/day	**Men/Women:** < 70 yrs old: 15 > 70 yrs old: 20	100	see IUs above
6	**Omega-3s, EPA + DHA** mg/day	**Men:** 1600 **Women:** 1100	N/A	1000–3000
7	**Theanine**	N/A	N/A	200–250 mg 2x/day or 200–500 mg before sleep

The chart on the next page gives you a quick reference for species of probiotics and plants that help feed your calm.

	ELEMENT	SPECIES
8	Probiotics	• *Lactobacillus acidophilus* • *Lactobacillus casei* • *Lactobacillus plantarum* • *Lactobacillus helveticus* • *Lactobacillus rhamnosus* • *Bifidobacterium breve* • *Bifidobacterium infantis* • *Bifidobacterium lactis* • *Bifidobacterium longum*
9	Adaptogens	• Asian ginseng (*Panax ginseng*) • American ginseng (*Panax quinquefolius*) • Schisandra (*Schisandra chinenis*) • Rhodiola (*Rhodiola rosea*, Arctic root) • Eleuthero (*Eleutherococcus senticosus*, Siberian ginseng) • Maca (*Lepidium meyenii*, Peruvian ginseng) • Licorice root (*Glycyrrhiza glabra*, G. *uralensis*)* • Holy basil (*Ocimum sanctum*, O. *tenuifloru*, *tulsi*) • Ashwagandha (*Withania somnifera*, Indian ginseng)
10	Nervine herbs	• Passionflower (*Passiflora incarnata*) • Chamomile (*Matricaria recutita*) • Lemongrass (*Cymbopogon citratus*) • Kava** (*Piper methysticum*, aka kava kava) • Valerian (*Valeriana officinalis*) • Hops (*Humulus lupulus*)

* Licorice can be toxic and cause an increase in blood pressure when consumed at high levels. It is included here because it appears in small amounts in anti-anxiety adaptogen mixes, but it isn't advised as a stand-alone high-dose adaptogen taken for extended periods.

**See Chapter 20: How Nervine Herbs Help in Part Two for a discussion about the kava controversy.

Part Six

Bringing It All Together

Every day is another chance
to get stronger,
to eat better,
to live healthier,
and to be the best version of you.

– Unknown

Bringing It All Together offers some prompts to help you reflect on the ideas presented throughout the book and gives you a place to track your learning and insights, build your knowledge without feeling overwhelmed, digest what you've read, and make a plan of action to make your life better.

It can also provide a record for you to refer back to as you experiment with making changes to boost your stress resilience and feed your calm.

For some of your notes, you may want to record page numbers for the source information so you can easily find it later.

You may want to put a paperclip or other marker on the edge of this page or the journaling page you're currently working on for quick reference.

_____

_____

_____

_____

_____

_____

_____

_____

_____

_____

_____

_____

_____

Part One: Your Body on Stress

Note connections between body systems mentioned and your symptoms related to anxiety or other health issues and any other insights from Part One.

1	**Adrenal gland**
2	**Nerves**
3	**Neurotransmitters**
4	**Relaxation**
5	**Gut**
6	**Glucose**

Part Two: What Helps Your Calm

Note connections between the 10 elements mentioned and your symptoms related to anxiety or other health issues. Also note if any mentioned causes of deficiency for particular elements resonate as being present in your life and any other insights from Part Two that could impact your plan to feed your calm and build stress resilience.

1	Magnesium
2	Zinc
3	B Vitamins
4	Vitamin C
5	Vitamin D
6	Omega-3 Fats

7	**Amino Acids** (protein amino acids plus theanine, 5-HTP, GABA)
8	**Probiotics**
9	**Adaptogens**
10	**Nervine Herbs**

Part Three: What Hurts Your Calm

Note connections between the five foods and food components mentioned and your symptoms related to anxiety or other health issues.

Use the prompts on the next page to make a plan of action to reduce or eliminate foods that may be hurting your calm. (**Note of Encouragement:** A plan is never set in stone. It's a starting point for experimenting to find out what works and doesn't work for you. Plans are meant to be revised as you learn from using your plan.)

1	Caffeine
2	Alcohol
3	Processed Foods
4	GMO Foods
5	Foods you are sensitive to

What food changes (reductions, eliminations, substitutions, testing, experimenting) **might be particularly helpful to you?**

_____

_____

_____

_____

_____

_____

_____

What steps are involved in making those changes?

_____

_____

_____

_____

_____

_____

_____

_____

Your plan of action to reduce or eliminate foods that may be hurting your calm:

_____

_____

_____

_____

_____

_____

Part Four: Stress Resilience Foods

Note any of the general eating advice that you would like to adopt, why you want to make the change, and how you can make the change happen.

1	Focus on real food
2	Eat protein throughout the day
3	Eat your vegetables
4	Have some fruit but don't overdo it
5	Eat a variety of foods
6	Eat organic and pasture-raised if and when you can
7	Reduce regular salt but include sea salt or Real Salt™

Note which of the 12 stress resilience foods are of particular interest to you and why (e.g., which contain the elements that you have noted earlier as potentially helpful, which fit your lifestyle, and which you are willing to change your lifestyle to accommodate).

1	Water
2	Wild-caught Salmon, Sardines, Herring
3	Oysters
4	Pasture-Raised Eggs
5	Pasture-Raised Meat (poultry, beef, pork, lamb, game)
6	Sprouted Lentils and Beans

7	**Cruciferous Vegetables** (broccoli, cauliflower, Brussels sprouts, cabbage, kale, collard greens, bok choy, arugula)
8	**Sweet Peppers**
9	**Fermented Foods**
10	**Seaweed**
11	**Berries and Cherries**
12	**Sprouted Rice and Quinoa**

Additional thoughts and your plan of action to incorporate your chosen stress resilience foods into your diet:

_____

_____

_____

_____

_____

_____

_____

_____

_____

_____

_____

_____

_____

_____

_____

_____

_____

_____

_____

_____

_____

_____

_____

_____

_____

_____

_____

_____

Part Five: Stress Resilience Supplements

Note which of the 10 stress resilience supplements are of particular interest to you, why, and how to take them (e.g., which contain the elements that you have noted earlier as potentially helpful, which would cover nutrients you aren't getting in food, and which are higher priorities than others, as well as what are the best forms and how or when to take the supplement).

1	**Magnesium**
2	**Zinc**
3	**B Vitamins**
4	**Vitamin C**
5	**Vitamin D$_3$**

6	**Omega-3 Fats, EPA and DHA**
7	**Theanine**
8	**Probiotics**
9	**Adaptogens**
10	**Nervine Herbs**

Additional thoughts and your plan of action to incorporate your chosen stress supplements into your routine:

Additional insights, thoughts, notes, plans . . .

_____
_____
_____
_____
_____
_____
_____
_____
_____
_____
_____
_____
_____
_____
_____
_____
_____
_____
_____
_____
_____

I'm rooting for you!

Life is an experiment. Make a plan. Put it into action.
And make adjustments using the new knowledge
from your experiment.

Here's to a calmer, more stress resilient you.

Appendix: Lab Tests

There are many lab tests that can help you figure out if you are deficient in individual nutrients, establish a baseline of where you start before making changes to your diet or adding supplements, and/or assess how well changes in diet and supplementation are improving your numbers. I won't go into all the possible tests that might be helpful to you, but I'll mention a few testing considerations and resources.

Check with your doctor or lab for instructions on how long to abstain from supplementation before providing test samples.

Magnesium

Dr. Carolyn Dean, author of *The Magnesium Miracle*, recommends avoiding the common magnesium test that measures serum levels because she finds it unreliable. She recommends measuring the magnesium in your red blood cells (RBC) instead. She says that you want to aim for the optimum magnesium RBC level of 6.0 to 6.5 mg/dL.[1]

For me personally, I had the RBC test done and it came out very close to the optimum level, but I know from how I feel when I keep up with daily magnesium supplementation versus slacking off that I need to be taking it regularly as a supplement. My experience makes me question the importance of testing for magnesium, but if you are going to do a lab test for magnesium, the RBC test seems like the way to go.

Vitamin D

Vitamin D is fat soluble. That means that, unlike water-soluble vitamins and minerals, you store it in your body and can accumulate too much if you over-supplement. (Your body won't let your vitamin D get too high from sunlight, but you can take in too much from supplements.) Testing to assess initial baseline levels and then testing again during supplementation can help determine how much to take and prevent overdoing intake. It can also help you determine if your need for supplements fluctuates seasonally.

There are two vitamin D tests currently being offered: 1,25(OH)D and 25(OH)D. The test for 25(OH)D—also known as 25-hydroxyvitamin D—is believed by many to be the better marker of overall D status. Some doctors, such as Dr. Ben Lynch N.D., promote performing both tests even though the 1,25(OH)D is *not* sufficient by itself.[2]

There are many online resources offering finger-prick test kits for Vitamin D. One example is the test kit found on Dr. Mercola's eStore.[3]

Cortisol

Your cortisol level is supposed to rise in the morning to help you feel energetic and dip in the evening to help you sleep. If you don't get that dip in the evening, it can interfere with sleep.

A cortisol blood test will only give you a general picture of your level at that time. A better way to test your levels is the diurnal cortisol saliva test. It uses four saliva samples during a 24-hour period (morning, noon, evening, and nighttime) so that the fluctuations in your levels can be assessed.

LiveWellTesting.com's ZRT Cortisol (Stress Hormone) Full Day Saliva Home Test Kit is an example of this type of test.[4]

Omega-3s

OmegaQuant.com offers a variety of at-home finger prick tests that assess your DHA+EPA in relation to other fats. The tests can be ordered on their website.[5]

References

Introduction

1. Leslie E. Korn, Nutrition Essentials for Mental Health: A Complete Guide to the Food-Mood Connection (New York: W. W. Norton, 2016), 10.

Part One: Your Body on Stress

Chapter 2. The Adrenals, Your Stress Glands

1. R. M. Sapolsky, "How Do Glucocorticoids Influence Stress Responses? Integrating Permissive, Suppressive, Stimulatory, and Preparative Actions," *Endocrine Reviews* 21 (2000): 55–89.
2. Sapolsky, "Glucocorticoids"; Constantine Tsigos and George P. Chrousos, "Hypothalamic–Pituitary–Adrenal Axis, Neuroendocrine Factors and Stress," *Journal of Psychosomatic Research* 53, no. 4 (2002): 865–87.
3. Sapolsky, "Glucocorticoids"; Tsigos and Chrousos, "Hypothalamic–Pituitary–Adrenal Axis"; Christine Heim, Ulrike Ehlert, and Dirk H. Hellhammer, "The Potential Role of Hypocortisolism in the Pathophysiology of Stress-Related Bodily Disorders," *Psychoneuroendocrinology* 25, no. 1 (2000): 1–35.
4. Eli Puterman et al., "Physical Activity Moderates Effects of Stressor-Induced Rumination on Cortisol Reactivity," *Psychosomatic Medicine* 73, no. 7 (2011): 604–611.
5. Puterman et al., "Physical Activity"; J. M. Kaye and S. L. Lightman, "Psychological Stress and Endocrine Axes," in *Human Psychoneuroimmunology*, eds. M. R. Irwin and K. Vedhara (Oxford: Oxford University Press, 2007): 25–52; Sapolsky, "Glucocorticoids."
6. Heim, Ehlert, and Hellhammer, "Hypocortisolism in Pathophysiology"; Gregory E. Miller, Edith Chen, and Eric S. Zhou, "If It Goes Up, Must It Come Down? Chronic Stress and the Hypothalamic–Pituitary–Adrenocortical Axis in Humans," *Psychological Bulletin* 133, no. 1 (2007): 25–45.
7. James L. Wilson, *Adrenal Fatigue: The 21st Century Stress Syndrome* (Petaluma, CA: Smart Publications, 2001).
8. Wilson, Adrenal Fatigue; K. E. Hannibal and M. D. Bishop, "Chronic Stress, Cortisol Dysfunction, and Pain: A Psychoneuroendocrine Rationale for Stress Management in Pain Rehabilitation," *Physical Therapy* 94, no. 12 (2014): 1816–1825.
9. Heim, Ehlert, and Hellhammer, "Hypocortisolism"; Miller, Chen, and Zhou, "If It Goes Up"; Hannibal and Bishop, "Chronic Stress"; Ulrike Ehlert, Jens Gaab, and Markus Heinrichs, "Psychoneuroendocrinological Contributions to the Etiology of Depression, Posttraumatic Stress Disorder, and Stress-Related Bodily Disorders: The Role of the Hypothalamus–Pituitary–Adrenal Axis," *Biological Psychology* 57, no. 1–3 (2001): 141–152; Charles L. Raison and Andrew H. Miller, "When Not Enough Is Too Much: The Role of Insufficient Glucocorticoid Signaling in the Pathophysiology of Stress-Related Disorders," *American Journal of Psychiatry* 160, no. 9 (2003): 1554–1565.
10. Miller, Chen, and Zhou, "If It Goes Up."

Chapter 3. Stress Gets on Your Nerves

1. Francesca Calabrese et al., "Brain-Derived Neurotrophic Factor: A Bridge between Inflammation and Neuroplasticity," *Frontiers in Cellular Neuroscience* 8 (2014).
2. Felicity Ng et al., "Oxidative Stress in Psychiatric Disorders: Evidence Base and Therapeutic Implications," *The International Journal of Neuropsychopharmacology* 11, no. 06 (2008).
3. Giancarlo Lucca et al., "Increased Oxidative Stress in Submitochondrial Particles into the Brain of Rats Submitted to the Chronic Mild Stress Paradigm," *Journal of Psychiatric Research* 43, no. 9 (2009): 864–869.
4. Lucca et al., "Increased Oxidative Stress"; Ng et al., "Oxidative Stress in Psychiatric Disorders"; Jaouad Bouayed, Hassan Rammal, and Rachid Soulimani, "Oxidative Stress and Anxiety: Relationship and Cellular Pathways," *Oxidative Medicine and Cellular Longevity* 2, no. 2 (2009): 63–67; Iiris Hovatta, Juuso Juhila, and Jonas Donner, "Oxidative Stress in Anxiety and Comorbid Disorders," *Neuroscience Research* 68, no. 4 (2010): 261–275; S. Moylan et al., "Exercising the Worry Away: How Inflammation, Oxidative and Nitrogen Stress Mediates the Beneficial Effect of Physical Activity on Anxiety Disorder Symptoms and Behaviours," *Neuroscience & Biobehavioral Reviews* 37, no. 4 (2013): 573–584.
5. S. Salim, G. Chugh, and M. Asghar, "Inflammation in Anxiety," in *Advances in Protein Chemistry and Structural Biology: Inflammation in Neuropsychiatric Disorders*, ed. R. Donev (Oxford: Academic, 2012).
6. Salim, Chugh, and Asghar, "Inflammation in Anxiety"; Charles L. Raison, Lucile Capuron, and Andrew H. Miller, "Cytokines Sing the Blues: Inflammation and the Pathogenesis of Depression," *Trends in Immunology* 27, no. 1 (2006): 24–31; Andrew H. Miller, Vladimir Maletic, and Charles L. Raison, "Inflammation and Its Discontents: The Role of Cytokines in the Pathophysiology of Major Depression," *Biological Psychiatry* 65, no. 9 (2009): 732–741.
7. Aoife O'Donovan et al., "Clinical Anxiety, Cortisol and Interleukin-6: Evidence for Specificity in Emotion–Biology Relationships," *Brain, Behavior, and Immunity* 24, no. 7 (2010): 1074–1077.

Chapter 4. Neurotransmitters Tell Your Body to Calm Down or Rev Up

1. Evert Boonstra et al., "Neurotransmitters as Food Supplements: The Effects of GABA on Brain and Behavior," *Frontiers in Psychology* 6 (2015).

Chapter 6. What's Gut Got to Do with It?

1. P. C. Konturek, T. Brzozowski, and S. J. Konturek, "Stress and the Gut: Pathophysiology, Clinical Consequences, Diagnostic Approach and Treatment Options," *Journal of Physiology and Pharmacology* 62 (2011): 591–9.
2. John R. Kelly et al., "Breaking Down the Barriers: The Gut Microbiome, Intestinal Permeability and Stress-Related Psychiatric Disorders," *Frontiers in Cellular Neuroscience* 9 (2015).

3. Ruth A. Luna and Jane A. Foster, "Gut Brain Axis: Diet Microbiota Interactions and Implications for Modulation of Anxiety and Depression," *Current Opinion in Biotechnology* 32 (2015): 35–41.
4. E. A. Mayer et al., "Gut Microbes and the Brain: Paradigm Shift in Neuroscience," *Journal of Neuroscience* 34, no. 46 (2014): 15490–15496.
5. J. A. Bravo et al., "Ingestion of Lactobacillus Strain Regulates Emotional Behavior and Central GABA Receptor Expression in a Mouse Via the Vagus Nerve," *Proceedings of the National Academy of Sciences* 108, no. 38 (2011): 16050–16055; Huiying Wang et al., "Effect of Probiotics on Central Nervous System Functions in Animals and Humans: A Systematic Review," *Journal of Neurogastroenterology and Motility* 22, no. 4 (2016): 589–605; Timothy G. Dinan et al., "Collective Unconscious: How Gut Microbes Shape Human Behavior," *Journal of Psychiatric Research* 63 (2015): 1–9.

Chapter 7. The Glucose Balancing Act
1. David Kennedy, "B Vitamins and the Brain: Mechanisms, Dose and Efficacy—A Review," *Nutrients* 8, no. 2 (2016): 68.
2. C. Dean, *The Magnesium Miracle: Discover the Essential Nutrient That Will Lower the Risk of Heart Disease, Prevent Stroke and Obesity, Treat Diabetes, and Improve Mood and Memory* (New York: Ballantine Books, 2014), 48.
3. R. M. Sapolsky, "How Do Glucocorticoids Influence Stress Responses? Integrating Permissive, Suppressive, Stimulatory, and Preparative Actions," *Endocrine Reviews* 21, no. 1 (2000): 55–89.
4. Andre Kleinridders et al., "Insulin Resistance in Brain Alters Dopamine Turnover and Causes Behavioral Disorders," *Proceedings of the National Academy of Sciences* 112, no. 11 (2015): 3463–3468.

Part Two: What Helps Your Calm

Chapter 10. How Magnesium Helps
1. Jeroen H. De Baaij, Joost G. J. Hoenderop, and René J. M. Bindels. "Magnesium in Man: Implications for Health and Disease," *Physiological Reviews* 95, no. 1 (2015): 1–46.
2. C. Dean, *The Magnesium Miracle: Discover the Essential Nutrient That Will Lower the Risk of Heart Disease, Prevent Stroke and Obesity, Treat Diabetes, and Improve Mood and Memory* (New York: Ballantine Books, 2014), xxi.
3. Dean, *Magnesium Miracle.*
4. Uwe Gröber, Joachim Schmidt, and Klaus Kisters, "Magnesium in Prevention and Therapy," *Nutrients* 7, no. 9 (2015): 8199–8226.
5. Torsten Bohn, "Dietary Factors Influencing Magnesium Absorption in Humans," *Current Nutrition & Food Science* 4, no. 1 (2008): 53–72; Dean, *Magnesium Miracle.*

6. Dean, *Magnesium Miracle*, liii.
7. Kuanrong Li et al., "Associations of Dietary Calcium Intake and Calcium Supplementation with Myocardial Infarction and Stroke Risk and Overall Cardiovascular Mortality in the Heidelberg Cohort of the European Prospective Investigation into Cancer and Nutrition Study (EPIC-Heidelberg)," *Heart* 98, no. 12 (2012): 920–925; M. J. Bolland et al., "Effect of Calcium Supplements on Risk of Myocardial Infarction and Cardiovascular Events: Meta-Analysis," *The BMJ* (2010): c3691; M. J. Bolland et al., "Calcium Supplements with or without Vitamin D and Risk of Cardiovascular Events: Reanalysis of the Women's Health Initiative Limited Access Dataset and Meta-Analysis," *The BMJ* (2011): d2040; R. Chan, J. Leung, and J. Woo, "Dietary and Supplemental Calcium Intake and Mortality," *JAMA Internal Medicine* 173, no. 19 (2013): 1840; Q. Xiao et al., "Dietary and Supplemental Calcium Intakes in Relation to Mortality from Cardiovascular Diseases in the NIH-AARP Diet and Health Study," *JAMA Internal Medicine* 173 (2013): 639–646.
8. J. J. Anderson, K. J. Roggenkamp, and C. M. Suchindran, "Calcium Intakes and Femoral and Lumbar Bone Density of Elderly U.S. Men and Women: National Health and Nutrition Examination Survey 2005–2006 Analysis," *The Journal of Clinical Endocrinology & Metabolism* 97, no. 12 (2012): 4531–4539; Heike A. Bischoff-Ferrari et al., "Calcium Intake and Hip Fracture Risk in Men and Women: A Meta-Analysis of Prospective Cohort Studies and Randomized Controlled Trials," *American Journal of Clinical Nutrition* 86, no. 6 (2007): 1780–1790.
9. Dean, Magnesium Miracle, xlix.
10. Yasmin Ismail, Abbas A. Ismail, and Adel A. Ismail, "The Underestimated Problem of Using Serum Magnesium Measurements to Exclude Magnesium Deficiency in Adults: A Health Warning Is Needed for 'Normal' Results," *Clinical Chemistry and Laboratory Medicine* 48, no. 3 (2010); Dean, *Magnesium Miracle*, 217-223.
11. S. B. Sartori, R. Landgraf, and N. Singewald, "The Clinical Implications of Mouse Models of Enhanced Anxiety," *Future Neurology* 6, no. 4 (2011): 531–571; S. B. Sartori et al., "Magnesium Deficiency Induces Anxiety and HPA Axis Dysregulation: Modulation by Therapeutic Drug Treatment," *Neuropharmacology* 62, no. 1 (2012): 304–312; Marijke C. Laarakker, Hein A. Van Lith, and Frauke Ohl, "Behavioral Characterization of A/J and C57BL/6J Mice Using a Multidimensional Test: Association between Blood Plasma and Brain Magnesium-Ion Concentration with Anxiety," *Physiology & Behavior* 102, no. 2 (2011): 205–219.
12. Bettina Pyndt Jørgensen et al., "Dietary Magnesium Deficiency Affects Gut Microbiota and Anxiety-Like Behaviour in C57BL/6N mice," *Acta Neuropsychiatrica* 27, no. 05 (2015): 307–311.

13. Ewa Poleszak et al., "Antidepressant- and Anxiolytic-Like Activity of Magnesium in Mice," *Pharmacology Biochemistry and Behavior* 78, no. 1 (2004): 7–12.
14. Ewa Poleszak et al., "Enhancement of Antidepressant-Like Activity by Joint Administration of Imipramine and Magnesium in the Forced Swim Test: Behavioral and Pharmacokinetic Studies in Mice," *Pharmacology Biochemistry and Behavior* 81, no. 3 (2005): 524–529.
15. Teymoor Yary et al., "Dietary Magnesium Intake and the Incidence of Depression: A 20-Year Follow-Up Study," *Journal of Affective Disorders* 193 (2016): 94–98.
16. E. K. Tarleton and B. Littenberg, "Magnesium Intake and Depression in Adults," *Journal of the American Board of Family Medicine* 28, no. 2 (2015): 249–256.
17. D. Sluimers, N. L. Willemse, and M. L. Landsmeer, "Re: Magnesium Intake and Depression in Adults," *Journal of the American Board of Family Medicine* 28, no. 5 (2015): 683–683.
18. E. K. Tarleton and B. Littenberg, "Response: Re: Magnesium Intake and Depression in Adults," *Journal of the American Board of Family Medicine* 28, no. 5 (2015): 683–684.
19. N. B. Boyle, C. L. Lawton, and L. Dye, "The Effects of Magnesium Supplementation on Subjective Anxiety," *Magnesium Research* 29, no. 3 (2016): 120.
20. David O. Kennedy et al., "Effects of High-Dose B Vitamin Complex with Vitamin C and Minerals on Subjective Mood and Performance in Healthy Males," *Psychopharmacology* 211, no. 1 (2010): 55–68.
21. Douglas Carroll et al., "The Effects of an Oral Multivitamin Combination with Calcium, Magnesium, and Zinc on Psychological Well-Being in Healthy Young Male Volunteers: A Double-Blind Placebo-Controlled Trial," *Psychopharmacology* 150, no. 2 (2000): 220–225.
22. L. Schlebusch et al., "A Double-Blind, Placebo-Controlled, Double-Centre Study of the Effects of an Oral Multivitamin-Mineral Combination on Stress," *South African Medical Journal* 90, no. 12 (2000): 1216–1223.
23. Con Stough et al., "The Effect of 90 Day Administration of a High Dose Vitamin B-Complex on Work Stress," *Human Psychopharmacology: Clinical and Experimental* 26, no. 7 (2011): 470–476.
24. Dean, *Magnesium Miracle*; De Baaij, Hoenderop, and Bindels, "Magnesium in Man"; Gröber, Schmidt, and Kisters, "Magnesium in Prevention and Therapy."

Chapter 11. How Zinc Helps

1. Shannon D. Gower-Winter and Cathy W. Levenson, "Zinc in the Central Nervous System: From Molecules to Behavior," *BioFactors* 38, no. 3 (2012): 186–193.

2. Cathy W. Levenson and Deborah Morris, "Zinc and Neurogenesis: Making New Neurons from Development to Adulthood," *Advances in Nutrition* 2, no. 2 (2011): 96–100.

3. C. J. Frederickson, K. Jae-Young, and A. I. Bush, "The Neurobiology of Zinc in Health and Disease," *Nature Reviews Neuroscience* 6 (2005): 449; Gower-Winter and Levenson, "Central Nervous System."

4. A. J. Russo, "Analysis of Plasma Zinc and Copper Concentration, and Perceived Symptoms, in Individuals with Depression, Post Zinc and Anti-Oxidant Therapy," *Nutrition and Metabolic Insights* 4 (2011): NMI.S6760.

5. Johnathan R. Nuttall and Patricia I. Oteiza, "Zinc and the Aging Brain," *Genes & Nutrition* 9, no. 1 (2013): 379.

6. Wolfgang Maret and Harold H. Sandstead, "Zinc Requirements and the Risks and Benefits of Zinc Supplementation," *Journal of Trace Elements in Medicine and Biology* 20, no. 1 (2006): 3–18; Harold H. Sandstead, "Causes of Iron and Zinc Deficiencies and Their Effects on Brain," *Journal of Nutrition* 130, no. 2 (2000): 347S-349S; Rosalind S. Gibson, Janet C. King, and Nicola Lowe, "A Review of Dietary Zinc Recommendations," *Food and Nutrition Bulletin* 37, no. 4 (2016): 443–460; Marica Brnić et al., "Influence of Phytase, EDTA, and Polyphenols on Zinc Absorption in Adults from Porridges Fortified with Zinc Sulfate or Zinc Oxide," *Journal of Nutrition* 144, no. 9 (2014): 1467–1473; Barbara Troesch et al., "Absorption Studies Show that Phytase from Aspergillus niger Significantly Increases Iron and Zinc Bioavailability from Phytate-Rich Foods," *Food and Nutrition Bulletin* 34, no. 2, supplement 1 (2013): S90–S101.

7. Simone Hagmeyer, Jasmin C. Haderspeck, and Andreas M. Grabrucker, "Behavioral Impairments in Animal Models for Zinc Deficiency," *Frontiers in Behavioral Neuroscience* 8 (2015): 443.

8. K. Młyniec et al., "Essential Elements in Depression and Anxiety, Part I," *Pharmacological Reports* 66, no. 4 (2014): 534–544.

9. M. Joshi et al., "Effect of Zinc in Animal Models of Anxiety, Depression and Psychosis," *Human & Experimental Toxicology* 31, no. 12 (2012): 1237–1243.

10. M. Islam et al., "Comparative Analysis of Serum Zinc, Copper, Manganese, Iron, Calcium, and Magnesium Level and Complexity of Interelement Relations in Generalized Anxiety Disorder Patients," *Biological Trace Element Research* 154 (2013): 21.

11. A. J. Russo, "Decreased Zinc and Increased Copper in Individuals with Anxiety," *Nutrition and Metabolic Insights* 4 (2011): NMI.S6349.

12. Ozgur Oner et al., "Effects of Zinc and Ferritin Levels on Parent and Teacher Reported Symptom Scores in Attention Deficit Hyperactivity Disorder," *Child Psychiatry & Human Development* 41, no. 4 (2010): 441–447; Michael Huss, Andreas Völp, and Manuela Stauss-Grabo, "Supplementation of Polyunsaturated Fatty Acids, Magnesium and Zinc in Children Seeking Medical Advice for Attention-Deficit/Hyperactivity Problems: An

Observational Cohort Study," *Lipids in Health and Disease* 9, no. 1 (2010): 105; John W. Crayton and William J. Walsh, "Elevated Serum Copper Levels in Women with a History of Post-Partum Depression," *Journal of Trace Elements in Medicine and Biology* 21, no. 1 (2007): 17–21; A. Prasad et al., "Zinc Status and Serum Testosterone Levels of Healthy Adults," *Nutrition* 12, no. 5 (1996): 344–8; Qingqing Chu et al., "A Potential Role for Zinc Transporter 7 in Testosterone Synthesis in Mouse Leydig Tumor Cells," *International Journal of Molecular Medicine* 37, no. 6 (2016): 1619–1626; Elise C. Cope, Deborah R. Morris, and Cathy W. Levenson, "Improving Treatments and Outcomes: An Emerging Role for Zinc in Traumatic Brain Injury," *Nutrition Reviews* 70, no. 7 (2012): 410–413; Sandstead, "Iron and Zinc Deficiencies"; Gower-Winter and Levenson, "Central Nervous System"; Hagmeyer, Haderspeck, and Grabrucker, "Behavioral Impairments."

13. Nuttall and Oteiza, "Zinc and Aging Brain."
14. Gower-Winter and Levenson, "Central Nervous System."

Chapter 12. How B Vitamins Help

1. David O. Kennedy, "B Vitamins and the Brain: Mechanisms, Dose and Efficacy—A Review," *Nutrients* 8, no. 2 (2016): 86.
2. Kennedy, "B Vitamins and the Brain," 68–96; Patricia O. Chocano-Bedoya et al., "Dietary B Vitamin Intake and Incident Premenstrual Syndrome," *The American Journal of Clinical Nutrition* 93, no. 5 (2011): 1080–1086; James L. Wilson, *Adrenal Fatigue: The 21st Century Stress Syndrome* (Petaluma, CA: Smart Publications, 2001): 198-200; "Cognitive Function In Depth," Linus Pauling Institute, Oregon State University, February 2011; "Vitamin B12," Linus Pauling Institute, Oregon State University, updated January 2014.
3. Kennedy, "B Vitamins and the Brain."
4. Wilson, *Adrenal Fatigue*, 199.
5. Sara-Jayne Long and David Benton, "Effects of Vitamin and Mineral Supplementation on Stress, Mild Psychiatric Symptoms, and Mood in Nonclinical Samples," *Psychosomatic Medicine* 75, no. 2 (2013): 144–153.
6. C. Hallert et al., "Clinical Trial: B Vitamins Improve Health in Patients with Coeliac Disease Living on a Gluten-Free Diet," *Alimentary Pharmacology & Therapeutics* 29, no. 8 (2009): 811–816.
7. K. Morita et al., "Low Serum Concentrations of Vitamin B6 and Iron Are Related to Panic Attack and Hyperventilation Attack," *Acta Medica Okayama* 67, no. 2 (2013): 99–104.
8. Neeraj Kumar et al., "Dietary Pyridoxine Potentiates Thermal Tolerance, Heat Shock Protein and Protect Against Cellular Stress of Milkfish (Chanos Chanos) under Endosulfan-Induced Stress," *Fish & Shellfish Immunology* 55 (2016): 407–414.

9. David O. Kennedy et al., "Effects of High-Dose B Vitamin Complex with Vitamin C and Minerals on Subjective Mood and Performance in Healthy Males," *Psychopharmacology* 211, no. 1 (2010): 55–68; Douglas Carroll et al., "The Effects of an Oral Multivitamin Combination with Calcium, Magnesium, and Zinc on Psychological Well-Being in Healthy Young Male Volunteers: A Double-Blind Placebo-Controlled Trial," *Psychopharmacology* 150, no. 2 (2000): 220–225; L. Schlebusch et al., "A Double-Blind, Placebo-Controlled, Double-Centre Study of the Effects of an Oral Multivitamin-Mineral Combination on Stress," *South African Medical Journal*, 90, no. 12 (2000): 1216–1223; Con Stough et al., "The Effect of 90 Day Administration of a High Dose Vitamin B-Complex on Work Stress," *Human Psychopharmacology: Clinical and Experimental* 26, no. 7 (2011): 470–476.

10. S. Samieipoor et al., "Effects of Vitamin B6 on Premenstrual Syndrome: A Systematic Review and Meta-Analysis," *Journal of Chemical and Pharmaceutical Science* 9, no. 3 (2016): 1346–1353.

11. E. Ebrahimi et al., "Effects of Magnesium and Vitamin B6 on the Severity of Premenstrual Syndrome Symptoms," *Journal of Caring Sciences* 1, no. 4 (2012): 183–189.

12. A. Coppen and J. Bailey, "Enhancement of the Antidepressant Action of Fluoxetine by Folic Acid: A Randomised, Placebo Controlled Trial," *Journal of Affective Disorders* 60, no. 2 (2000): 121–130.

13. A. Mesripour, V. Hajhashemi, and A. Kuchak, "Effect of Concomitant Administration of Three Different Antidepressants with Vitamin B6 on Depression and Obsessive Compulsive Disorder in Mice Models," *Research in Pharmaceutical Sciences* 12, no. 1 (2017): 46.

14. Abderrahim Oulhaj et al., "Omega-3 Fatty Acid Status Enhances the Prevention of Cognitive Decline by B Vitamins in Mild Cognitive Impairment," *Journal of Alzheimer's Disease* 50, no. 2 (2016): 547–557; Fredrik Jernerén et al., "Brain Atrophy in Cognitively Impaired Elderly: The Importance of Long-Chain Ω-3 Fatty Acids and B Vitamin Status in a Randomized Controlled Trial," *American Journal of Clinical Nutrition* 102, no. 1 (2015): 215–221.

15. "Folate: Fact Sheet for Health Professionals," Office of Dietary Supplements, National Institutes of Health, updated October 4, 2018.

16. Swati B. Patil and Md. K. Khan, "Germinated Brown Rice As a Value Added Rice Product: A Review," *Journal of Food Science and Technology* 48, no. 6 (2011): 661–667.

Chapter 13. How Vitamin C Helps

1. Fiona E. Harrison and James M. May, "Vitamin C Function in the Brain: Vital Role of the Ascorbate Transporter SVCT2," *Free Radical Biology and Medicine* 46, no. 6 (2009): 719–730; David O. Kennedy et al., "Effects of High-Dose B Vitamin Complex with Vitamin C and Minerals on Subjective Mood and

Performance in Healthy Males," *Psychopharmacology* 211, no. 1 (2010): 55–68; Jaouad Bouayed, Hassan Rammal, and Rachid Soulimani, "Oxidative Stress and Anxiety: Relationship and Cellular Pathways," *Oxidative Medicine and Cellular Longevity* 2, no. 2 (2009): 63–67; Iiris Hovatta, Juuso Juhila, and Jonas Donner, "Oxidative Stress in Anxiety and Comorbid Disorders," *Neuroscience Research* 68, no. 4 (2010): 261–275.

2. Sebastian J. Padayatty, "Human Adrenal Glands Secrete Vitamin C in Response to Adrenocorticotrophic Hormone," *American Journal of Clinical Nutrition* 86, no. 1 (2007): 145–149.

3. James M. May et al., "Ascorbic Acid Efficiently Enhances Neuronal Synthesis of Norepinephrine from Dopamine," *Brain Research Bulletin* 90 (2013): 35–42.

4. Nicholas L. Doulas, Andreas Constantopoulos, and Basil Litsios, "Effect of Ascorbic Acid on Guinea Pig Adrenal Adenylate Cyclase Activity and Plasma Cortisol," *Journal of Nutrition* 117, no. 6 (1987): 1108–1114.

5. E. Peters, R. Anderson, and A. Theron, "Attenuation of Increase in Circulating Cortisol and Enhancement of the Acute Phase Protein Response in Vitamin C-Supplemented Ultramarathoners," *International Journal of Sports Medicine* 22, no. 02 (2001): 120–126; Andres E. Carrillo, René J. Murphy, and Stephen S. Cheung, "Vitamin C Supplementation and Salivary Immune Function Following Exercise-Heat Stress," *International Journal of Sports Physiology and Performance* 3, no. 4 (2008): 516–530; Glen Davison, Michael Gleeson, and Shaun Phillips, "Antioxidant Supplementation and Immunoendocrine Responses to Prolonged Exercise," *Medicine & Science in Sports & Exercise* 39, no. 4 (2007): 645–652.

6. Deepanwita Das, Chaitali Sen, and Anupam Goswami, "Effect of Vitamin C on Adrenal Suppression by Etomidate Induction in Patients Undergoing Cardiac Surgery: A Randomized Controlled Trial," *Annals of Cardiac Anaesthesia* 19, no. 3 (2016): 410.

7. Stuart Brody et al., "A Randomized Controlled Trial of High Dose Ascorbic Acid for Reduction of Blood Pressure, Cortisol, and Subjective Responses to Psychological Stress," *Psychopharmacology* 159, no. 3 (2001): 319–324.

8. Manar A. Angrini and Julian C. Leslie, "Vitamin C Attenuates the Physiological and Behavioural Changes Induced by Long-Term Exposure to Noise," *Behavioural Pharmacology* 23, no. 2 (2012): 119–125.

9. Bruna Puty et al., "Ascorbic Acid Protects Against Anxiogenic-Like Effect Induced by Methylmercury in Zebrafish: Action on the Serotonergic System," *Zebrafish* 11, no. 4 (2014): 365–370.

10. Robert N. Hughes, Nicola J. Hancock, and Rikki M. Thompson, "Anxiolysis and Recognition Memory Enhancement with Long-Term Supplemental Ascorbic Acid (Vitamin C) in Normal Rats: Possible Dose Dependency and Sex Differences," *Journal of Psychiatry and Brain Functions* 2, no. 1 (2015): 4.

11. Ricardo W.Binfaré et al., "Ascorbic Acid Administration Produces an Antidepressant-Like Effect: Evidence for the Involvement of Monoaminergic Neurotransmission," *Progress in Neuro-Psychopharmacology and Biological Psychiatry* 33, no. 3 (2009): 530–540.

12. Zohreh Mazloom, Maryam Ekramzadeh, and Najmeh Hejazi, , "Efficacy of Supplementary Vitamins C and E on Anxiety, Depression and Stress in Type 2 Diabetic Patients: A Randomized, Single-Blind, Placebo-Controlled Trial," *Pakistan Journal of Biological Sciences* 16, no. 22 (2013): 1597–1600.

13. Michelle Zhang et al., "Vitamin C Provision Improves Mood in Acutely Hospitalized Patients," *Nutrition* 27, no. 5 (2011): 530–533.

14. Ivaldo J. Lima de Oliveira et al., "Effects of Oral Vitamin C Supplementation on Anxiety in Students: A Double-Blind, Randomized, Placebo-Controlled Trial," *Pakistan Journal of Biological Sciences* 18, no. 1 (2015): 11–18.

15. Saeedeh Alsadat Moosavirad et al., "Protective Effect of Vitamin C, Vitamin B12 and Omega-3 on Lead-Induced Memory Impairment in Rat," *Research in Pharmaceutical Sciences* 11, no. 5 (2016): 390.

16. Stine Hansen, Pernille Tveden-Nyborg, and Jens Lykkesfeldt, "Does Vitamin C Deficiency Affect Cognitive Development and Function?" *Nutrients* 6, no. 9 (2014): 3818–3846.

17. . Jens Lykkesfeldt et al., "Ascorbate Is Depleted by Smoking and Repleted by Moderate Supplementation: A Study in Male Smokers and Nonsmokers with Matched Dietary Antioxidant Intakes," *American Journal of Clinical Nutrition* 71, no. 2 (2000): 530–536.

18. T. Duarte, M. Cooke, and G. Jones, "Gene Expression Profiling Reveals New Protective Roles for Vitamin C in Human Skin Cells," *Free Radical Biology and Medicine* 46, no. 1 (2009): 78–87.

19. D. F. Garcia-Diaz et al., "Vitamin C in the Treatment and/or Prevention of Obesity," *Journal of Nutritional Science & Vitaminology* 60, no. 6 (2014): 367–379.

20. Stuart Brody, "High-Dose Ascorbic Acid Increases Intercourse Frequency and Improves Mood: A Randomized Controlled Clinical Trial," *Biological Psychiatry* 52, no. 4 (2002): 371–374.

Chapter 14. How Vitamin D Helps

1. Rhonda P. Patrick and Bruce N. Ames, "Vitamin D and the Omega-3 Fatty Acids Control Serotonin Synthesis and Action, Part 2: Relevance for ADHD, Bipolar Disorder, Schizophrenia, and Impulsive Behavior," *FASEB Journal* 29, no. 6 (2015): 2207–2222; M. Wrzosek, J. Lukaszkiewicz, and A. Jakubczyk, "Vitamin D and the Central Nervous System," *Pharmacology Reports* 65 (2013): 271–8.

2. Vijay Ganji et al., "Serum Vitamin D Concentrations Are Related to Depression in Young Adult US Population: The Third National Health and Nutrition Examination Survey," *International Archives of Medicine* 3, no. 1 (2010): 29.

3. Y. Milaneschi et al., "The Association between Low Vitamin D and Depressive Disorders," *Molecular Psychiatry* 19, no. 4 (2013): 444–451.

4. Maria Polak et al., "Serum 25-Hydroxyvitamin D Concentrations and Depressive Symptoms among Young Adult Men and Women," *Nutrients* 6, no. 11 (2014): 4720–4730.

5. Simon Spedding, "Vitamin D and Depression: A Systematic Review and Meta-Analysis Comparing Studies with and without Biological Flaws," *Nutrients* 6, no. 4 (2014): 1501–1518.

6. Jane Maddock et al., "Vitamin D and Common Mental Disorders in Mid-Life: Cross-Sectional and Prospective Findings," *Clinical Nutrition* 32, no. 5 (2013): 758–764.

7. M. Bičíková et al., "Vitamin D in Anxiety and Affective Disorders," *Physiological Research* 64, Supplement 2 (2015): S101–S103.

8. D. J. Armstrong et al., "Vitamin D Deficiency Is Associated with Anxiety and Depression in Fibromyalgia," *Clinical Rheumatology* 26, no. 4 (2006): 551–554.

9. Chaowen Wu et al., "Association between Serum Levels of Vitamin D and the Risk of Post-Stroke Anxiety," *Medicine* 95, no. 18 (2016): e3566.

10. Allan V. Kalueff et al., "Increased Anxiety in Mice Lacking Vitamin D Receptor Gene," *NeuroReport* 15, no. 8 (2004): 1271–1274.

11. Julia Fedotova, Svetlana Pivina, and Anastasia Sushko, "Effects of Chronic Vitamin D3 Hormone Administration on Anxiety-Like Behavior in Adult Female Rats after Long-Term Ovariectomy," *Nutrients* 9, no. 1 (2017): 28.

12. T. J. Littlejohns et al., "Vitamin D and the Risk of Dementia and Alzheimer Disease," *Neurology* 83, no. 10 (2014): 920–928.

13. Ghazaleh Valipour, Parvane Saneei, and Ahmad Esmaillzadeh, "Serum Vitamin D Levels in Relation to Schizophrenia: A Systematic Review and Meta-Analysis of Observational Studies," *Journal of Clinical Endocrinology & Metabolism* 99, no. 10 (2014): 3863–3872.

14. Madeeha Kamal, Abdulbari Bener, and Mohammad S. Ehlayel, "Is High Prevalence of Vitamin D Deficiency a Correlate for Attention Deficit Hyperactivity Disorder?" *ADHD Attention Deficit and Hyperactivity Disorders* 6, no. 2 (2014): 73–78.

15. Khaled Saad et al., "Vitamin D Status in Autism Spectrum Disorders and the Efficacy of Vitamin D Supplementation in Autistic Children," *Nutritional Neuroscience* 19, no. 8 (2015): 346–351; Junyan Feng et al., "Clinical Improvement Following Vitamin D3 Supplementation in Autism Spectrum Disorder," *Nutritional Neuroscience* 20, no. 5 (2016): 284–290.

16. Z. Lu et al., "An Evaluation of the Vitamin D3 Content in Fish: Is the Vitamin D Content Adequate to Satisfy the Dietary Requirement for Vitamin D?" *Journal of Steroid Biochemistry and Molecular Biology* 103, no. 3–5 (2007): 642–644.

17. Julia Kühn et al., "Free-Range Farming: A Natural Alternative to Produce Vitamin D-Enriched Eggs," *Nutrition* 30, no. 4 (2014): 481–484.

18. D. B. Haytowitz, "Vitamin D in Mushrooms," Nutrient Data Laboratory, Beltsville Human Nutrition Research Center, accessed May 3, 2017, https://www.ars.usda.gov/ARSUserFiles/80400525/Articles/AICR09_Mushroom_VitD.pdf.

19. Victoria F. Logan et al., "Long-Term Vitamin D3 Supplementation Is More Effective Than Vitamin D2 in Maintaining Serum 25-Hydroxyvitamin D Status over the Winter Months," *British Journal of Nutrition* 109, no. 06 (2012): 1082–1088; Muhammad M. Hammami and Ahmed Yusuf, "Differential Effects of Vitamin D2 and D3 Supplements on 25-Hydroxyvitamin D Level Are Dose, Sex, and Time Dependent: A Randomized Controlled Trial," *BMC Endocrine Disorders* 17, no. 1 (2017); Laura Tripkovic et al., "Comparison of Vitamin D2 and Vitamin D3 Supplementation in Raising Serum 25-Hydroxyvitamin D Status: A Systematic Review and Meta-Analysis," *American Journal of Clinical Nutrition* 95, no. 6 (2012): 1357–1364.

20. Kühn et al., "Free-Range Farming."

Chapter 15. How Omega-3 Fats Help

1. R. Grant and J. Guest, "Role of Omega-3 PUFAs in Neurobiological Health" in *The Benefits of Natural Products for Neurodegenerative Diseases, Advances in Neurobiology* vol. 12, eds. M. Essa, M. Akbar, and G. Guillemin (Cham, Switzerland: Springer, 2016): 247–274; Christian P. Müller et al., "Brain Membrane Lipids in Major Depression and Anxiety Disorders," *Biochimica et Biophysica Acta (BBA): Molecular and Cell Biology of Lipids* 1851, no. 8 (2015), 1052–1065; Rhonda P. Patrick and Bruce N. Ames, "Vitamin D and the Omega-3 Fatty Acids Control Serotonin Synthesis and Action, Part 2: Relevance for ADHD, Bipolar Disorder, Schizophrenia, and Impulsive Behavior," *FASEB Journal* 29, no. 6 (2015): 2207–2222; Genevieve Young and Julie Conquer, "Omega-3 Fatty Acids and Neuropsychiatric Disorders," *Reproduction Nutrition Development* 45, no. 1 (2005): 1–28; Eric E. Noreen et al., "Effects of Supplemental Fish Oil on Resting Metabolic Rate, Body Composition, and Salivary Cortisol in Healthy Adults," *Journal of the International Society of Sports Nutrition* 7, no. 1 (2010): 31; Jacques Delarue et al., "Fish Oil Attenuates Adrenergic Overactivity without Altering Glucose Metabolism During an Oral Glucose Load in Haemodialysis Patients," *British Journal of Nutrition* 99, no. 05 (2007).

2. H. Gerster, "Can Adults Adequately Convert Alpha-Linolenic Acid (18:3n-3) to Eicosapentaenoic Acid (20:5n-3) and Docosahexaenoic Acid (22:6n-3)?" *International Journal for Vitamin and Nutrition Research* 68, no. 3 (1998): 159–173.

3. Young and Conquer, "Omega-3 Fatty Acids."

4. Young and Conquer, "Omega-3 Fatty Acids."

5. Andrew L. Stoll, The Omega-3 Connection: The Groundbreaking Omega-3 Antidepression Diet and Brain Program (New York: Simon & Schuster,

2001), 40; M. Haag, "Essential Fatty Acids and the Brain," *Canadian Journal of Psychiatry* 48, no. 3 (2003): 195–203.

6. A. P. Simopoulos, "Omega-6/Omega-3 Essential Fatty Acid Ratio and Chronic Diseases," *Food Reviews International* 20, no. 1 (2004): 77–90.

7. Simopoulos, "Omega-6/Omega-3."

8. Joanne J. Liu et al., "Omega-3 Polyunsaturated Fatty Acid (PUFA) Status in Major Depressive Disorder with Comorbid Anxiety Disorders," *Journal of Clinical Psychiatry* 74, no. 07 (2013): 732–738.

9. Pnina Green et al., "Red Cell Membrane Omega-3 Fatty Acids Are Decreased in Nondepressed Patients with Social Anxiety Disorder," *European Neuropsychopharmacology* 16, no. 2 (2006): 107–113.

10. G. Fontani et al., "Cognitive and Physiological Effects of Omega-3 Polyunsaturated Fatty Acid Supplementation in Healthy Subjects," *European Journal of Clinical Investigation* 35, no. 11 (2005): 691–699.

11. Janice K. Kiecolt-Glaser et al., "Omega-3 Supplementation Lowers Inflammation and Anxiety in Medical Students: A Randomized Controlled Trial," *Brain, Behavior, and Immunity* 25, no. 8 (2011): 1725–1734.

12. Laure Buydens-Branchey, Marc Branchey, and Joseph R. Hibbeln, "Associations between Increases in Plasma N-3 Polyunsaturated Fatty Acids Following Supplementation and Decreases in Anger and Anxiety in Substance Abusers," *Progress in Neuro-Psychopharmacology and Biological Psychiatry* 32, no. 2 (2008): 568–575.

13. Erik Messamore and Robert K. McNamara, "Detection and Treatment of Omega-3 Fatty Acid Deficiency in Psychiatric Practice: Rationale and Implementation," *Lipids in Health and Disease* 15, no. 1 (2016).

14. Sharon Rabinovitz, "Effects of Omega-3 Fatty Acids on Tobacco Craving in Cigarette Smokers: A Double-Blind, Randomized, Placebo-Controlled Pilot Study," *Journal of Psychopharmacology* 28, no. 8 (2014): 804–809.

15. Müller et al., "Brain Membrane Lipids."

16. M. E. Sublette et al., "Meta-Analysis of the Effects of Eicosapentaenoic Acid (EPA) in Clinical Trials in Depression," *Journal of Clinical Psychiatry* 72, no. 12 (2011): 1577–1584; R. J. Mocking et al., "Meta-Analysis and Meta-Regression of Omega-3 Polyunsaturated Fatty Acid Supplementation for Major Depressive Disorder," *Translational Psychiatry* 6, no. 3 (2016): e756–e756.

17. Giuseppe Grosso et al., "Role of Omega-3 Fatty Acids in the Treatment of Depressive Disorders: A Comprehensive Meta-Analysis of Randomized Clinical Trials," *PLoS ONE* 9, no. 5 (2014): e96905.

18. Mocking et al., "Meta-Analysis and Meta-Regression."

19. Sublette et al., "Meta-Analysis of Effects of EPA."

20. Mocking et al., "Meta-Analysis and Meta-Regression."

21. Patrick and Ames, "Vitamin D"; Young and Conquer, "Omega-3 Fatty Acids"; Kuan-Pin Su, Yutaka Matsuoka, and Chi-Un Pae, "Omega-3 Polyunsaturated

Fatty Acids in Prevention of Mood and Anxiety Disorders," *Clinical Psychopharmacology and Neuroscience* 13, no. 2 (2015): 129–137.

22. A. P. Simopoulos, "Evolutionary Aspects of Diet, the Omega-6/Omega-3 Ratio and Genetic Variation: Nutritional Implications for Chronic Diseases," *Biomedicine & Pharmacotherapy* 60, no. 9 (2006): 502–507.

23. "Omega-3 Fatty Acids: Fact Sheet for Health Professionals," Office of Dietary Supplements, National Institutes of Health, updated November 21, 2018, https://ods.od.nih.gov/factsheets/Omega3FattyAcids-HealthProfessional/.

24. Messamore and McNamara, "Detection and Treatment of Omega-3 Deficiency."

25. Sublette et al., "Meta-Analysis of Effects of EPA."; Mocking et al., "Meta-Analysis and Meta-Regression"; Grosso et al., "Role of Omega-3 Fatty Acids."

26. Brenda C. Davis and Penny M. Kris-Etherton, "Achieving Optimal Essential Fatty Acid Status in Vegetarians: Current Knowledge and Practical Implications," *American Journal of Clinical Nutrition* 78, no. 3 (2003): S640.

27. Jeffery A. Foran et al., "Quantitative Analysis of the Benefits and Risks of Consuming Farmed and Wild Salmon," *Journal of Nutrition* 135, no. 11 (2005): 2639–2643.

Chapter 16. How Protein Amino Acids Help

1. George J. Siegel, *Basic Neurochemistry: Molecular, Cellular and Medical Aspects* (Amsterdam: Elsevier Academic Press, 2011).

2. P. Humphries, E. Pretorius, and H. Naudé, "Direct and Indirect Cellular Effects of Aspartame on the Brain," *European Journal of Clinical Nutrition* 62, no. 4 (2007): 451–462.

3. E.A.T. Evers et al., "The Effects of Acute Tryptophan Depletion on Brain Activation During Cognition and Emotional Processing in Healthy Volunteers," *Current Pharmaceutical Design* 16, no. 18 (2010): 1998–2011; Trisha Jenkins et al., "Influence of Tryptophan and Serotonin on Mood and Cognition with a Possible Role of the Gut-Brain Axis," *Nutrients* 8, no. 1 (2016): 56.

4. Laurence Slutsker, "Eosinophilia-Myalgia Syndrome Associated with Exposure to Tryptophan from a Single Manufacturer," *JAMA: The Journal of the American Medical Association* 264, no. 2 (1990): 213–217.

5. John D. Fernstrom, "Can Nutrient Supplements Modify Brain Function?" *American Journal of Clinical Nutrition* 71, no. 6 (2000): 1669S–1673S.

6. T. C. Birdsall, "5-Hydroxytryptophan: A Clinically-Effective Serotonin Precursor," *Alternative Medicine Review* 3 (1998): 271–280.

7. "Serotonin Syndrome Disease Reference Guide," Drugs.com, accessed December 15, 2018, https://www.drugs.com/mcd/serotonin-syndrome.

8. Nobuhiro Kawai et al., "The Sleep-Promoting and Hypothermic Effects of Glycine Are Mediated by NMDA Receptors in the Suprachiasmatic Nucleus," *Neuropsychopharmacology* 40, no. 6 (2014): 1405–1416.

9. Makoto Bannai et al., "The Effects of Glycine on Subjective Daytime Performance in Partially Sleep-Restricted Healthy Volunteers," *Frontiers in Neurology* 3 (2012); Wataru Yamadera et al., "Glycine Ingestion Improves Subjective Sleep Quality in Human Volunteers, Correlating with Polysomnographic Changes," *Sleep and Biological Rhythms* 5, no. 2 (2007): 126–131.

10. Kentaro Inagawa et al., "Assessment of Acute Adverse Events of Glycine Ingestion at High Doses in Human Volunteers," *Journal of Urban Life Health Association* 50 no. 1 (2006): 27–32.

11. C. R. Markus et al., "Evening Intake of α-Lactalbumin Increases Plasma Tryptophan Availability and Improves Morning Alertness and Brain Measures of Attention," *American Journal of Clinical Nutrition* 81, no. 5 (2005): 1026–1033.

12. C. R. Markus, Berend Olivier, and Edward H. De Haan, "Whey Protein Rich in α-Lactalbumin increases the Ratio of Plasma Tryptophan to the Sum of the Other Large Neutral Amino Acids and Improves Cognitive Performance in Stress-Vulnerable Subjects," *American Journal of Clinical Nutrition* 75, no. 6 (2002): 1051–1056; C. R. Markus et al., "The Bovine Protein α-Lactalbumin Increases the Plasma Ratio of Tryptophan to the Other Large Neutral Amino Acids, and in Vulnerable Subjects Raises Brain Serotonin Activity, Reduces Cortisol Concentration, and Improves Mood under Stress," *American Journal of Clinical Nutrition* 71, no. 6 (2000): 1536–1544.

13. Craig Hudson, Susan Hudson, and Joan MacKenzie, "Protein-Source Tryptophan As an Efficacious Treatment for Social Anxiety Disorder: A Pilot Study," *Canadian Journal of Physiology and Pharmacology* 85, no. 9 (2007): 928–932.

14. Jonathan P. Roiser et al., "The Effect of Acute Tryptophan Depletion on the Neural Correlates of Emotional Processing in Healthy Volunteers," *Neuropsychopharmacology* 33, no. 8 (2007): 1992–2006.

15. Eduard Maron, Jakov Shlik, and David J. Nutt, "Tryptophan Research in Panic Disorder," *International Journal of Tryptophan Research* 1 (2008): IJTR.S929.

Chapter 17. How Non-Protein Amino Acids Help

1. Janet Bryan, "Psychological Effects of Dietary Components of Tea: Caffeine and L-Theanine," *Nutrition Reviews* 66, no. 2 (2008): 82–90.

2. Bryan, "Psychological Effects"; David White et al., "Anti-Stress, Behavioural and Magnetoencephalography Effects of an L-Theanine-Based Nutrient Drink: A Randomised, Double-Blind, Placebo-Controlled, Crossover Trial," *Nutrients* 8, no. 1 (2016): 53.

3. T. C. Birdsall, "5-Hydroxytryptophan: A Clinically-Effective Serotonin Precursor," *Alternative Medicine Review* 3 (1998): 271–280.

4. Birdsall, "5-Hydroxytryptophan."

5. Mathew H. Gendle, Erica L. Young, and Alexandra C. Romano, "Effects of Oral 5-Hydroxytryptophan on a Standardized Planning Task: Insight into Possible Dopamine/Serotonin Interactions in the Forebrain," *Human Psychopharmacology: Clinical and Experimental* 28, no. 3 (2013): 270–273; Mathew H. Gendle and Abbe C. Golding, "Oral Administration of 5-Hydroxytryptophan (5-HTP) Impairs Decision Making under Ambiguity but Not under Risk: Evidence from the Iowa Gambling Task," *Human Psychopharmacology: Clinical and Experimental* 25, no. 6 (2010): 491–499.

6. Adham M. Abdou et al., "Relaxation and Immunity Enhancement Effects of γ-Aminobutyric acid (GABA) Administration in Humans," *BioFactors* 26, no. 3 (2006): 201–208; A. E. Fayed, "Review Article: Health Benefits of Some Physiologically Active Ingredients and Their Suitability As Yoghurt Fortifiers," *Journal of Food Science and Technology* 52, no. 5 (2014): 2512–2521.

7. Evert Boonstra et al., "Neurotransmitters as Food Supplements: The Effects of GABA on Brain and Behavior," *Frontiers in Psychology* 6 (2015): 1520.

8. Julia Ross, *The Mood Cure: The 4-Step Program to Rebalance Your Emotional Chemistry and Rediscover Your Natural Sense of Well-Being* (New York: Viking, 2004), p. 89.

9. White et al., "Anti-Stress, Behavioural and Magnetoencephalography Effects."

10. Keiko Unno et al., "Ingestion of Theanine, an Amino Acid in Tea, Suppresses Psychosocial Stress in Mice," *Experimental Physiology* 98, no. 1 (2012): 290–303.

11. Birdsall, "5-Hydroxytryptophan."

12. Koen Schruers et al., "Acute L-5-Hydroxytryptophan Administration Inhibits Carbon Dioxide-Induced Panic in Panic Disorder Patients," *Psychiatry Research* 113, no. 3 (2002): 237–243.

13. A. Yoto et al., "Oral Intake of γ-Aminobutyric Acid Affects Mood and Activities of Central Nervous System During Stressed Condition Induced by Mental Tasks," *Amino Acids* 43, no. 3 (2011): 1331–1337.

14. Birdsall, "5-Hydroxytryptophan."

15. Pradeep J. Nathan et al., "The Neuropharmacology of L-Theanine (N-Ethyl-L-Glutamine)," *Journal of Herbal Pharmacotherapy* 6, no. 2 (2006): 21–30.

16. Emma K. Keenan et al., "How Much Theanine in a Cup of Tea? Effects of Tea Type and Method of Preparation," *Food Chemistry* 125, no. 2 (2011): 588–94.

17. Guoqiang Chen et al., "Rapid and Selective Quantification of L-Theanine in Ready-to-Drink Teas from Chinese Market Using SPE and UPLC-UV," *Food Chemistry* 135, no.2 (2012): 402–07.

18. Klára Boros, Dezső Csupor, and Nikoletta Jedlinszki, "Theanine and Caffeine Content of Infusions Prepared from Commercial Tea Samples," *Pharmacognosy Magazine* 12, no. 45 (2016): 75–79.

19. White et al., "Anti-Stress, Behavioural and Magnetoencephalography Effects."

20. Radhika Dhakal, Vivek K. Bajpai, and Kwang-Hyun Baek, "Production of GABA (γ-aminobutyric acid) by Microorganisms: A Review," *Brazilian Journal of Microbiology* 43, no. 4 (2012): 1230–1241.

21. D. Karladee and S. Suriyong, "γ-Aminobutyric Acid (GABA) Content in Different Varieties of Brown Rice During Germination," *Science Asia* 38 no. 1 (2012): 13–17.

Chapter 18. How Probiotics Help

1. Ron Sender, Shai Fuchs, and Ron Milo, "Revised Estimates for the Number of Human and Bacteria Cells in the Body," *PLOS Biology* 14, no. 8 (2016): e1002533.
2. Marika Mikelsaar et al., "Do Probiotic Preparations for Humans Really Have Efficacy?" *Microbial Ecology in Health and Disease* 22, no. 1 (2011): 10128.
3. Amar Sarkar et al., "Psychobiotics and the Manipulation of Bacteria–Gut–Brain Signals," *Trends in Neurosciences* 39, no. 11 (2016): 763–781.
4. Patrice D. Cani and Nathalie M. Delzenne, "The Gut Microbiome As Therapeutic Target," *Pharmacology & Therapeutics* 130, no. 2 (2011): 202–212; John R. Kelly et al., "Breaking Down the Barriers: The Gut Microbiome, Intestinal Permeability and Stress-Related Psychiatric Disorders," *Frontiers in Cellular Neuroscience* 9 (2015): 392; Huiying Wang et al., "Effect of Probiotics on Central Nervous System Functions in Animals and Humans: A Systematic Review," *Journal of Neurogastroenterology and Motility* 22, no. 4 (2016): 589–605.
5. Wang et al., "Effect of Probiotics."
6. Alison C. Bested, Alan C. Logan, and Eva M. Selhub, "Intestinal Microbiota, Probiotics and Mental Health: From Metchnikoff to Modern Advances: Part III – Convergence toward Clinical Trials," *Gut Pathogens* 5, no. 1 (2013): 4; Timothy G. Dinan et al., "Collective Unconscious: How Gut Microbes Shape Human Behavior," *Journal of Psychiatric Research* 63 (2015): 1–9.
7. Cani and Delzenne, "Gut Microbiome."
8. Kelly et al., "Breaking Down Barriers."
9. Wang et al., "Effect of Probiotics."
10. Kelly et al., "Breaking Down Barriers"; Wang et al., "Effect of Probiotics."
11. Amy Langdon, Nathan Crook, and Gautam Dantas, "The Effects of Antibiotics on the Microbiome throughout Development and Alternative Approaches for Therapeutic Modulation," *Genome Medicine* 8, no. 1 (2016); F. Imhann et al., "Proton Pump Inhibitors Affect the Gut Microbiome, Gut 65 (2016): 740–748; Alexander R. Moschen, Verena Wieser, and Herbert Tilg, "Dietary Factors: Major Regulators of the Gut's Microbiota," *Gut and Liver* 6, no. 4 (2012): 411–416; G. Vassallo et al., "Review Article: Alcohol and Gut Microbiota— The Possible Role of Gut Microbiota Modulation in the Treatment of Alcoholic Liver Disease," *Alimentary Pharmacology & Therapeutics* 41, no. 10 (2015): 917–927; Simon R. Knowles, Elizabeth A. Nelson, and Enzo A. Palombo, "Investigating the Role of Perceived Stress on Bacterial Flora Activity and Salivary Cortisol Secretion: A Possible Mechanism Underlying Susceptibility to Illness," *Biological Psychology* 77, no. 2 (2008): 132–137; Michael T. Bailey et al., "Exposure to a Social Stressor Alters the Structure of the Intestinal Microbiota:

Implications for Stressor-Induced Immunomodulation," *Brain, Behavior, and Immunity* 25, no. 3 (2011): 397–407; P. C. Konturek, T. Brzozowski, and S. J. Konturek, "Stress and the Gut: Pathophysiology, Clinical Consequences, Diagnostic Approach and Treatment Options," *Journal of Physiology and Pharmacology* 62 (2011): 591–9; Kelly et al., "Breaking Down Barriers."

12. J. C. O'Horo et al., "Treatment of Recurrent Clostridium difficile Infection: A Systematic Review," *Infection* 42, no. 1 (2013): 43–59.

13. "Fecal Transplantation (Bacteriotherapy)," Gastroenterology and Hepatology, Johns Hopkins Medicine, accessed December 31, 2018, http://www.hopkinsmedicine.org/gastroenterology_hepatology/clinical_services/advanced_endoscopy/fecal_transplantation.html.

14. L. J. Brandt, "Fecal Transplantation for the Treatment of Clostridium difficile Infection," *Gastroenterology & Hepatology* 8, no. 3 (2012): 191–194.

15. Wei-Hsien Liu et al., "Alteration of Behavior and Monoamine Levels Attributable to Lactobacillus Plantarum PS128 in Germ-Free Mice," *Behavioural Brain Research* 298 (2016): 202–209.

16. Daniel J. Davis et al., "Lactobacillus plantarum Attenuates Anxiety-Related Behavior and Protects Against Stress-Induced Dysbiosis in Adult Zebrafish," *Scientific Reports* 6, no. 1 (2016).

17. J. A. Bravo et al., "Ingestion of Lactobacillus Strain Regulates Emotional Behavior and Central GABA Receptor Expression in a Mouse Via the Vagus Nerve," *Proceedings of the National Academy of Sciences* 108, no. 38 (2011): 16050–16055.

18. Michaël Messaoudi et al., "Assessment of Psychotropic-Like Properties of a Probiotic Formulation (Lactobacillus helveticus R0052 and Bifidobacterium longum R0175) in Rats and Human Subjects," *British Journal of Nutrition* 105, no. 05 (2010): 755–764.

19. Akito Kato-Kataoka et al., "Fermented Milk Containing Lactobacillus casei Strain Shirota Preserves the Diversity of the Gut Microbiota and Relieves Abdominal Dysfunction in Healthy Medical Students Exposed to Academic Stress," *Applied and Environmental Microbiology* 82, no. 12 (2016): 3649–3658.

20. A. V. Rao et al., "A Randomized, Double-Blind, Placebo-Controlled Pilot Study of a Probiotic in Emotional Symptoms of Chronic Fatigue Syndrome," *Gut Pathogens* 1, no. 1 (2009): 6.

21. Matthew R. Hilimire, Jordan E. DeVylder, and Catherine A. Forestell, "Fermented Foods, Neuroticism, and Social Anxiety: An Interaction Model," *Psychiatry Research* 228, no. 2 (2015): 203–208.

22. Kirsten Tillisch et al., "Consumption of Fermented Milk Product with Probiotic Modulates Brain Activity," *Gastroenterology* 144, no. 7 (2013): 1394–1401.e4.

23. G. De Palma et al., "Transplantation of Fecal Microbiota from Patients with Irritable Bowel Syndrome Alters Gut Function and Behavior in Recipient Mice," *Science Translational Medicine* 9, no. 379 (2017): eaaf6397.

24. Borja Sánchez et al., "Probiotics, Gut Microbiota, and Their Influence on Host Health and Disease," *Molecular Nutrition & Food Research* 61, no. 1 (2016): 1600240.
25. Sánchez et al., "Probiotics"; Ravinder Nagpal et al., "Probiotics, Their Health Benefits and Applications for Developing Healthier Foods: A Review," FEMS Microbiology Letters 334, no. 1 (2012): 1–15; A. A. Amara and A. Shibl, "Role of Probiotics in Health Improvement, Infection Control and Disease Treatment and Management," *Saudi Pharmaceutical Journal* 23, no. 2 (2015): 107–114.
26. Cani and Delzenne, "Gut Microbiome."
27. Wang et al., "Effect of Probiotics."
28. Wang et al., "Effect of Probiotics"; Mikelsaar et al., "Probiotic Preparations."

Chapter 19. How Adaptogens Help

1. Vinod S. Pawar and Hugar Shivakumar, "A Current Status of Adaptogens: Natural Remedy to Stress," *Asian Pacific Journal of Tropical Disease* 2 (2012): S480–S490.
2. Pawar and Shivakumar, "Status of Adaptogens"; David Winston and Steven Maimes, *Adaptogens: Herbs for Strength, Stamina, and Stress Relief* (Rochester, VT: Healing Arts Press, 2007).
3. Winston and Maimes, *Adaptogens*: 142-146; Alexander Panossian and Georg Wikman, "Evidence-Based Efficacy of Adaptogens in Fatigue, and Molecular Mechanisms Related to their Stress-Protective Activity," *Current Clinical Pharmacology* 4, no. 3 (2009): 198–219; S. Lee and D. Rhee, "Short Review: Effects of Ginseng on Stress-Related Depression, Anxiety, and the Hypothalamic–Pituitary–Adrenal Axis," *Journal of Ginseng Research* 41, no.4 (2017): 589–594.
4. A. Pengelly and K. Bennett, "Appalachian Plant Monographs: *Panax quinquefolius* L., American Ginseng," September 2011, available at https://www.frostburg.edu/fsu/assets/File/ACES/panax%20quinquefolius%20-%20final(2).pdf; Winston and Maimes, *Adaptogens*, 130–134.
5. Winston and Maimes, *Adaptogens*, 157-161; A. Panossian and H. Wagner, "Stimulating Effect of Adaptogens: An Overview with Particular Reference to Their Efficacy Following Single Dose Administration," *Phytotherapy Research* 19, no. 10 (2005): 819–838.
6. Gustavo F. Gonzales, "Ethnobiology and Ethnopharmacology of Lepidium meyenii (Maca), a Plant from the Peruvian Highlands," *Evidence-Based Complementary and Alternative Medicine* 2012 (2012): 1–10.
7. Sharanbasappa Durg et al., "Withania somnifera (Ashwagandha) in Neurobehavioural Disorders Induced by Brain Oxidative Stress in Rodents: A Systematic Review and Meta-Analysis," *Journal of Pharmacy and Pharmacology* 67, no. 7 (2015): 879–899; Winston and Maimes, Adaptogens, 138–141.
8. Marc Maurice Cohen, "Tulsi—Ocimum sanctum: A Herb for All Reasons," *Journal of Ayurveda and Integrative Medicine* 5, no. 4 (2014): 251–259; Winston and Maimes, *Adaptogens*, 167–171.

9. Winston and Maimes, *Adaptogens*, 174–178.
10. Hesham R. Omar et al., "Licorice Abuse: Time to Send a Warning Message," *Therapeutic Advances in Endocrinology and Metabolism* 3, no. 4 (2012): 125–138, https://doi.org/10.1177/2042018812454322.
11. Panossian and Wikman, "Evidence-Based Efficacy"; Alexander G. Panossian, "Adaptogens in Mental and Behavioral Disorders," *Psychiatric Clinics of North America* 36, no. 1 (2013): 49–64; Winston and Maimes, Adaptogens, 191–194.
12. Alexander Panossian and Georg Wikman, "Pharmacology of Schisandra chinensis Bail.: An overview of Russian Research and Uses in Medicine," *Journal of Ethnopharmacology* 118, no. 2 (2008): 183–212; Panossian and Wikman, "Evidence-Based Efficacy"; Winston and Maimes, *Adaptogens*, 195–198.
13. Winston and Maimes, Adaptogens, 61–62; Pawar and Shivakumar, "Status of Adaptogens"; Panossian and Wagner, "Stimulating Effect."
14. Winston and Maimes, *Adaptogens*, 129–204.
15. Winston and Maimes, *Adaptogens*.
16. Alexander Panossian and Georg Wikman, "Effects of Adaptogens on the Central Nervous System and the Molecular Mechanisms Associated with Their Stress—Protective Activity," *Pharmaceuticals* 3, no. 1 (2010): 188–224; Panossian and Wikman, "Evidence-Based Efficacy"; Panossian and Wikman, "Pharmacology"; Panossian, "Adaptogens."
17. Jian-Ming Lu, Qizhi Yao, and Changyi Chen, "Ginseng Compounds: An Update on their Molecular Mechanisms and Medical Applications," *Current Vascular Pharmacology* 7, no. 3 (2009): 293–302; Pengelly and Bennett, "Appalachian Plant Monographs."
18. Durg et al., "Withania somnifera."
19. Alexander Panossian et al., "The Adaptogens Rhodiola and Schizandra Modify the Response to Immobilization Stress in Rabbits by Suppressing the Increase of Phosphorylated Stress-activated Protein Kinase, Nitric Oxide and Cortisol," *Drug Target Insights* 2 (2007): 39–54.
20. Deepak Rai et al., "Anti-Stress Effects of Ginkgo biloba and Panax ginseng: A Comparative Study," *Journal of Pharmacological Sciences* 93, no. 4 (2003): 458–464.
21. M. Chatterjee, "Comparative Evaluation of Bacopa monniera and Panax quniquefolium in Experimental Anxiety and Depressive Models in Mice," *Indian Journal of Experimental Biology* 48 (2010): 306–313.
22. Ram C. Saxena et al., "Efficacy of an Extract of Ocimum tenuiflorum (OciBest) in the Management of General Stress: A Double-Blind, Placebo-Controlled Study," *Evidence-Based Complementary and Alternative Medicine* 2012 (2012): 1–7.
23. Nicole A. Brooks et al., "Beneficial Effects of Lepidium meyenii (Maca) on Psychological Symptoms and Measures of Sexual Dysfunction in Postmenopausal Women Are Not Related to Estrogen or Androgen Content," *Menopause* 15, no. 6 (2008): 1157–1162.

24. K. Chandrasekhar, Jyoti Kapoor, and Sridhar Anishetty, "A Prospective, Randomized Double-Blind, Placebo-Controlled Study of Safety and Efficacy of a High-Concentration Full-Spectrum Extract of Ashwagandha Root in Reducing Stress and Anxiety in Adults," *Indian Journal of Psychological Medicine* 34, no. 3 (2012): 255.

25. A. A. Spasov et al., "A Double-Blind, Placebo-Controlled Pilot Study of the Stimulating and Adaptogenic Effect of Rhodiola rosea SHR-5 Extract on the Fatigue of Students Caused by Stress During an Examination Period with a Repeated Low-Dose Regimen," *Phytomedicine* 7, no. 2 (2000): 85–89.

26. V. A. Shevtsov et al., "A Randomized Trial of Two Different Doses of a SHR-5 Rhodiola rosea Extract Versus Placebo and Control of Capacity for Mental Work," *Phytomedicine* 10, no. 2–3 (2003): 95–105.

27. Enrico De Andrade et al., "Study of the Efficacy of Korean Red Ginseng in the Treatment of Erectile Dysfunction," *Asian Journal of Andrology* 9, no. 2 (2007): 241–244; Dai-Ja Jang et al., "Red Ginseng for Treating Erectile Dysfunction: A Systematic Review," *British Journal of Clinical Pharmacology* 66, no. 4 (2008): 444–450.

28. Kyung-Jin Oh et al., "Effects of Korean Red Ginseng on Sexual Arousal in Menopausal Women: Placebo-Controlled, Double-Blind Crossover Clinical Study," *Journal of Sexual Medicine* 7, no. 4 (2010): 1469–1477.

29. Gonzales, "Ethnobiology and Ethnopharmacology."

30. Cohen, "Tulsi—Ocimum sanctum."

31. Hao Liu et al., "Discovering Anti-Osteoporosis Constituents of Maca (Lepidium meyenii) by Combined Virtual Screening and Activity Verification," *Food Research International* 77 (2015): 215–220.

32. Jin-Kang Zhang et al., "Protection by Salidroside against Bone Loss via Inhibition of Oxidative Stress and Bone-Resorbing Mediators," *PLoS ONE* 8, no. 2 (2013): e57251.

33. Prabhakara R. Nagareddy and M. Lakshmana, "Withania somnifera Improves Bone Calcification in Calcium-Deficient Ovariectomized Rats," *Journal of Pharmacy and Pharmacology* 58, no. 4 (2006): 513–519.

34. Muhammad H. Siddiqi et al., "Ginseng Saponins and the Treatment of Osteoporosis: Mini Literature Review," *Journal of Ginseng Research* 37, no. 3 (2013): 261–268.

35. Mi H. Kim et al., "Ameliorative Effects of Schizandra chinensis on Osteoporosis Via Activation of Estrogen Receptor (ER)-α/-β," *Food and Function* 5, no. 7 (2014): 1594–1601.

36. Winston and Maimes, *Adaptogens*: 253–268.

Chapter 20. How Nervine Herbs Help

1. Kurt Appel et al., "Modulation of the γ-Aminobutyric Acid (GABA) System by Passiflora incarnata L," *Phytotherapy Research* 25, no. 6 (2010): 838–843; J. K. Srivastava, E. Shankar, and S. Gupta, "Chamomile: A Herbal Medicine of the Past with a Bright Future (Review)," *Molecular Medicine Reports* 3, no. 6 (2010): 895–901; Celso A. Costa et al., "The GABAergic System Contributes to the Anxiolytic-Like Effect of Essential Oil from Cymbopogon citratus (Lemongrass)," *Journal of Ethnopharmacology* 137, no. 1 (2011): 828–836; Han C. Chua et al., "Kavain, the Major Constituent of the Anxiolytic Kava Extract, Potentiates GABAA Receptors: Functional Characteristics and Molecular Mechanism," *PLoS ONE* 11, no. 6 (2016): e0157700; Lourdes Franco et al., "The Sedative Effect of Non-Alcoholic Beer in Healthy Female Nurses," *PLoS ONE* 7, no. 7 (2012): e37290.

2. Niteeka Maroo, Avijit Hazra, and Tapas Das, "Efficacy and Safety of a Polyherbal Sedative-Hypnotic Formulation NSF-3 in Primary Insomnia in Comparison to Zolpidem: A Randomized Controlled Trial," *Indian Journal of Pharmacology* 45, no. 1 (2013): 34.

3. Jerome Sarris, Emma LaPorte, and Isaac Schweitzer, "Kava: A Comprehensive Review of Efficacy, Safety, and Psychopharmacology," *Australian & New Zealand Journal of Psychiatry* 45, no. 1 (2011): 27–35.

4. S. Akhondzadeh et al., "Passionflower in the Treatment of Generalized Anxiety: A Pilot Double-Blind Randomized Controlled Trial with Oxazepam," *Journal of Clinical Pharmacy and Therapeutics* 26, no. 5 (2001): 363–367.

5. L. P. Dantas et al., "Effects of Passiflora incarnata and Midazolam for Control of Anxiety in Patients Undergoing Dental Extraction," *Medicina Oral Patología Oral y Cirugia Bucal* 22, no. 1 (2016): e95–e101.

6. Pınar Aslanargun et al., "Passiflora incarnata Linneaus as an Anxiolytic before Spinal Anesthesia," *Journal of Anesthesia* 26, no. 1 (2011): 39–44.

7. Jay D. Amsterdam et al., "A Randomized, Double-Blind, Placebo-Controlled Trial of Oral Matricaria recutita (Chamomile) Extract Therapy for Generalized Anxiety Disorder," *Journal of Clinical Psychopharmacology* 29, no. 4 (2009): 378–382; Jay D. Amsterdam et al., "Chamomile (Matricaria recutita) May Have Antidepressant Activity in Anxious Depressed Humans: An Exploratory Study," *Alternative Therapies in Health and Medicine* 18, no. 5 (2012): 44–49.

8. M. Rahimi et al., "The Effect of Chamomile Tea on Dyspnoea and Anxiety Among Patients with Heart Failure," *CONNECT: The World of Critical Care Nursing* 10, no. 1 (2016): 5–8.

9. David Arome, Chinedu Enegide, and Solomon Fidelis Ameh, "Pharmacological Evaluation of Anxiolytic Property of Aqueous Root Extract of Cymbopogon citratus in Mice," *Chronicles of Young Scientists* 5, no. 1 (2014): 33–38.

10. M. M. Blanco et al., "Neurobehavioral Effect of Essential Oil of Cymbopogon citratus in Mice," *Phytomedicine* 16, no. 2–3 (2009): 265–270.

11. Tiago C. Goes et al., "Effect of Lemongrass Aroma on Experimental Anxiety in Humans," *Journal of Alternative and Complementary Medicine* 21, no. 12 (2015): 766–773.

12. S. Salter and S. Brownie, "Treating Primary Insomnia: The Efficacy of Valerian and Hops," *Australian Family Physician* 39, no. 6 (2010): 433.

13. Franco et al., "Sedative Effect."

14. Maroo, Hazra, and Das, "Efficacy and Safety."

15. R. J. Boerner et al., "Kava-Kava Extract LI 150 Is as Effective as Opipramol and Buspirone in Generalised Anxiety Disorder: An 8-Week Randomized, Double-Blind Multi-Centre Clinical Trial in 129 Out-Patients," *Phytomedicine* 10 (2003): 38–49.

16. M. H. Pittler, "Kava Extract Versus Placebo for Treating Anxiety," *Cochrane Database of Systematic Reviews*, 6 (2010).

17. Srivastava, Shankar, and Gupta, "Chamomile."

18. Goes et al., " Lemongrass Aroma"; Yuk-Lan Lee et al., "A Systematic Review on the Anxiolytic Effects of Aromatherapy in People with Anxiety Symptoms," *Journal of Alternative and Complementary Medicine* 17, no. 2 (2011): 101–108; T. Komori et al., "The Sleep-Enhancing Effect of Valerian Inhalation and Sleep-Shortening Effect of Lemon Inhalation," *Chemical Senses* 31, no. 8 (2006): 731–737.

Part Three: What Hurts Your Calm

Chapter 23. How Caffeine Hurts

1. Anne Procyk, "Nutritional and Integrative Interventions for Mental Health Disorders" PESI Seminar, Seattle, WA, (May 27, 2016).

Chapter 24. How Alcohol Hurts

1. J. P. Smith and C. I. Randall, "Anxiety and Alcohol Use Disorders: Comorbidity and Treatment Considerations," *Alcohol Research Current Reviews* 34, no. 4 (2012): 414.

2. Ian M. Colrain, Christian L. Nicholas, and Fiona C. Baker, "Alcohol and the Sleeping Brain," in *Handbook of Clinical Neurology: Vol. 125 Alcohol and the Nervous System*, eds. Edith V. Sullivan and Adolf Pfefferbaum (Amsterdam: Elsevier, 2014): 415–431.

Chapter 25. How Processed Foods Hurt

1. Felice N. Jacka et al., "A Prospective Study of Diet Quality and Mental Health in Adolescents," *PLoS ONE* 6, no. 9 (2011): e24805; Felice N. Jacka, Arnstein Mykletun, and Michael Berk, "Moving towards a Population Health Approach to the Primary Prevention of Common Mental Disorders," *BMC Medicine* 10

(2012): 149; Adrienne O'Neil et al., "Relationship between Diet and Mental Health in Children and Adolescents: A Systematic Review," *American Journal of Public Health* 104, no. 10 (2014): e31–e42.

2. Jacka et al., "Prospective Study."
3. Emily E. Noble, Ted M. Hsu, and Scott E. Kanoski, "Gut to Brain Dysbiosis: Mechanisms Linking Western Diet Consumption, the Microbiome, and Cognitive Impairment," *Frontiers in Behavioral Neuroscience* 11 (2017): 9; P. Humphries, E. Pretorius, and H. Naudé, "Direct and Indirect Cellular Effects of Aspartame on the Brain," *European Journal of Clinical Nutrition* 62, no. 4 (2007): 451–462.
4. Noble, Hsu, and Kanoski, "Gut to Brain Dysbiosis."
5. Leon Ferder, Marcelo D. Ferder, and Felipe Inserra, "The Role of High-Fructose Corn Syrup in Metabolic Syndrome and Hypertension," *Current Hypertension Reports* 12, no. 2 (2010): 105–112.
6. Humphries, Pretorius, and Naudé, "Direct and Indirect Cellular Effects."
7. World Health Organization, *Eliminating Trans Fats in Europe: A Policy Brief* (Copenhagen: World Health Organization, Regional Office for Europe, 2015), 2, accessed January 2, 2019, http://www.euro.who.int/__data/assets/pdf_file/0010/288442/Eliminating-trans-fats-in-Europe-A-policy-brief.pdf?ua=1.
8. C. S. Pase et al., "Influence of Perinatal Trans Fat on Behavioral Responses and Brain Oxidative Status of Adolescent Rats Acutely Exposed to Stress," *Neuroscience* 247 (2013): 242–252; C. S. Pase et al., "Prolonged Consumption of Trans Fat Favors the Development of Orofacial Dyskinesia and Anxiety-Like Symptoms in Older Rats," *International Journal of Food Sciences and Nutrition* 65, no. 6 (2014): 713–719; Fábio T. Kuhn et al., "Influence of Trans Fat and Omega-3 on the Preference of Psychostimulant Drugs in the First Generation of Young Rats," *Pharmacology Biochemistry and Behavior* 110 (2013): 58–65.
9. Pase et al., "Influence of Perinatal Trans Fat," 242.
10. Almudena Sánchez-Villegas et al., "Dietary Fat Intake and the Risk of Depression: The SUN Project," *PLoS ONE* 6, no. 1 (2011): e16268.
11. "Are You or Your Family Eating Toxic Food Dyes?" Mercola.com, February 24, 2011, http://articles.mercola.com/sites/articles/archive/2011/02/24/are-you-or-your-family-eating-toxic-food-dyes.aspx.
12. L. E. Arnold, Nicholas Lofthouse, and Elizabeth Hurt, "Artificial Food Colors and Attention-Deficit/Hyperactivity Symptoms: Conclusions to Dye for," *Neurotherapeutics* 9, no. 3 (2012): 599–609.
13. Donna McCann et al., "Food Additives and Hyperactive Behaviour in 3-Year-Old and 8/9-Year-Old Children in the Community: A Randomised, Double-Blinded, Placebo-Controlled Trial," *The Lancet* 370, no. 9598 (2007): 1560–1567.
14. McDonald's UK, Our Food: Ingredient Listing, updated January 2012, accessed January 2, 2019, http://www.mcdonalds.co.uk/content/dam/McDonaldsUK/Food/Category/Nutrients/OurFood-Booklet.pdf.

15. McDonald's USA, *McDonald's USA Ingredients Listing for Popular Menu Items*, accessed January 2, 2019, http://s3.amazonaws.com/us-east-prod-dep-share-s3/dna/pushlive/ingredientslist.pdf.

16. U.S. Food and Drug Administration, Center for Food Safety and Applied Nutrition, "Background Document for the Food Advisory Committee: Certified Color Additives in Food and Possible Association with Attention Deficit Hyperactivity Disorder in Children March 30–31, 2011," accessed January 2, 2019, https://foodpoisoningbulletin.com/wp-content/uploads/FAC-Color-Additives-ADHD.pdf.

17. National Toxicology Program, "Butylated Hydroxyanisole" in Report on Carcinogens, Fourteenth Edition (Research Triangle Park, NC: U.S. Department of Health and Human Services, 2016), accessed January 2, 2019, https://ntp.niehs.nih.gov/ntp/roc/content/profiles/butylatedhydroxyanisole.pdf.

18. V. Labrador et al., "Cytotoxicity of Butylated Hydroxyanisole in Vero Cells," *Cell Biology and Toxicology* 23, no. 3 (2006): 189–199.

19. Xiaoheng Li et al., "Effects of Butylated Hydroxyanisole on the Steroidogenesis of Rat Immature Leydig Cells," *Toxicology Mechanisms and Methods* 26, no. 7 (2016): 511–519; Linxi Li et al., "Butylated Hydroxyanisole Potently Inhibits Rat and Human 11β-Hydroxysteroid Dehydrogenase Type 2," *Pharmacology* 97, no. 1–2 (2015): 10–17; A. Pop et al., "Evaluation of the Possible Endocrine Disruptive Effect of Butylated Hydroxyanisole, Butylated Hydroxytoluene and Propyl Gallate in Immature Female Rats," *Farmacia* 61, no. 1 (2013): 202–211.

20. G. Petersen, D. Rasmussen, and K. Gustavson, *Study on Enhancing the Endocrine Disrupter Priority List with a Focus on Low Production Volume Chemicals* (Hørsholm, Denmark: DHI Water and Environment, 2007), accessed January 2, 2019, http://ec.europa.eu/environment/chemicals/endocrine/pdf/final_report_2007.pdf.

21. Ivana Klopčič and Marija Sollner Dolenc, "Endocrine Activity of AVB, 2MR, BHA and Their Mixtures," *Toxicological Sciences*, 156, no. 1 (2017): 240–251.

22. R. S. Lanigan and T. A. Yamarik, "Final Report on the Safety Assessment of BHT," *International Journal of Toxicology* 21, no. 2_suppl (2002): 19–94.

23. Alexandra E. Turley, Joseph W. Zagorski, and Cheryl E. Rockwell, "The Nrf2 Activator tBHQ Inhibits T Cell Activation of Primary Human CD4 T Cells," *Cytokine* 71, no. 2 (2015): 295.

Chapter 26. How GMO Foods Hurt

1. "Food, Genetically Modified," World Health Organization, accessed December 16, 2018, http://www.who.int/topics/food_genetically_modified/en/.

2. David Johnson and Siobhan O'Connor, "These Charts Show Every Genetically Modified Food People Already Eat in the U.S.," Time, April 30, 2015, http://time.com/3840073/gmo-food-charts/.

3. "Food, Genetically Modified," World Health Organization, accessed December 16, 2018, http://www.who.int/topics/food_genetically_modified/en/.
4. David Johnson and Siobhan O'Connor, "These Charts Show Every Genetically Modified Food People Already Eat in the U.S.," Time, April 30, 2015, http://time.com/3840073/gmo-food-charts/.
5. Amy Dean and Jennifer Armstrong, "Genetically Modified Foods," American Academy of Environmental Medicine, May 8, 2009, https://www.aaemonline.org/gmo.php.
6. Dean and Armstrong, "Genetically Modified Foods."

Chapter 27. How Foods You Are Sensitive to Hurt
1. Food Allergen Labelling and Consumer Protection Act of 2004, Pub. Law 108-282, Title II, https://www.fda.gov/Food/GuidanceRegulation/GuidanceDocumentsRegulatoryInformation/Allergens/ucm106187.htm.
2. C. Catassi, "Gluten Sensitivity," Annals of Nutrition and Metabolism 67, no. 2 (2015): 16–26.

Part Four: Stress Resilience Foods

Chapter 30. Why Not Phytates and Oxalates?
1. Torsten Bohn et al., "Phytic Acid Added to White-Wheat Bread Inhibits Fractional Apparent Magnesium Absorption in Humans," American Journal of Clinical Nutrition 79, no. 3 (2004): 418–423; Torsten Bohn, "Dietary Factors Influencing Magnesium Absorption in Humans," Current Nutrition & Food Science 4, no. 1 (2008): 53–72; Ulrich Schlemmer et al., "Phytate in Foods and Significance for Humans: Food Sources, Intake, Processing, Bioavailability, Protective Role and Analysis," Molecular Nutrition & Food Research 53, no. S2 (2009): S330–S375; Torsten Bohn et al., "Fractional Magnesium Absorption Is Significantly Lower in Human Subjects from a Meal Served with an Oxalate-Rich Vegetable, Spinach, As Compared with a Meal Served with Kale, a Vegetable with a Low Oxalate Content," British Journal of Nutrition 91, no. 04 (2004): 601; S. N. Bsc, "Oxalate Content of Foods and Its Effect on Humans," Asia Pacific Journal of Clinical Nutrition 8, no. 1 (1999): 64–74.
2. Rosalind S. Gibson, Janet C. King, and Nicola Lowe, "A Review of Dietary Zinc Recommendations," Food and Nutrition Bulletin 37, no. 4 (2016): 451.
3. Coothan K. Veena et al., "Mitochondrial Dysfunction in an Animal Model of Hyperoxaluria: A Prophylactic Approach with Fucoidan," European Journal of Pharmacology 579, no. 1-3 (2008): 330–336; Ming-Chieh Ma, Yih-Sharng Chen, and Ho-Shiang Huang, "Erythrocyte Oxidative Stress in Patients with Calcium Oxalate Stones Correlates with Stone Size and Renal Tubular Damage," Urology 83, no. 2 (2014): 510.e9-510.e17; Saeed R.

Khan, "Hyperoxaluria-Induced Oxidative Stress and Antioxidants for Renal Protection," *Urological Research* 33, no. 5 (2005): 349–357; F. D. Khand et al., "Mitochondrial Superoxide Production During Oxalate-Mediated Oxidative Stress in Renal Epithelial Cells," *Free Radical Biology and Medicine* 32, no. 12 (2002): 1339–1350.

4. Stef Robijn et al., "Hyperoxaluria: A Gut–Kidney Axis?" *Kidney International* 80, no. 11 (2011): 1146–1158; L. H. Markiewicz et al., "Diet Shapes the Ability of Human Intestinal Microbiota to Degrade Phytate: In Vitro Studies," *Journal of Applied Microbiology* 115, no. 1 (2013): 247–259.

5. "Oxalate content of Foods," Harvard T. H. Chan School of Public Health Nutrition Department's File Download Site, accessed December 16, 2018, https://regepi.bwh.harvard.edu/health/Oxalate/files.

6. Weiwen Chai and Michael Liebman, "Effect of Different Cooking Methods on Vegetable Oxalate Content," *Journal of Agricultural and Food Chemistry* 53, no. 8 (2005): 3027–3030.

7. Muhammad S. Akhtar et al., "Effect of Cooking on Soluble and Insoluble Oxalate Contents in Selected Pakistani Vegetables and Beans," *International Journal of Food Properties* 14, no. 1 (2011): 241–249.

Chapter 31. Water

1. Barry Popkin, Kristen D'Anci, and Irwin Rosenberg, "Water, Hydration, and Health," *Nutrition Reviews* 68, no. 8 (2010): 439–58; Kristen E. D'Anci et al., "Voluntary Dehydration and Cognitive Performance in Trained College Athletes," Perceptual and Motor Skills 109, no. 1 (2009): 251–269; Lawrence E. Armstrong et al., "Mild Dehydration Affects Mood in Healthy Young Women," *Journal of Nutrition* 142, no. 2 (2011): 382–388; Matthew S. Ganio et al., "Mild Dehydration Impairs Cognitive Performance and Mood of Men," *British Journal of Nutrition* 106, no. 10 (2011): 1535–1543.

Chapter 32. Wild-Caught Salmon, Sardines, and Herring

1. Neila Chaari et al., "Neuropsychological Effects of Mercury Exposure Among Dentists in Monastir City," *Recent Patents on Inflammation & Allergy Drug Discovery* 9, no. 2 (2016): 151–158; Jean-Paul Bourdineaud et al., "Deleterious Effects in Mice of Fish-Associated Methylmercury Contained in a Diet Mimicking the Western Populations' Average Fish Consumption," *Environment International* 37, no. 2 (2011): 303–313.

2. NRDC, "Mercury in Fish," https://www.nrdc.org/sites/default/files/walletcard.pdf.

3. M. C. Hamilton et al., "Lipid Composition and Contaminants in Farmed and Wild Salmon," *Environmental Science & Technology* 39, no. 22 (2005): 8622–8629; Jeffery A. Foran et al., "Risk-Based Consumption Advice for

Farmed Atlantic and Wild Pacific Salmon Contaminated with Dioxins and Dioxin-like Compounds," *Environmental Health Perspectives* 113, no. 5 (2005): 552–556; R. A. Hites, "Global Assessment of Organic Contaminants in Farmed Salmon," *Science* 303, no. 5655 (2004): 226–229.

Chapter 34. Pasture-Raised Eggs
1. Julia Kühn et al., "Free-Range Farming: A Natural Alternative to Produce Vitamin D-Enriched Eggs," *Nutrition* 30, no. 4 (2014): 481–484.
2. H. D. Karsten et al., "Vitamins A, E and Fatty Acid Composition of the Eggs of Caged Hens and Pastured Hens," *Renewable Agriculture and Food Systems* 25, no. 01 (2010): 45–54.

Chapter 35. Pasture-Raised Meat
1. C. A. Daley et al., "A Review of Fatty Acid Profiles and Antioxidant Content in Grass-Fed and Grain-Fed Beef," *Nutrition Journal* 9, no. 10 (2010); N. Hall, H. Schönfeldt, and B. Pretorius, "Fatty Acids in Beef from Grain- and Grass-Fed Cattle: The Unique South African Scenario," *South African Journal of Clinical Nutrition* 29, no. 2 (2016): 55–62.

Chapter 36. Sprouted Lentils and Beans
1. Marica Brnić et al., "Influence of Phytase, EDTA, and Polyphenols on Zinc Absorption in Adults from Porridges Fortified with Zinc Sulfate or Zinc Oxide," *Journal of Nutrition* 144, no. 9 (2014): 1467–1473; Barbara Troesch et al., "Absorption Studies Show that Phytase from Aspergillus niger Significantly Increases Iron and Zinc Bioavailability from Phytate-Rich Foods," *Food and Nutrition Bulletin* 34, no. 2_suppl1 (2013): S90–S101; Harold H. Sandstead, "Causes of Iron and Zinc Deficiencies and Their Effects on Brain," *Journal of Nutrition* 130, no. 2 (2000): 347S–349S; Rosalind S. Gibson, Janet C. King, and Nicola Lowe, "A Review of Dietary Zinc Recommendations," *Food and Nutrition Bulletin* 37, no. 4 (2016): 443–460; Rosalind S. Gibson, Leah Perlas, and Christine Hotz, "Improving the Bioavailability of Nutrients in Plant Foods at the Household Level," *Proceedings of the Nutrition Society* 65, no. 02 (2006): 160–168.
2. Loren Cordain et al., "Modulation of Immune Function by Dietary Lectins in Rheumatoid Arthritis," *British Journal of Nutrition* 83, no. 3 (2000): 207–217.

Chapter 37. Cruciferous Vegetables
1. Yu Jiang et al., "Cruciferous Vegetable Intake Is Inversely Correlated with Circulating Levels of Proinflammatory Markers in Women," *Journal of the Academy of Nutrition and Dietetics* 114, no. 5 (2014): 700–708.e2.
2. Shuhui Wu et al., "Sulforaphane Produces Antidepressant- and Anxiolytic-Like Effects in Adult Mice," *Behavioural Brain Research* 301 (2016): 55–62.

3. Wu et al., "Sulforaphane."
4. Nagisa Mori et al., "Cruciferous Vegetable Intake Is Inversely Associated with Lung Cancer Risk among Current Nonsmoking Men in the Japan Public Health Center (JPHC) Study," *Journal of Nutrition* 147, no. 5 (2017): 841–849.
5. Xiaojiao Liu and Kezhen Lv, "Cruciferous Vegetables Intake Is Inversely Associated with Risk of Breast Cancer: A Meta-Analysis," *The Breast* 22, no. 3 (2013): 309–313.
6. Ben Liu et al., "Cruciferous Vegetables Intake and Risk of Prostate Cancer: A Meta-Analysis," *International Journal of Urology* 19, no. 2 (2011): 134–141.
7. Peter Felker, Ronald Bunch, and Angela M. Leung, "Concentrations of Thiocyanate and Goitrin in Human Plasma, Their Precursor Concentrations in Brassica Vegetables, and Associated Potential Risk for Hypothyroidism," *Nutrition Reviews* 74, no. 4 (2016): 248–258.
8. Young A. Cho and Jeongseon Kim, "Dietary Factors Affecting Thyroid Cancer Risk: A Meta-Analysis," *Nutrition and Cancer* 67, no. 5 (2015): 811–817.

Chapter 38. Sweet Peppers

1. Anouk Kaulmann and Torsten Bohn, "Carotenoids, Inflammation, and Oxidative Stress—Implications of Cellular Signaling Pathways and Relation to Chronic Disease Prevention," *Nutrition Research* 34, no. 11 (2014): 907–929.
2. Nicole T. Stringham, Philip V. Holmes, and James M. Stringham, "Supplementation with Macular Carotenoids Reduces Psychological Stress, Serum Cortisol, and Sub-Optimal Symptoms of Physical and Emotional Health in Young Adults," *Nutritional Neuroscience* 21, no. 4 (2017): 286–296.

Chapter 40. Seaweed

1. Christine Dawczynski, Rainer Schubert, and Gerhard Jahreis, "Amino Acids, Fatty Acids, and Dietary Fibre in Edible Seaweed Products," *Food Chemistry* 103, no. 3 (2007): 891–899.
2. Fumio Watanabe et al., "Vitamin B12-Containing Plant Food Sources for Vegetarians," *Nutrients* 6, no. 5 (2014): 1861–1873.
3. David Brownstein, *Iodine: Why You Need It, Why You Can't Live Without It* (West Bloomfield, MI: Medical Alternatives Press, 2014), 91.
4. Brownstein, *Iodine*.

Chapter 41. Berries and Cherries

1. Elizabeth E. Devore et al., "Dietary Intakes of Berries and Flavonoids in Relation to Cognitive Decline," Annals of Neurology 72, no. 1 (2012): 135–143; Mary A. Lila, "Anthocyanins and Human Health: An In Vitro Investigative Approach," *Journal of Biomedicine and Biotechnology* 2004, no. 5 (2004): 306–313.

2. M. M. Rahman et al., "Effects of Anthocyanins on Psychological Stress-Induced Oxidative Stress and Neurotransmitter Status," *Journal of Agricultural and Food Chemistry* 56, no. 16 (2008): 7545–7550.

3. Sonya Lunder, "Pesticides + Poison Gases = Cheap, Year-Round Strawberries," Environmental Working Group, April 10, 2018, https://www.ewg.org/foodnews/strawberries.php.

Chapter 42. Sprouted Rice and Quinoa

1. Swati B. Patil and Md. K. Khan, "Germinated Brown Rice As a Value Added Rice Product: A Review," *Journal of Food Science and Technology* 48, no. 6 (2011): 661–667; Bo Lönnerdal, "Dietary Factors Influencing Zinc Absorption," *Journal of Nutrition* 130, no. 5 (2000): 1378S–1383S.

2. D. Karladee and S. Suriyong, "γ-Aminobutyric Acid (GABA) Content in Different Varieties of Brown Rice During Germination," *Science Asia* 38 no. 1 (2012): 13–17.

Part Five: Stress Resilience Supplements

Chapter 44. Supplement Tips and My Top 10 List

1. Medscape.com, https://reference.medscape.com/drug-interactionchecker; WebMD.com, https://www.webmd.com/interaction-checker/default.htm.

Chapter 45. Magnesium

1. C. Dean, *The Magnesium Miracle: Discover the Essential Nutrient That Will Lower the Risk of Heart Disease, Prevent Stroke and Obesity, Treat Diabetes, and Improve Mood and Memory* (New York: Ballantine Books, 2014), 239–250; Mark Sircus, Transdermal Magnesium Therapy: A New Modality for the Maintenance of Health (Bloomington, IN: iUniverse, 2011), 160.

2. Dean, Magnesium Miracle; Sircus, *Transdermal Magnesium Therapy*; G. Toft, H. B. Ravn, and V. E. Hjortdal, "Intravenously and Topically Applied Magnesium in the Prevention of Arterial Thrombosis," Thrombosis Research 99, no. 1 (2000): 61–69; N. C. Chandrasekaran et al., "Permeation of Topically Applied Magnesium Ions through Human Skin Is Facilitated by Hair Follicles," *Magnesium Research* 29 no. 2 (2016): 35–42; Deborah J. Engen et al., "Effects of Transdermal Magnesium Chloride on Quality of Life for Patients with Fibromyalgia: A Feasibility Study," *Journal of Integrative Medicine* 13, no. 5 (2015): 306–313; Dennis Goodman, *Magnificent Magnesium: Your Essential Key to a Healthy Heart and More* (Garden City Park, NY: Square One, 2014), 144-145.

3. Mark Sircus, "Magnesium Chloride Product Analysis," Dr. Sircus (blog), December 8, 2009, http://drsircus.com/magnesium/magnesium-chloride-product-analysis/.

4. Sircus, Transdermal Magnesium Therapy, 164.
5. M. Firoz and M. Graber, "Bioavailability of US Commercial Magnesium Preparations," Magnesium Research 14 no. 4 (2001): 257–62; Ragner Rylander, "Bioavailability of Magnesium Salts: A Review," *Journal of Pharmacy and Nutrition Sciences* 4 (2014): 57–59; Nazan Uysal et al., "Timeline (Bioavailability) of Magnesium Compounds in Hours: Which Magnesium Compound Works Best?" *Biological Trace Element Research* 187 (2018): 128.
6. Inna Slutsky et al., "Enhancement of Learning and Memory by Elevating Brain Magnesium," *Neuron* 65, no. 2 (2010): 165–177.
7. Dean, Magnesium Miracle, lviii.
8. Sheldon Saul Hendler and David M. Rorvik, *PDR for Nutritional Supplements* (Montvale, NJ: Thomson Reuters, 2008), 410.
9. Leslie E. Korn, *Nutrition Essentials for Mental Health: A Complete Guide to the Food-Mood Connection* (New York: W. W. Norton, 2016), 267.

Chapter 46. Zinc

1. Rita Wegmüller et al., "Zinc Absorption by Young Adults from Supplemental Zinc Citrate Is Comparable with That from Zinc Gluconate and Higher than from Zinc Oxide," *Journal of Nutrition* 144, no. 2 (2013): 132–136; S. A. Barrie et al., "Comparative Absorption of Zinc Picolinate, Zinc Citrate and Zinc Gluconate in Humans," *Agents and Actions* 21, no. 1–2 (1987): 223–228; Danping Huang et al., "Different Zinc Sources Have Diverse Impacts on Gene Expression of Zinc Absorption Related Transporters in Intestinal Porcine Epithelial Cells," *Biological Trace Element Research* 173, no. 2 (2016): 325–332; P. Gandia et al., "A Bioavailability Study Comparing Two Oral Formulations Containing Zinc (Zn Bis-Glycinate vs. Zn Gluconate) after a Single Administration to Twelve Healthy Female Volunteers," *International Journal for Vitamin and Nutrition Research* 77, no. 4 (2007): 243–248; A. Mahmood et al., "Zinc Carnosine, a Health Food Supplement That Stabilises Small Bowel Integrity and Stimulates Gut Repair Processes," *Gut* 56, no. 2 (2007): 168–175; Tori Hudson, "Nutrient Profile: Zinc-Carnosine: A Combination of Zinc and L-Carnosine Improves Gastric Ulcers," *Natural Medicine Journal* 5, no. 11 (2013), accessed December 16, 2018, https://www.naturalmedicinejournal.com/journal/2013-11/nutrient-profile-zinc-carnosine.
2. Bo Lönnerdal, "Dietary Factors Influencing Zinc Absorption," *Journal of Nutrition* 130, no. 5 (2000): 1378S–1383S.
3. Sheldon Saul Hendler and David M. Rorvik, *PDR for Nutritional Supplements* (Montvale, NJ: Thomson Reuters, 2008), 735.

Chapter 47. B Vitamins

1. Maurizio Fava and David Mischoulon, "Folate in Depression," *Journal of Clinical Psychiatry* 70, no. suppl 5 (2009): 12–17.
2. Bernard F. Cole, John A. Baron, and Leila A. Mott, "Folic Acid and Prevention of Colorectal Adenomas—Reply," JAMA 298, no. 12 (2007): 1397; Marta Ebbing, "Cancer Incidence and Mortality after Treatment with Folic Acid and Vitamin B12," *JAMA* 302, no. 19 (2009): 2119.
3. Sheldon Saul Hendler and David M. Rorvik, *PDR for Nutritional Supplements* (Montvale, NJ: Thomson Reuters, 2008), 614.
4. *PDR*, 552.
5. *PDR*, 447.
6. *PDR*, 483.
7. *PDR*, 641.
8. *PDR*, 88.
9. *PDR*, 234.
10. *PDR*, 652.
11. David Kennedy, "B Vitamins and the Brain: Mechanisms, Dose and Efficacy—A Review," *Nutrients* 8, no. 2 (2016): 68.

Chapter 48. Vitamin C

1. Leslie E. Korn, *Nutrition Essentials for Mental Health: A Complete Guide to the Food-Mood Connection* (New York: W. W. Norton, 2016), 227.
2. Sheldon Saul Hendler and David M. Rorvik, *PDR for Nutritional Supplements* (Montvale, NJ: Thomson Reuters, 2008), 665.

Chapter 49. Vitamin D3

1. Ulrike Lehmann et al., "Efficacy of Fish Intake on Vitamin D Status: A Meta-Analysis of Randomized Controlled Trials," *American Journal of Clinical Nutrition* 102, no. 4 (2015): 837–847.
2. Laura Tripkovic et al., "Comparison of Vitamin D2 and Vitamin D3 Supplementation in Raising Serum 25-Hydroxyvitamin D Status: A Systematic Review and Meta-Analysis," *American Journal of Clinical Nutrition* 95, no. 6 (2012): 1357–1364; Victoria F. Logan et al., "Long-Term Vitamin D3 Supplementation Is More Effective Than Vitamin D2 in Maintaining Serum 25-Hydroxyvitamin D Status over the Winter Months," *British Journal of Nutrition* 109, no. 06 (2012): 1082–1088.
3. Leslie E. Korn, *Nutrition Essentials for Mental Health: A Complete Guide to the Food-Mood Connection* (New York: W. W. Norton, 2016), 267.

Chapter 50. Omega-3 Fats, EPA and DHA

1. R. J. Mocking et al., "Meta-Analysis and Meta-Regression of Omega-3 Polyunsaturated Fatty Acid Supplementation for Major Depressive Disorder," *Translational Psychiatry* 6, no. 3 (2016): e756–e756.
2. Erik Messamore and Robert K. McNamara, "Detection and Treatment of Omega-3 Fatty Acid Deficiency in Psychiatric Practice: Rationale and Implementation," *Lipids in Health and Disease* 15, no. 1 (2016): 6.
3. Sheldon Saul Hendler and David M. Rorvik, *PDR for Nutritional Supplements* (Montvale, NJ: Thomson Reuters, 2008), 213.

Chapter 51. Theanine

1. James F. Balch, Mark Stengler, and Robin Young Balch, *Prescription for Natural Cures: A Self-Care Guide for Treating Health Problems with Natural Remedies Including Diet, Nutrition, Supplements, and Other Holistic Methods,* Revised Edition (Nashville, TN: Turner Publishing Company, 2016), 53.
2. Balch, Stengler, and Young Balch, *Prescription for Natural Cures,* 412.

Chapter 52. Probiotics

1. Marika Mikelsaar et al., "Do Probiotic Preparations for Humans Really Have Efficacy?" Microbial Ecology in Health and Disease 22, no. 1 (2011): 10128; Huiying Wang et al., "Effect of Probiotics on Central Nervous System Functions in Animals and Humans: A Systematic Review," *Journal of Neurogastroenterology and Motility* 22, no. 4 (2016): 589–605.

Chapter 53. Adaptogens

1. Hesham R. Omar et al., "Licorice Abuse: Time to Send a Warning Message," *Therapeutic Advances in Endocrinology and Metabolism* 3, no. 4 (2012): 125–138.
2. David Winston and Steven Maimes, *Adaptogens: Herbs for Strength, Stamina, and Stress Relief* (Rochester, VT: Healing Arts Press, 2007), 121.

Appendix: Lab Tests

1. C. Dean, *The Magnesium Miracle: Discover the Essential Nutrient That Will Lower the Risk of Heart Disease, Prevent Stroke and Obesity, Treat Diabetes, and Improve Mood and Memory* (New York: Ballantine Books, 2014), xxxviii.
2. "Vitamin D, Infections and Chronic Disease," DrBenLynch.com, https://www.drbenlynch.com/vitamin-d-infections/.
3. Dr. Mercola, https://shop.mercola.com/product/1090/1/vitamin-d-test-kit-for-consumer-sponsored-research.
4. LiveWellTesting.com, https://livewelltesting.com/zrt-cortisol-stress-hormone-full-day-saliva-home-test-kit/.
5. OmegaQuant, https://omegaquant.com.

Index

muscle relaxation, 45, **127**, 208
mushrooms vitamin D, 76–78
myelin sheath, 24, 60

N

nerves, 17, 23–28, 29, **40**, 98, **127**, 197
   B vitamins and, 60, 217
   illustrations, *24, 31*
   magnesium and, 45, 208
   neurotransmitters and, 30–32
   omega-3 fats and, 79, 80, 227
   vagus nerve, 36
   vitamin C and, 65, 223
   vitamin D and, 71, 225
   zinc and, 56, 215
   See also myelin sheath; vagus nerve
nervine herbs
   food sources, 126
   how help, 43, 120–125, **127**
   research, 122–125
   supplements, 206, 229, 234–235, **238**
   vs. isolated nutrients, 111–112
   See also individual nervine herbs
neurotransmitters, 17, 29–32, **40**, **127**
   B vitamins and, 60, 217
   excitatory, 29–30, 216
   illustration, *31*
   inhibitory, 29–30
   insulin resistance and, 39
   magnesium and, 45, 208, 212, 213
   nervine herbs and, 120
   non-protein amino acids and, 96–101
   omega-3 fats and, 79, 80, 227
   probiotics and, 103–104
   processed foods and, 144, 147, 150
   protein amino acids and, 87–89
   synapse, 30, *31*
   vitamin D and, 71, 225

zinc and, 56, 215, 216
   See also individual neurotransmitters
niacin. *See* B vitamins: B3
nightshades, 192
non-essential defined, 86
Non-GMO Project Verified, 158
non-protein amino acids. *See*
      5-HTP; amino acids; GABA;
      theanine
nootropic supplements, 136
noradrenaline, 18, 29, **40**, 65
nuts
   Big 8 allergens, 161, **164**
   omega fats, 79, 85
   phytates in, 54, 57, 174
   protein in, 94
   supplements and, 213, 216

O

Ocimum sanctum, O. tenuiflorum.
      See holy basil
omega-3 fats
   ALA, 79, 84–85, 181
   B vitamins and, 60, 63
   bonuses, 83
   DHA, defined, 79
   EPA, defined, 79
   EPA/DHA omega mix, 82
   food sources, 84–**85**, 177, 179,
      180, 181, 186, 187, **200**
   how help, 43, 79–83, **127**
   lab tests, 259
   processed foods and, 148
   recommended amounts, 83–84
   research, 80–82
   supplements, 206, 227–**228**, **237**
omega-6 fats, 79, 80, 85, 187

summer squash, **55**
Swiss chard, 54, 174, 213

T

TBHQ (tBHQ), 153–155, **164**
tea
  adaptogen, 233,
  green, 96, 101, 136
  iced, 145
  nervine herb, 120, 123, 126, 142, 235
  theanine in, 96, 101
  See also caffeine
testosterone, 58, 154
theanine
  bonuses, 100
  food sources, 101
  how helps, 96, **127**
  research, 99
  supplements, 206, 229, 234, 235, **237**
thiamine. *See* B vitamins: B1
thyroid
  cruciferous veggies and, 190–191
  seaweed and, 196
trans fats, 80, 144, 147–149
traumatic brain injury, 58
tryptophan
  5-HTP contains, 96–97
  Acute Tryptophan Depletion, 89
  controversy, 90
  depletion, 89, 93
  essential amino acid, 87
  food sources, 94–**95**, 177, 179,
    180, 185, 186, 188, **200–201**
  how helps, 87–90
  probiotics enhance levels, 103
  RDA, 93
  research, 91–93
turkey. *See* chicken

U

UL defined, 44
ulcerative colitis, 34
ulcers, peptic, 34, 109

V

vagus nerve, 34, 36, 98
valerian (*Valeriana officinalis*), 120,
    124–125, 234, **238**. *See also*
    nervine herbs
vegetarians, 64, 84, 168, 220
vitamins. *See also* B vitamins;
    vitamin C; vitamin D
  fat soluble, 75, 225, 257
  water soluble, 61, 75
vitamin C
  adrenal glands and, 65–67
  ascorbic acid, 223
  bonuses, 68–69
  brain and, 65
  cortisol and, 67
  food sources, 69–**70**, 189, 192,
    197, **201**
  how helps, 43, 65–69, **127**
  multivitamin/mineral research, 51
  recommended amounts, 69
  research, 58, 67–68
  smoking increases need, 69
  supplements, 206, 217, 223–**224**,
    233, **237**
vitamin D
  bonuses, 74
  D_2 vs. D_3, 76, 78, 225
  food sources, 76–**78**, 177, **200**
  how helps, 43, 71–74, **127**
  lab tests, 225, 257–258
  magnesium and, 47
  (continued next page)

Vitamin D (continued)
  in mushrooms, 77–78
  recommended amounts, 75
  research, 73–74
  sun source tips, 71–72
  supplements, 206, 225–**226**, **237**

W

water, 138, 172, 176, 199, **200**
weight gain, 20, 53
wheat, 161–163, **164**
Withania somnifera See ashwagandha

Y

yellow dye #5, #6, #10, **152**, **164**
yerba mate, 136, **164**
yogurt
  B vitamins in, **64**
  glycine/tryptophan in, **95**
  magnesium in, **55**
  probiotics in, 105, 110, 193–194
  sugar in, 145
  zinc in, **59**

Z

zinc
  bonuses, 58
  deficiency causes, 57
  food sources, 59, 179, 185, 186,
        188, 195,197, 198, **200**, **201**
  how helps, 43, 56–58, **127**
  multivitamin/mineral research, 51
  oxalates/phytates and, 173–174
  recommended amounts, 59
  research, 57–58
  supplements, 206, 215–**216**, **236**
  zinc-copper interaction, 56–57
zucchini, 55

Made in the USA
Columbia, SC
07 December 2020

26753485R00176